LOT 2

LOT 2

The Language of Thought Revisited

Jerry A. Fodor

CLARENDON PRESS · OXFORD

OXFORD

UNIVERSITY PRESS

Great Clarendon Street, Oxford OX2 6DP

Oxford University Press is a department of the University of Oxford.
It furthers the University's objective of excellence in research, scholarship,
and education by publishing worldwide in

Oxford New York

Auckland Cape Town Dar es Salaam Hong Kong Karachi
Kuala Lumpur Madrid Melbourne Mexico City Nairobi
New Delhi Shanghai Taipei Toronto

With offices in

Argentina Austria Brazil Chile Czech Republic France Greece
Guatemala Hungary Italy Japan Poland Portugal Singapore
South Korea Switzerland Thailand Turkey Ukraine Vietnam

Oxford is a registered trademark of Oxford University Press
in the UK and in certain other countries

Published in the United States
by Oxford University Press Inc., New York

© Jerry A. Fodor 2008

The moral rights of the author have been asserted
Database right Oxford University Press (maker)

First published 2008

British Library Cataloguing in Publication Data
Data available

Library of Congress Cataloging in Publication Data
Data available

Typeset by Laserwords Private Limited, Chennai, India
Printed in Great Britain
on acid-free paper by
CPI Antony Rowe, Chippenham, Wiltshire

ISBN 978–0–19–954877–4

10 9 8 7 6 5 4 3 2 1

To Ainsley, Isobel, and Lucinda

Acknowledgments

I want to thank Brian McLaughlin for very useful comments on earlier drafts of this material; and to apologize to Ainsley, Isobel, and Lucinda for there being only two pictures.

Contents

Abbreviations   viii

A Note on Notation   x

PART I: CONCEPTS   1

1. Introduction   3
2. Concept Pragmatism: Declined and Fell   25
3. LOT Meets Frege's Problem (Among Others)   50
4. Locality   101

PART II: MINDS   127

5. Nativism   129
6. Preconceptual Representation   169
7. The Metaphysics of Reference   196

References   221
Index   227

Abbreviations

AI	artificial intelligence
CTM	computational theory of mind
EB	echoic buffer
FINST	finger of instantiation
HF	hypothesis formation
IRS	inferential-role semantics
LF	logical form
LOT	language of thought
NP	noun phrase
PA	propositional attitude
PP	prepositional phrase
PT	physicalist thesis
RTM	representational theory of mind
STM	short-term memory
VP	verb phrase

writing, writing, writing all the time, spinning like a wheel, a machine—tomorrow, writing, the day after, more writing. Come holidays, come summer, still writing. When does he ever stop and rest, the poor wretch?

Ivan Goncharov

for two nights and three days now, I have not stirred from my desk or closed my eyes. ... I am neither eating nor sleeping. I do not even glance at the newspaper while I finish this article, which, when it is published, will cause a great stir in this land of ours, and not only here, the whole cultural world is following this debate with bated breath, and this time I believe I have succeeded in silencing the obscurantists once and for all! This time they will be forced to concur and say Amen, or at least to admit that they have nothing more to say, that they have lost their cause, their game is up. ... And how about you, my dears?

Amos Oz

A Note on Notation

I've been casual about notation except where it seemed that there is a real possibility of ambiguity. Where context fails to disambiguate, or threatens to do so, I generally follow conventions that are widely adhered to in cognitive science and the philosophy of mind: single quotes for expressions that are mentioned rather than used (the word 'dog' applies to dogs), capitals for the names of concepts (the word 'cat' expresses the concept CAT), and italics for semantic values construed broadly to include meanings, senses, referents, and the like (the word 'cat' refers to *cats;* the word 'cat' means *cat;* the word 'cat' expresses the property of *being a cat.*) There are, no doubt, residual equivocations; but I hope that none of the arguments depends on them.

PART I
Concepts

1

Introduction

This all started some years ago; more years ago than I now like to think about. In 1975 I published a book called *The Language of Thought* (hereinafter *LOT 1*). The event was not widely remarked. General celebration did not ensue. A day of national rejoicing was not proclaimed.[1] Since then, as each of its publishers was swallowed by a successor, *LOT 1* has drifted from home to home, like an orphan in a Dickens novel. Never mind; in philosophy you're doing well if you haven't been remaindered. As of this writing, *LOT 1* is still available (from the Harvard University Press (paperback only)). It sells a copy or two now and then, perhaps to nostalgic antiquarians, or perhaps simply by mistake. That being so, *LOT 1* seems as good a place as any to start upon the present enterprise, which is to say something about what's changed since back then, and something about what hasn't. This Introduction is a sort of critical review of *LOT 1* (constructive criticism only, as is always my wont) together with some proleptic glances towards stuff in the later chapters of the present volume.

When I wrote *LOT 1* I remember thinking (and not without a certain satisfaction) that it didn't contain a single new idea. I believed (quite wrongly, it seems to me in retrospect) that my enterprise was merely journalistic: I was writing an exposition of what I took to be an emerging, interdisciplinary consensus about

[1] On the other hand, I report with considerable pride that a very well-known philosopher of mind has chosen *LOT 1*, among all the books published in his field in the last fifty years, as the one he would most like to see burned. It's the nicest thing anybody ever said about my work.

how the mind works; the theory that was then just beginning to be called 'cognitive science'. I thought that, with luck, cognitive science might offer a serious alternative to the moribund behaviorism that was, at the time, the mainstream of thinking about the mind in both psychology and philosophy. A consummation devoutly to be wished that seemed to me, because, impressive though the methodological and ontological credentials of behaviorism might have appeared at the time, in practice it had made the study of the mind surprisingly boring. 'If only one didn't have to be a behaviorist', I said to myself in those days, 'one might be able to think of some quite interesting questions to ask about the mind; some of which might even turn out to have quite interesting answers.'[2] But no; however dreary the journey proved, the path of virtue lay in strict adherence to what were widely supposed to be the dictates of 'the' scientific method.[3] But, then as now, the trouble with cleaving to the path of virtue is that it's not much fun.

So, I thought I would report upon what was perhaps an emerging alternative: a cognitive science that was mentalistic rather than behavioristic. In doing so, I would claim only what many of my colleagues outside philosophy were coming to believe about the cognitive mind. That was how it seemed to me at the time. But I now think I must have fallen victim to an ambiguity of scope. True, the main theses of *LOT 1* were all second-hand. But, though each was to be found somewhere in the literature, nowhere in the literature were they all to be found. Each of the bits and pieces that I put together was endorsed by some of my colleagues, but none of my colleagues thought well of their conjunction. To the contrary,

---

[2] I remember a conversation with Jerrold Katz when we were in graduate school together. I had said something about how it was too bad that Skinner was right about psychology because there would be lots of exciting things for psychologists to do if he weren't. Jerry replied by asking whether, in the course of my studies, I had learned nothing at all about philosophy. That rebuttal struck me as conclusive at the time, and it still does.

[3] Oddly, we then supposed that there was just the one. I've gotten to know a number of scientists over the intervening years, and it's my impression that, like the rest of us, they mostly make up their methodology as they go along. The scientific method as I have come to understand it: *Try not to say anything false; try to keep your wits about you.*

most of them hated it. Most of them still do. Perhaps there wasn't a consensus emerging after all.

To take just one example (lots more to follow): *LOT 1* was hyper-realist about both 'propositional attitudes' and propositional-attitude explanations. Surely, I thought, it's been clear since Aristotle that explaining actions by attributing beliefs and desires to their agent is the very paradigm of how a mentalistic psychology does its thing. I did know, sort of vaguely, that some philosophers were prepared to live with beliefs and desires only as explanatory fictions: creatures like us behave 'as if' we had them, but that's an illusion to which a due skepticism about theoretical entities (either in psychology or in general) was the recommended antidote. Nobody's ontological scruples need be offended by the new kind of mentalism because instrumentalism ('beliefs and desires are merely *façons de parler*, and so, very likely, is everything else') would allow us to take back with one hand what we gave with the other. But that struck me as just cheating, and it still does. For better or worse, the ontology of the theories one accepts is *ipso facto* the ontology to which one is committed. Whatever theory it may be, the charge for liking it is lumping it.

Moreover, the language-of-thought hypothesis endorsed in *LOT 1* wasn't just any old hyper-realism about the mental; it was, in particular, a species of RTM (that is, of the representational theory of mind). Roughly, but near enough for present purposes, RTM is a claim about the metaphysics of cognitive mental states and processes: Tokens[4] of cognitive mental states are tokens of relations between creatures and their mental representations.[5] Tokens of mental processes are 'computations'; that is, causal chains of (typically inferential) operations on mental

---

[4] I shall unblushingly take the 'type'/'token' relation for granted: Types are abstracta of which tokens are the instances. Wanting to sneeze is an event type; my presently wanting to sneeze is a token of that type. This metaphysics could do with some sharpening, but I don't much doubt that its essence would survive the process.

[5] Or, if you prefer, they're relations between creatures, their mental representations, and propositions that their mental representations express.

representations. There is no tokening of a (cognitive) mental state or process (by a creature, at a time) unless there is a corresponding tokening of a mental representation (by that creature, at that time).[6]

RTM has been the main line of thought among mental realists, hyper- or otherwise, arguably since Plato and Aristotle, patently since Descartes and the British empiricists. But, clearly, mentalism per se doesn't entail RTM. Alternatives float to the surface of the mentalist tradition from time to time, especially in discussions of perception. It's possible, for example, to read the 'direct' realism of Reid (1983) and Gibson (1966) (and, recently, of McDowell 1994 and Putnam 2000) as ontologically committed to perceptual beliefs, and to mental processes that eventuate in their fixation, but as rejecting both the claim that perceiving requires mental representation and the claim that perception is, in any interesting sense, a species of inference. I don't find direct realism remotely plausible as epistemology, still less as psychology.[7] Be that as it may. What 'direct' realists aim for is mental realism without mental representation. No doubt, there must be *something* that intrudes between perception and its object; perhaps it's something neural. But nothing that does needs to be representational or even mental; so the story goes.

In short, one can find, in philosophy (and in psychology and on the omnibus to Clapham), kinds of theories that agree that typical mental states are representational (and are, to that extent,

---

[6] I don't care, and I don't see why psychology should, whether tokenings of propositional attitudes are *identical* to tokenings of mental representations or whether, for example, the former merely supervene upon the latter. I'm by no means convinced that such issues have much substance.

[7] As far as I can see, it entails that 'veridical' perceptions belong to a different natural kind from (e.g.) illusions, ambiguities, perceptual errors, and so forth. That may be acceptable for the purposes of epistemologists (I guess I'm not entirely clear what the purposes of epistemologists are); but it's wildly implausible for theories in the psychology of perception, where, as often as not, empirical findings about *mis*perceptions are the primary data that theories must accommodate. 'So much the worse for psychology of perception', you may say; but I do think that's high-handed. It's not permitted to dismiss an otherwise bona fide theoretical option because it implies an ontology that happens not to suit your taste.

versions of RTM), but that don't take propositional attitudes to be relations between minds and tokens of mental representations.[8] This is, perhaps, the least philosophically tendentious kind of mental realism: There are beliefs and there are instances of believing, but there aren't any ideas (in the sense of that term that's familiar from (e.g.) empiricist theorizing). In particular, there's nothing 'in the head' that expresses the proposition that a propositional attitude is an attitude towards.

In fact, some of the earliest forms of computational psychology (see e.g. Deutsch 1960) take mental processes to be causal chains of mental-state tokens, but don't view mental states as relations; a fortiori not as relations to mental representations.[9] This distinction turned out to matter as theories in psychology evolved. So, for example, connectionists label the nodes in their networks, and the label that is assigned to a node is supposed to specify the content that the activation of the node expresses. But connectionism has no truck with mental representations (mental images, sentences in Mentalese, or whatever); for, on the one hand, only the node *labels* in 'neural networks' have semantic content, and, on the other, the node labels play no role in mental processes according to the standard formulations.[10] Hence the notorious inability of connectionists to acknowledge the productivity, systematicity, and compositionality of thought (to say nothing of the role of logical form in processes of inference).[11]

So, maybe RTM looked like an emerging consensus in the early days of cognitive science only if you didn't look too closely. On

---

[8] Analogously, there are philosophical views according to which sensory states are real enough, but aren't constituted by relations between creatures and sensations. (You can be in pain without there being a pain that you are in, so to speak.)

[9] According to a very ancient paper of mine (1968), the causal processes underlying such performances as, for example, tying one's shoes often consist of events of devising and executing plans, programs, and the like which are explicitly represented in the mind. (See also Miller et al. 1960.) That kind of theory (which Ryle 1949 stigmatized as 'intellectualist', to say nothing of 'Cartesian') was both computational about mental processes *and* realist about mental representations.

[10] If nodes differ *only* in their labels, they are *ipso facto* identical in their causal powers.

[11] For extensive elaboration of this sort of point, see Fodor and Pylyshyn (1988).

balance, the nearest approximation to the view of cognition that *LOT 1* had in mind was perhaps the sort of computationalism that was pervasive in AI. From *LOT 1*'s perspective, AI was right in taking mental states to be relations to mental representations, and also in its view about what mental representations are like: not pictures, or maps, but formulas in a language-like medium that functions both to express the intentional content of mental states and to provide the domain of mental processes. Even here, however, the match between *LOT 1* and what cognitive scientists were coming to believe was far from perfect. 'Classical' versions of AI (in contrast to connectionist versions) did hold more or less explicitly that the life of the mind consists primarily in the execution of programs; in effect, in constructing plans and carrying them out. And, like the kind of cognitive science that *LOT 1* favored, it didn't endorse Cartesian dualism. (Functionalism was in the air. According to functionalists, mental states are individuated by what they do, not by what they're made of; so it really doesn't matter (much) whether minds and bodies are the same kinds of substances.) But from *LOT 1*'s perspective, its emphasis on planning and action led classical AI to miss a truism: that the mind's main concern is not acting but thinking, and that paradigmatic thinking is directed to ascertaining truths. *What minds do is think about things.*

This is the tip of quite a lot of iceberg. Cognitive science didn't, as it turned out, develop in the way that *LOT 1* thought it would. Rather, the mainstream view, not just in AI but in philosophy and cognitive psychology, is now a kind of pragmatism: What's essential to thought is not its relation to the things in the world that it represents but its relations to the actions (the 'behaviors') that it guides. So, Patricia Churchland (who is not particularly identified with the kind of cognitive science that is practiced in AI) says that 'looked at from an evolutionary point of view, the principle function of nervous systems is to get the body parts where they should be in order that the organism may survive... Truth, whatever that is, definitely takes the hindmost' (1987).[12] Descartes would have had a fit.[13]

In my view, pragmatism is perhaps the worst idea that philosophy ever had; there will be much more to that effect as we go along. But the pragmatists' way of thinking about thinking was arguably *the* defining feature of anglophone philosophical psychology throughout the first half of the twentieth century, and, to a remarkable extent, it persists even now. According to the pragmatist analysis, philosophy and psychology had inherited a Cartesianism that assumed, first, that the main use of minds is in thinking true thoughts, and, second, that the truth of a thought consists in its correspondence to the aspect of the world that it's a thought about. The paradoxical and unintended upshot of these Cartesian assumptions was to make the putative mind/world relation itself seem problematic and prey to skeptical doubts.

The trouble is (so the pragmatist analysis continues) that it's part of the Cartesian view that the mind can't, as it were, *see* its correspondence to the world (or lack thereof). There is no place outside its experience of the world from which the mind can evaluate the putative correspondence between them. Accordingly, nothing changes in experience if the correspondence drops out. Indeed, nothing changes in experience if *the world* drops out. In effect, 'correspondence' and 'the world' make their living doing one another's wash: 'Correspondence' is just what Cartesians choose to call the purported relation between true thoughts and the world; and 'the world' is just what Cartesians choose to call whatever it is that the truth of a thought consists in

[12] This is, of course, 'West Coast' or 'let's pretend' evolutionary theory. In fact, nothing at all is known about how cognition evolved; and, quite possibly, nothing much ever will be. 'Tough luck', as R. C. Lewontin remarked.

[13] A plausible alternative view is that the mind exhibits a biological division of labor between truth-seeking, cognitive mechanisms, that function to determine how the world is, and planning mechanisms, that decide what to do in that sort of world. A really fascinating example, discussed by Pigliucci and Kaplan (2006: 147–8), suggests that some such functional differentiation may be in place in evolutionarily quiet creatures, including certain primitive plants. (!)

its corresponding to. The gears connect with one another, but not with anything else. That being so, we can (and should) do without them.

The sum and substance is: It's a short slide from holding that truth is a matter of correspondence of thought to the world to some or other variety of epistemic skepticism about empirical beliefs. The exact connection between the two theses has never been made fully articulate,[14] but the philosophical anxiety it gave rise to was real all the same. (Inarticulate worrying is what philosophers do at night instead of sleeping. The least you can say for the unexamined life is that it doesn't give you insomnia.)

The pragmatists undertook to cut this knot. Abilities are prior to theories, they say. Competence is prior to content. In particular, *knowing how* is the paradigm cognitive state and it is prior to *knowing that* in the order of intentional explanation.[15] Therefore, don't think of thinking as being *about* the world; think of thinking as being *in* the world. Do not say that the world is what makes your thoughts true (or false); say that the world is what makes your actions succeed or fail. Skepticism obligingly dissolves: Maybe you can't tell whether your beliefs are true, but certainly you can often tell whether your plans succeed. Often enough, it *hurts* when they don't.

---

[14] It looks to me as though the argument depends on inferring a metaphysical conclusion (truth does not consist of mind-world correspondence) from an epistemological premise (if truth consists of mind-world correspondence, we can't know 'for sure' whether our beliefs are true). I have spent the last forty years or so asserting that such inferences are invalid; indeed, ill-advised. Well, they are.

[15] There are all sorts of ways of formulating this basic principle of pragmatism; but, as far as I can tell, they are all either useless, or incoherent, or false. In the present case the issue is whether 'knows how to…', 'is able to…', etc. are themselves intensional contexts. (If Granny knows how to suck eggs, and eggs are what dinosaurs liked to eat, does it follow that Granny knows how to suck what dinosaurs liked to eat?) If 'knows how to…' is intensional, then beliefs and abilities are *both* individuated by their content, and the intensionality of the one is not less obscure than the intensionality of the other. But if 'knows how to…' is transparent, then there are all sorts of things that one knows how to do that one knows nothing about at all. For example, on the transparent reading, Granny's knowing how to suck what dinosaurs liked to eat, is *not* contingent on her knowing what dinosaurs liked to eat. In neither case does the putative priority of knowing how to knowing that help to clarify either.

And so forth. Once again it's miles from clear what such intuitions amount to, but their impact on both cognitive psychology and the philosophy of mind was simply undeniable. One sees it in the work of (among philosophers) Dewey, Wittgenstein, Quine, Ryle, Sellars, Putnam, Rorty, Dummett, Brandom, McDowell, and among such neo-Gibsonians/Heideggerians as Dreyfus (1978). You need only shake a stick. And, in cognitive psychology the thesis that *thought is the internalization of action* is what connects the likes of William James to the reflexologists and ethologists; and the reflexologists and ethologists to Vygotsky and Piaget; and Vygotsky and Piaget to Bruner and the 'New Look'; and the 'New Look' to Gibson and...[16] 'But bear with me | My heart is in the coffin there ... | And I must pause till it come back to me.'

According to *Lot 2*, pragmatism is in the very air that our cognitive science breathes. It's the bad cold that we've all come down with. It's what must be overcome; preferably by next Tuesday. By contrast, the polemics in *LOT 1* had a variety of philosophical targets: *LOT 1* didn't like reductionism, and it didn't like behaviorism, and it didn't like empiricism, and it didn't like operationalism; and, by and large, it didn't like them pretty indiscriminately. In retrospect, the views *LOT 1* disapproved of seem to have been a mixed bag; in fact, with just a little philosophical fancy footwork, it is possible to embrace more or less any of them compatible with rejecting most or all of the others. If, for example, one thinks of empiricism as simply the denial of nativism, there is no obvious reason why a mentalist has to be an empiricist: Hume and Quine were examples to the contrary, since (each in his own way) they both understood that learning presupposes a lot of innate endowment. And, even if you read 'nativism' narrowly (namely, as positing unlearned *beliefs*), there is a position in logical space for the kind of mentalist who is ontologically committed to propositional attitudes, but takes them

---

[16] Conversely, the thread that connects such 'Neocartesians' as, for example, Chomsky with Descartes is the thesis that *action is the externalization of thought* (of 'practical reasoning' in particular).

to be *dispositions*: '*Of course* there are beliefs and desires; but they aren't quite the sorts of things you think they are. In fact, they are dispositions to behave.' (This is the usual philosophical game of 'I can say anything you can say; but I won't mean what you do when I say it'. Cf. Berkeley: '*Of course* there are tables and chairs; but they're a lot like afterimages'.)

So, one of the ways *LOT 2* differs from *LOT 1* is in the single-mindedness with which it identifies pragmatism as the enemy par excellence of Cartesian realism about mental states.[17] Maybe a touch of sophistry will serve to reconcile realism with empiricism, or with operationalism, or even with ('logical') behaviorism. But the disagreement between pragmatism and the kind of cognitive science that *LOT 2* has in mind is absolute. From *LOT 2*'s Cartesian point of view, the genius of pragmatism is to get all of its explanatory priorities backward: Cartesians think that thought is prior to perception (because perception is, *inter alia*, a kind of inference). Pragmatists think the opposite. Cartesians think that concepts are prior to percepts (because inference requires, *inter alia*, subsuming a percept under a concept).[18] Pragmatists think the opposite. Cartesians think that thought is prior to action (because acting requires planning, and planning is a species of reasoning). Pragmatists think the opposite. Cartesians think that concept individuation is prior, in the order of analysis, to concept possession. Pragmatists think the opposite. Cartesians think that action is the externalization of thought. Pragmatists think that thought is the internalization of action. In effect, pragmatism is Cartesianism read from right to left. There are lots of issues that a sufficiently shameless philosopher of mind can contrive to have both ways; but not the issue between pragmatists and Cartesians.

[17] Almost exclusively, in what follows, 'pragmatism' means pragmatism about *content* rather than pragmatism about *truth*. These two issues are closely connected if you suppose that content is largely a matter of truth-conditions. I *am*, in fact, inclined to suppose that; but it won't be assumed in any of the discussion to follow.

[18] 'If it's a dog, then it barks'; i.e. if the concept DOG applies to it, so does the concept BARKER.

And pragmatism can't be true; not, at least, the kind of pragmatism according to which the distinctive function of the mind is guiding action. (There are, of course, other kinds of pragmatism; much more about them later.) *Pace* Churchland, it simply couldn't be true that the Ur-form of thinking is thinking what to do or where to go. To the contrary, the ability to think the kind of thoughts that have truth-values is, in the nature of the case, prior to the ability to plan a course of action. The reason is perfectly transparent: Acting on plans (as opposed to, say, merely behaving reflexively or just thrashing about[19]) requires being able to think about the world.[20] You can't think a plan of action unless you can think how the world would be if the action were to succeed; and thinking *the world will be such and such if all goes well* is thinking the kind of thing that can be true or false.

You can't think up a plan unless you can think about how the world would be if the plan succeeds. Notice, however, it *doesn't go the other way around*. You may perfectly well be able to think about the goal of a plan even if you can't think the plan. That's because you may be able to think the goal of a plan even if you can't think of it *as* the goal of the plan.[21] Planning to get painted blue requires

---

[19] It's a typical pragmatist thesis that thinking is somehow continuous with reflexive behavior. (This is a species of the idea that thought is the internalization of behavior.) But that can't be right; 'reacts reflexively to ...' is transparent; it belongs to the notion of a reflex that to respond to *x*s reflexively is *not* to respond to them 'under a description'. By contrast, 'thinks that *x* is F' is opaque to the substitution of coextensive predicates at the 'F' position: Thoughts have intensional objects, reflexes don't. So thoughts can't be reflexes; not even sublimated reflexes. (This sort of argument will recur again and again through the chapters that follow.)

[20] By contrast, it's entirely plausible that being caused, in some way or other, by thinking about the world *is* what makes the difference between acting and merely behaving reflexively or merely thrashing about. (No doubt defending this claim would require holding that lots of thoughts are unconscious. But the reasons for holding that are legion in any case.) Note, however, that the causal connection between the thinking and the acting can be quite indirect; as, for example, in the case where iteration transmutes considered actions into habits.

[21] Cognitive science consists mostly of working out the distinction between *representing as* and merely *representing*; which is to say that cognitive science is mostly about intentional states *as such*. Some day psychologists will come to understand that this is so. The next day the Messiah will come.

the ability to represent oneself as painted blue,[22] but being able to represent oneself as painted blue doesn't require being able to plan to get oneself painted blue. Still less does it require *knowing how* to get oneself painted blue. You might, for example, wish ever so much that you were painted blue without having the slightest idea of how to bring that about. Indeed, you might think that there is *nothing at all* that you can do that would eventuate in your being blue; being blue is just an impossible dream. Still, you can think of yourself as painted blue.[23]

Thought about the world is prior to thought about how to change the world. Accordingly, *knowing that* is prior to *knowing how*. Descartes was right and Ryle was wrong. Why, after all these years, does one still have to say these things?[24]

So, to repeat, pragmatism can't be true: In the order of explanation, thinking about being painted blue is part and parcel of acting so as to get yourself painted blue *and not vice versa*. That is, as one laughingly says, a conceptual point; so, *pace* Churchland once again, it must hold 'from an evolutionary point of view' as from every other.[25] (Or maybe it's not a conceptual point; maybe it's a metaphysical point. The same conclusion follows on either assumption.)

As previously remarked, because this kind of argument purports to warrant the Cartesian priority of thinking to acting, it typifies a

---

[22] In, as one says, 'some world or other'. The present issue isn't the status of possible-world semantics; it's whether planning that ... is prior to thinking that....

[23] How, indeed, *could* one think that it's impossible to get oneself painted blue without *thereby* thinking of oneself as painted blue?

[24] I'll tell you why; it's because (for theorists like Ryle) planned behavior isn't construed as behavior that's the outcome of a mental process. Rather, it's behavior that's performed in certain ways (heedfully, or carefully, or with due consideration, or whatever). The trouble with this conceptual analysis (as with all the other conceptual analyses I've ever heard of) is that it fails in both directions.

[25] This is, by the way, fully compatible with the evolutionary thesis that the contribution thought makes to guiding action is what the cognitive mind was, in the first instance, 'selected for'. The way to hold that thesis, in light of the present considerations, is to say that the mind typically contributes to the success of actions *by providing relevant true beliefs* on which the actions are predicated. If I'm dubious about this sort of evolutionary story (and I am, very) that's not because of my aversion to pragmatism. It's because I doubt that there is any sense to be made of the notion 'selection for'. That, however, is another story; and I tell it elsewhere. (See Fodor 2008.)

lot that you will find later in the book. It is Cartesian in another way too: it assumes that relations among the contents of mental states are in play in typical propositional-attitude explanations. In the present case, it's part of the mentalist story about *how* thoughts guide action that there is a certain relation that typically holds between the content of the agent's beliefs and the content of his desires. The practical syllogism itself cries out that this is so. According to the tradition, the 'conclusion' of a practical syllogism is an action, and the reasoning that results in the action goes more or less as follows:

Thinks: I want P
Thinks: P only if Q

Acts to bring it about that Q

What connects the major and minor premise of a practical syllogism, and the minor premise to the conclusion, is their overlapping contents: P is both the intentional object of a certain desire, and the intentional object of a certain thought. Q is a constituent of a thought and of the description under which an action is intended. It's in virtue of this relation between their contents that beliefs and desires eventuate in actions.[26]

The last several pages were a digression. (For better or worse, there will be many more such as we go along.) The discussion it strayed from was about some respects in which the cognitive science LOT *1* recommended was a scarecrow kind of construction, made out of bits and pieces taken from theories other bits and pieces of which it rejected. So, in particular, LOT *1* appropriated the classical AI view that mental processes are defined over representations in Mentalese; but it very much did not approve the (more or less standard) AI view of the semantics of Mentalese which was, in the then current terminology, 'procedural' (see e.g. Miller and

---

[26] Of course, this depends on reading the practical syllogism as providing not just a *norm* of rational actions but also an account of its etiology. There are arguments lying around that it would be wrong to do so, but none of them is defensible.

Johnson-Laird 1987).[27] Nor did *LOT 1* endorse the ontology of AI, which was solipsistic more often than not. Roughly, the idea in *LOT 1* was that psychology should be *noncommittal* as to whether there is anything in the world that isn't mental.[28] *LOT 1* kept mum about most of that; but, for better or worse, its author declined to do so. There ensued a series of papers that tried, in one way or other, to avoid a conclusion that now strikes me as inevitable: that pure referentialism is the kind of semantics that RTM requires;[29] that is, one that says that reference is the only primitive mind-world semantic property.[30] In particular, Chapter 3 is mostly about why Frege was wrong to hold (if, indeed, he did hold) that semantics requires a notion of the sense of a concept as well as a notion of its referent.

The arguments that Frege got that wrong are rather tedious: they consist in nibbling away at the intuitions that Frege's arguments for senses rest on. (I have come to think that the Frege argument for senses rests on *nothing but* appeals to intuitions; if so, that is itself a reason for viewing it askance. What's so good about saving intuitions?) Quibbling over examples is boring, but perhaps in this case it's worth the bother; large issues lurk in the background. For just one example: If referentialism is true and the content of a concept is its reference, we can simply stop worrying about Twin

[27] Roughly, the idea was that the meaning of a mental symbol is somehow a construct out of its 'use', which is in turn identified with its causal/inferential role in mental processes. This way of understanding the relation between concept individuation and concept possession is typical of pragmatist views of content. The discussion in Chapter 2 is largely an explanation of why I think it's wrong.

[28] Even these days it's not unheard of in cognitive science to opt for a real, honest-to-God, ontological kind of solipsism, according to which there just *isn't* anything that's not mental. Sometimes I think that maybe Jackendoff holds that; in my darkest moments I think that maybe even Chomsky does.

[29] Patently, the referentialist view that semantics is about a relation of reference that holds between symbols and the world is incompatible both with 'ontological' solipsism (the view that there isn't anything in the world) and 'methodological' solipsism (the view that it doesn't matter to semantics whether there is anything in the world).

[30] This, to be sure, is a very strong claim; but I'll only sketch the arguments here, since they are discussed at considerable length in my book *Concepts* (1998). The basic consideration is that none of the standard proposals about what senses might be both meets the conditions for compositionality and is independently viable.

Earth (another consummation devoutly to be wished). For, if there are no senses, then there is no question whether my twin and I have the same WATER concept. We straightforwardly don't, since, by assumption, our WATER concepts aren't even coextensive.[31] So: I believe that water is wet, but my twin doesn't; my twin believes that XYZ is wet, but I don't. *Punkt.* There is (much advertising to the contrary notwithstanding) no residual puzzle about why our quite different beliefs should nonetheless result in our performing arbitrarily similar actions. That's because it's entirely compatible with referentialism (and it's independently enormously plausible) that how one acts on one's beliefs depends not just on their content but also on what one believes about what one is thinking about. Well, what my Twin believes about XYZ is precisely what I believe about H_2O. So *of course* he acts in relation to the one just as I act in relation to the other. Exactly what was all the fuss about 'externalism' supposed to be a fuss about?

What with one thing and another, *LOT 1* had problems about the semantics of mental representations, many of which it simply failed to notice. It now seems to me that these problems traced back to a common cause: *LOT 1* failed, just about entirely, to recognize the centrality of compositionality in constraining theories about the semantics of mental representations; that is, the implications of the requirement that the content of a thought is entirely determined by its structure together with the content of its constituent concepts.[32] To spell out some of these implications is, accordingly, a main goal in *LOT 2.*

---

[31] A point that some of my early publications failed to get clear on. I was very young back then. Never mind; it is better to be young than to be right.

[32] Philosophers have noted that it's very hard to give a precise account of the compositionality constraint that makes it both nontrivial and proof against blatant counterexamples. I think they're right about that, but I do wonder why it worries them so. There is, as we're about to see, a variety of phenomena that appeals to compositionality are supposed to explain. (Productivity and systematicity are the most familiar of these, but we'll encounter others as we go along.) The interesting problem is not to decide what, exactly, counts as a representational system's being compositional; it's to constrict some not-wildly-counterintuitive notion of compositionality that allows us satisfactorily to explain these phenomena. Do not try to analyze concepts that you haven't got. Better still, do not try to analyze concepts at all.

For example, because it didn't think much about compositionality, *LOT 1* failed to see that (assuming, as I do, that Quine is right about there not being definitions, analyticities, and the like[33]) it's very likely that reference is the only semantic property that composes. If so, then the semantics of Mentalese *must* be referential. *LOT 1* missed the point about referentialism *because* it missed the point about compositionality.

For much the same reason, *LOT 1* failed to anticipate (and, a fortiori, failed to resolve) an issue that has proved central to the last several decades of cognitive science discussion; namely, the nature and identity of *concepts*. Very plausibly, the fact that the sentence 'Dogs bark' is compositional (that is, the fact that it means that dogs bark) places severe constraints on what one can say about the thought that dogs bark (i.e the thought that the sentence 'Dogs bark' is used to express). Qua version of RTM, *LOT 1* was committed to propositional attitudes being relational states, of which mental representations are one of the relata.[34] And I guess *LOT 1* sort of understood that whatever the representations are that the mind uses as the vehicles of thought, they must have some sort of internal semantic structure. In particular, the representation that the mind tokens when it entertains the thought that dogs

---

[33] Of course, Quine may *not* be right about definitions, analyticities, and the like. But, given the paucity of examples, it's a risky methodology to build semantics on the assumption. For lots of discussion see my *Concepts* (1998).

[34] Over the years there has been much unedifying discussion about whether RTM should say that thoughts are relations to mental representations *or* that they are relations to propositions. In fact, there's no reason why it shouldn't say both. What forces this issue is not RTM but naturalism, which declines to leave intensional entities and relations (reference, propositions, and the like) unreduced. I think that psychology ought to endorse naturalism if only because all the other sciences apparently do. But, in principle, a rational mental realist might perfectly well not agree.

Here's a different way to put much the same point: 'a semantic theory' can refer either to a specification of the semantic properties of the expressions in a language (perhaps an assignment of truth-conditions to its declarative sentences) or to an account of the metaphysical character of the (primitive) semantic properties and relations (perhaps a causal theory of reference or, for that matter, an onomatopoesis theory: 'slurp' refers to slurping because 'slurp' sounds like slurping.) Issues about naturalism arise in respect to theories of the second kind. But, in principle at least, not to theories of the first kind.

bark must be constituted (*inter alia*) by whatever representation it tokens when it entertains the concepts DOG and BARK. Insofar as *LOT 1* got this right, however, that was because it was duly impressed by Chomsky's point about the relation between the sentences and words (morphemes, lexical items, whatever) of natural languages: Just as the semantics of sentences are constructs out of the semantics of words, so the semantics of thoughts are constructions out of the semantics of the concepts that are their constituents.

But (at least as I read him at the time) for Chomsky the primary issue in this part of the woods was the productivity of language: that there are so many sentences rules out theories according to which sentences are semantic primitives.[35] Productivity precludes the idea (to which Quine, Wittgenstein, and Davidson, to say nothing of Skinner, all seem to have been attracted) that (short) sentences are the typical units of syntactic and semantic analysis. (Jane says 'Slab'; Tarzan brings slab). And productivity likewise precludes the idea, prevalent among behaviorists and associationists, that utterances of sentences are typically unstructured causal chains of word-length responses.

LOT 2 continues to agree with Chomsky about all of that, but with a certain change of focus. From my present perspective, the importance of the productivity(/systematicity) of language(/mind) isn't just that it's a useful stick with which to beat the wicked, but also that it points to compositionality as the issue par excellence in evaluating versions of RTM. Over the last couple of years I've become increasingly convinced that capturing the compositionality of thought is what RTM most urgently requires; not just because

[35] Various philosophers still want to assert, to the contrary, that the semantics of words are somehow constructs from the semantics of the sentences in which they occur (see e.g. Brandom, 2000; Block 1986). I think the arguments for saying that invariably depend on confusing issues about the ontology of representations with theories about the epistemology of translation and 'interpretation'. In any case, just as you would expect, such sentence-first semantic theories invariably get into terrible trouble when they try to explain productivity, systematicity, and the like.

compositionality is at the heart of the productivity and systematicity of thought, but also because it determines the relation
between thoughts and concepts. The key to the compositionality
of thoughts is that they have concepts as their constituents.

Much of the rest of this book consists of saying that sort of
thing over and over again: Referentialism must be right about the
content of intentional states because compositionality demands it;
atomism must be right about the individuation of concepts because
compositionality demands it; and thought must have constituent
structures because compositionality demands that too. What is
thus to be a main thesis of *LOT 2* was strikingly absent from
LOT 1: Most of what we know about concepts follows from the
compositionality of thoughts.[36]

The sum and substance of the discussion so far is that *LOT 1*
was arguably less good than I had hoped it would be; certainly it was less prescient than I had supposed it might be. 'B+
query' seems about right. But I'm loath to stop at that. For
example, warts and all, I think *LOT 1* was right to say that (at
least some) mental processes are computations on mental representations. And, likewise, it was right to think that there is
something radically fishy about the notion of concept learning
(more later). And, fair's fair, there are a number of other things
that it seems to me *LOT 1* also got just about right (and of which
the discussion in the present volume is therefore a conservative
extension). Traditional versions of RTM dried up not because of
their commitment to the 'Theory of Ideas' but because of their
associationism. By contrast, the foundation stone of our present
cognitive science—what makes it so profoundly different from,
say, the cognitive psychology in Hume—is Turing's suggestion
that cognitive processes are not associations but computations. And

---

[36] This isn't, of course, any sort of a priori truth. It's conceivable, for example, that
most of what we know about concepts will someday follow from what we know about
brains. The sound you'll hear, if you listen very carefully, will be of me not holding my
breath.

computation, in the sense Turing has in mind, requires a language of thought.[37,38]

Finally, and perhaps most important, I still think *LOT 1* was right about the proper relation between logical theories and theories of reasoning. The essence of that relation is that mental representations have 'logical form' ('logical syntax', as one sometimes says). From this point of view, what matters about the thought that *Granny left and Auntie stayed* is its being a conjunction, which means (according to RTM) that the logical syntax of the mental representation that you token when you think that thought is conjunctive. That the logical syntax of the thought is conjunctive (partially) determines, on the one hand, its truth-conditions and its behavior in inference and, on the other hand, its causal/computational role in mental processes. I think that this bringing of logic and logical syntax together with a theory of mental processes is the foundation of our cognitive science; in particular, the main argument for a language of thought is that, very, very plausibly, only something that is language-like can have a logical form.[39]

I continue to think that some such story as *LOT 1* told must be at least part of the truth about intentional mental states and processes. But *LOT 1* itself doubted that it is the whole truth;

[37] That mental representations must be language-like because they must be syntactically structured is a thesis that connectionism proposes to reject, thereby dispensing with the main thing that AI was right about. (Many connectionists don't understand that they are doing so because they persist in confusing the idea that mental representations typically have syntactic constituents with the idea that mental representations are typically 'distributed'.)

There is an anecdote about Evelyn Waugh that I hope is true: Waugh is told that Jones (a friend of his whom he particularly detested) has undergone an operation to remove a tumor that turned out to be benign. Waugh: 'It is a typical achievement of modern science to have located the one bit of Jones that was *not* malignant; and then to have removed it.'

[38] Historical footnote: It was once widely believed that there simply *can't be* a language of thought because it's true a priori that languages must be vehicles of communication. Thus Rush Rhees concludes his early paper 'Can there be a private language?' (1963) with the resounding observation that 'language is something that is spoken', by which I take him to mean that language is *essentially* something that is spoken. That is, I think, an extremely interesting claim, but Rhees offers no argument that it is true.

[39] 'Propositions have logical form.' Yes, but they don't have causal powers, and mental states do.

the last chapter was devoted to noticing some straws in the wind that strongly suggest that there's more to thinking than computing. That there is has become increasingly plausible in the intervening years. If so, then getting a serious psychology of intentionality to work is much more difficult than I once supposed that it would be. It's turned out over the years that many things are much more difficult than I had once supposed.

So, *LOT 2* is a sort of progress report on our continuing effort to inch towards a theory of the intentionality of cognition: what's been done, what still needs to be done, and what, as things stand, we have no idea at all of how to do. There remains plenty of tunnel at the end of the light. Tom Nagel once wrote that consciousness is what makes the philosophy of mind so hard. That's almost right. In fact, it's intentionality that makes the philosophy of mind so hard; consciousness is what makes it impossible.

Well, to round off these preliminaries, what follows often disagrees with *LOT 1*; and it often worries about questions that *LOT 1* hadn't heard of; and, no doubt, from time to time it gets wrong things that *LOT 1* got right. But I do want to emphasize that the methodological view hasn't changed at all. I'm after a theory of the cognitive mind. I don't care whether it's a philosophical theory or a psychological theory or both or neither, so long as it's true. And if true is too much to ask for, I'll settle for its being coherent and comporting with the evidence that we have so far. And if that is also too much to ask for, I'll settle for its being the best of the current alternatives. God knows, that isn't asking for much.

So, in particular, I don't view this as a project in 'analytic' philosophy, if that means analyzing either words, or concepts, or their uses. As far as I can tell, such projects have always failed, and my guess is that they always will. Accordingly, I don't adhere to the method of 'semantic ascent'. I won't, for example, pretend to be talking about 'mind' when I'm in fact talking about minds; or about 'thinking' when in fact I'm talking about thinking. And so forth. In my view, ascending semantically eventuates, pretty generally, in confusing theories about how things are with theories about how we speak or think of them. I don't need that. I am already quite confused enough to be getting on with.

OK, here we go.

SNARK. A moment of your time, if you please.

AUTHOR. Who might you be?

SNARK. I am Snark. I am a loathsome and irritating creature.

AUTHOR. So I see. Are you, by any chance, *the* Snark, the one who is famous from the poem?

SNARK. [*sighs*]. No, I'm afraid not. Are you, by any chance, *the* Fodor, the one who is famous from the travel books?

AUTHOR. [*sighs*]. No, I'm afraid not. Well, what can I do for you?

SNARK. I am here to dog (or more precisely to snark) your every footstep throughout the text that follows. I propose to confute your assertions, deconstruct your arguments, object to your theses, answer your rhetorical questions, trump your epigrams; in short, to make a proper nuisance of myself to the best of my ability. Also, I moonlight as an anonymous reader and am prepared to provide evaluations of the manuscript at the request of potential publishers.

AUTHOR. Favorable evaluations I hope?

SNARK. Don't bet the farm, sonny.

AUTHOR. Well, I'm sorry, but Granny already has the job. In fact, I'm expecting her momentarily. She usually turns up just after the Introduction.

SNARK. Not this time, however. She wishes me to tell you that she is indisposed.

AUTHOR. Not really ill, I hope?

SNARK. Rather, let us say, fed up. Granny no longer wishes to serve as your dialectal whipping person or as the butt of your cheap jokes. She finds these positions invidious. She has had enough of both and then some.

AUTHOR. And you are here in her stead?

SNARK. You may regard me as among her many avatars. Ontologically speaking.

AUTHOR. Do you charge a lot?

SNARK. In proportion to your royalties; which are, I assume, risible.

AUTHOR. Very well, then: Snark in for Granny. Why don't you go get yourself some lunch, and report for work in Chapter 2. By the way, what do snarks do for sustenance?

SNARK. We drink the heart's blood of authors.

AUTHOR. Just as I'd supposed. Well, off you go. Don't rush back; take your time; it's a long book.

2
Concept Pragmatism: Declined and Fell

2.1 Definitions in use and the circularity arguments

If RTM is true, then concepts are:

- constituents of beliefs
- the units of semantic evaluation
- a locus of causal interactions among mental representations
- formulas in Mentalese.

But what on earth does all that mean? And, supposing that there is something that it means, of what sort of things could it all be true? And how does all this bear on issues about pragmatism? All in good time.

In the beginning, psychologists, linguists, philosophers, and the man on the Clapham omnibus all agreed that (many) concepts have (or are) definitions (or, as I'll sometimes say, that many concepts are 'constituted by' their defining inferences[1]). Thus the concept BACHELOR is constituted by the defining inferences 'if something is a bachelor then it is an unmarried man' and

---

[1] 'Constituted by' glosses over a number of issues some of which I shall continue to gloss over; my excuse is that 'concepts *are* (or aren't) definitions' is the way the issue is usually framed in the cognitive-science literature. Probably the claim that's actually intended is about concept *possession*; something like: 'to have a concept is to know its definition'. That would be an instance of the characteristically pragmatist doctrine that concepts are to be analyzed by the conditions for having them rather than the other way around. Much more on this as we go along.

'if something is an unmarried man then it's a bachelor'; if you replace 'bachelor' with a word that expresses any concept other than BACHELOR, at least one of these inferences fails. This is all much as RTM might wish: If concepts are (something like) definitions, then having a concept should be (something like) mentally representing its definition. So mental representation is what underlies a whole batch of questions about concepts and their individuation; just as we Cartesians have said all along.

But then something went wrong: a widespread consensus emerged that no definitional account of concepts could be true. The trouble, in a nutshell, was that there aren't many definitions around. You can't for example, say what concept DOG is by filling in the blank in 'Something is a dog iff it is ...'; not, at least, if you want what fills the blank to be a definition of 'dog'; try it yourself and see.[2] So, cognitive scientists said to one another that there is much that we still don't know about concepts and that further research is required.

There are actually two questions here, and it's important to keep them distinct. First: Can the theory that concepts(/lexical meanings) are definitions be saved somehow or other, given the lack of convincing examples? Second: If having a concept isn't knowing its definition, what is it? Most of this chapter is about positions that are conservative about definitions (for a thing to be a C is to satisfy the definition of 'C') but pragmatist about concept possession (to have C is to have certain C-involving capacities). It's worth having a close look at these views, since something of the sort is practically ubiquitous in cognitive science.

To begin with, the rejection of definitions was never universal in cognitive science. There remained a cadre of unconvinced linguists (in the 'lexical semantics' tradition) who held some or other version of the thesis that there is a 'semantic level' of grammatical representation at which definable words are represented by their

---

[2] You can, to be sure, purchase a definition at the price of triviality; as in: 'Something is a dog iff it is a dog'.

definitions; at which, for example, 'kill' is represented as 'cause to die'. On this view, the concept KILL is a complex out of the (relatively) primitive concepts CAUSE and DIE (and, correspondingly, the meaning of the world 'kill' is a complex out of the meanings of the words 'cause' and 'die'). I don't propose to discuss lexical semantics; I've done so elsewhere (1998: chs. 3–4), and enough is enough.[3] But there is a recent vogue in the philosophical literature for reviving the definition construct in an altered version with 'definitions-in-use' playing the role of definitions-*tout-court*. This definition–in-use story deserves close scrutiny if only because it raises some Very Large Questions about the individuation of concepts and about what it is to have one, and about relations between natural-language semantics and logic. I propose to discuss it in some detail, starting with a word or two about old-style definitions just to remind you of the background.

2.1.1 *Definitions and the containment theory*

There were differences of opinion among friends of definitions about how many words can be defined, but it was common ground that not all of them can be. There must some basis of 'primitive', undefined terms in which the definitions of the others are couched. In consequence, a theorist who is committed to the claim that definition is an important notion in semantics must somehow explain how this basis is to be chosen. That turns out no small matter.

---

[3] As remarked in the text, a main trouble with old-style definitions is the lack of convincing examples. So, strictly speaking 'kill' isn't a synonym of 'cause to die'; (not, at least, if 'cause to die' means *cause to die*), since there are instances of the latter that aren't instances of the former. (Sam might cause Mary's death by getting somebody else to kill her.) What's true is only that (barring resurrection) if somebody killed Mary, then Mary is dead.

This example is not atypical. Attempts to define a term tend frequently to elicit necessary but not sufficient conditions for membership in its extension. I've heard linguists refer to this as the 'X problem'; they say that 'kill' means 'cause to die' *plus X*, and that the residual question ('We're working on it even as we speak') is therefore to fill in the X without rendering the equivalence trivial. (It's true, but not interesting, that 'Sam killed Mary' means *Sam caused Mary to die by killing her.*) This project has borne very little fruit so far; though, of course, you never know. The X problem will reappear in the text presently.

The anglophone tradition, in both philosophy and psychology, largely accepted the empiricist thesis that all concepts can be (indeed, must be) defined in a primitive basis of *sensory* concepts like (e.g.) RED or HOT or (maybe) ROUND. This empiricist semantics was in turn supposed to be grounded in an epistemology according to which all knowledge is experiential in the long run. I think, however, that even the friends of definitions now pretty generally agree that the empiricist project failed;[4] it was a cautionary example of what happens when you try to read your semantics off your epistemology. In fact, our concepts invariably overrun their experiential basis; trees and rocks aren't, after all, reducible to tree-experiences or rock-experiences. That should hardly seem surprising, since experiences are mind-dependent (no minds, no experiences), but trees and rocks are not. Also, you can climb trees and throw rocks, but you can't climb or throw sensations. And so forth. Empiricism couldn't but founder on such ontological truisms.

In contrast with the empiricist tradition, discussions of the primitive basis for conceptual(/lexical) reductions in cognitive science often favor the idea that it consists not just sensory concepts but also of some very abstract 'metaphysical' concepts like CAUSE, AGENT, ACTION, FACT, EVENT, etc. (see e.g. Carey 1985; Jackendoff 1993). As far as I know, however, there are no serious proposals for cashing the 'etc.'.[5] For one thing, it's very unclear what makes some concepts metaphysical and others not. For another thing, neither sensory concepts nor the putative metaphysical ones generally behave in the ways that primitive concepts presumably ought to. For example, I suppose that (all else equal) a primitive concept ought to be more accessible in 'performance' tasks than the concepts that it is used to define; or,

---

[4] However, see Prinz (2002).

[5] Nor are there any serious proposals as to what properties these abstract concepts should be understood to express. Suppose 'John eats' says of John that he is the agent of an eating. What, then, is the property of agency that is thereby ascribed to John? I don't have the sense that lexical semanticists worry much about this sort of question, but I wonder why they don't.

at a minimum, that primitive concepts should be acquired no later than the complex concepts of which they are constituents. By these sorts of criteria, however, the psychological data do not support the thesis that the primitives are *either* sensory *or* very abstract, *or* a combination of the two.

To the contrary, it appears that the most accessible concepts, both in perceptual classification and in ontogeny, are 'middle level' ones (Rosch 1973). In fact, it appears that children generally learn sensory concepts relatively late, whether the criterion of learning is the ability to sort or the ability to name. Likewise, a dog is, I suppose, a kind of animal; but subjects are faster at classifying a dog as a dog than in classifying the same dog as an animal. A killing is, I suppose, a kind of event; but there is surely less consensus about what's an event than about what's a killing. Subjects who agree about how many passengers the plane crash killed may have no clear intuitions about how many events the crash consisted in. (One for each wing that fell off? One for each engine that failed? One for each passenger who died? One for each passenger who didn't die? And so forth.) And God only knows at what stage of cognitive development the concept EVENT becomes available; I'm not at all sure that I've even got one.[6]

Finally, and again no small matter, inferences that definitions license are supposed to have a special kind of modal force. If 'X = A + B' is true by definition, then 'Xs are A' and 'Xs are B' are supposed to be conceptually(/linguistically) necessary; they're supposed to be 'analytic', as philosophers say. It was a virtue of the old-style definitional account of concepts that it seemed to explain why this is so. Scanting details, the basic idea was that analytic (as opposed to nomological or logical) necessities are engendered by *containment relations* between complex concepts and their constituents. 'Bachelors are unmarried' is conceptually

---

[6] A case could be made that concepts like EVENT, AGENT, CAUSE, ACTION, THING, and so forth are asymptotically close to empty; in effect, that they function as place-holders for bona fide predicates. Quite plausibly, to say 'He flew out the window; what an odd THING to HAPPEN!' is just to say 'He flew out the window; how odd!'.

necessary because the concept UNMARRIED is literally contained in the concept BACHELOR.

Wanting to draw a connection between analyticity and constituency was, I think, profoundly rightheaded. For, notice, the containment theory works pretty well for analyticities that involve *phrases*: 'brown cow → brown' is intuitively analytic; plausibly, that's because 'brown' is a constituent of 'brown cow'. But the containment story often seems not so plausible when it's applied *within lexical items*. Thus, to stick with the canonical example, it's supposed that the concept KILL is the concept CAUSE TO DIE; that is, that KILL is a structured object of which the concept DIE is literally a constituent; likewise, that the concept DOG is a structured object of which the concept ANIMAL is literally a constituent, and so forth. But then what is one to make of the concept RED? On the one hand, the inference 'red → colored' would certainly seem to be as plausible a candidate for analyticity as most. On the other hand, there isn't any X such that 'colored and X → red' (except, of course, 'red'). This is presumably an extreme case of the 'X-problem' that was mentioned in note 3.

So the containment theory of analyticity confronted a dilemma: On the one hand, it really is very plausible that 'brown cow → brown' is analytic because 'brown' is a constituent of 'brown cow'. On the other hand, the recurrence of the X-problem suggests that if 'red → colored' is analytic, that isn't because *colored* is a constituent of the meaning of 'RED'. It looks like we will have to deny either that analyticity derives from containment or that 'red → colored' is analytic.

If those are indeed the options, the second seems the better of the two. It isn't, after all, implausible that 'red → colored' is a fact about what redness is, not about what 'red' means.[7] The moral of the persistence of the X-problem may be that God knew what he was doing when he made the lexicon. 'Brown cow' looks to be a

---

[7] The sort of point would seem to be quite general (excepting only 'logical' words like 'and', 'or', 'some', etc., of which more presently). It seems thoroughly plausible that the fact that dogs are animals is a fact about dogs, not a fact about 'dog'.

complex symbol of which 'brown' is a part. Maybe that's because 'brown cow' *is* a complex symbol of which 'brown' is a part. 'Red' doesn't look like it's a complex symbol of which 'colored' is a part. Maybe that's because 'red' isn't a complex symbol, a fortiori not one of which 'colored' is a part. Appearances aren't always deceptive; perhaps the reason there appears not to be internal semantic structure in lexical items is that there isn't any.

In any case, it's common ground if 'red', 'kill', 'brown', etc. have constituent structure they do so only at the (putative) semantic level. The relevant generalization seems to be that (BACHELOR to the contrary notwithstanding) analyticity is unproblematic only where constituent structure seems unproblematic. Conversely, the fact that it's not obvious that 'cow → animal' is analytic is part and parcel of the fact that it's not obvious that ANIMAL is a constituent of COW.

If, in short, what you had in mind is that semantic constituency should come to the rescue of analyticity, thereby making the world safe for conceptual necessity, there's nothing much that has happened so far that you could find encouraging.[8] So much for the proposal to reduce linguistic(/conceptual) necessity to containment-at-the-semantic-level. It was the core of traditional definitional semantics, and, given the troubles it ran into, you might have thought that we'd seen the last of definitional semantics. But no; definitions are back in philosophical fashion.[9] Whatever comes around comes around again.

The motivation for the revival isn't far to seek: Many philosophers think that there are proprietary philosophical truths, a mark of

---

[8] On the other hand, a reconstruction of semantic necessity in terms of constituency would at least avoid the classical Quinean polemics, which at best are effective only against *epistemic* construals of analyticity.

[9] I'm not sure they ever went out of fashion in AI, presumably because of the remarkable tolerance of its practitioners for analyses that have bizarre modal consequences. I remember being told by one of them that 'x is dead' means something like *x's health is −10 on a scale from −1 to 10*; presumably, 'x is very ill' means something like *x's health is −9.7 on a scale from −1 to 10*. The guy who proposed this analysis was unmoved by the consequence that it allows you to recover from being dead. 'Poor Smith died this morning.' 'What a pity; how's he feeling now?'

which is that they are knowable a priori. Well, such philosophers are prone to reason, if there are a priori truths there ought to be some story about what it is that makes them a priori; and, if there are definitions, there is indeed a story to tell. A priori truths derive from the analysis of concepts(/from the definitions of terms). Accordingly, philosophers can discover a priori truths by a process of lexical/conceptual analysis. Since there would seem to be no other plausible account of apriority on offer,[10] we need definitions on pain of technological unemployment among analytic philosophers. So there had better be definitions. It is possible, in certain moods, to find this line of argument very convincing; especially towards the end of the month.

2.1.2 Definitions-in-use

We've just been noticing the traditionally close relation between saying that there are definitions and saying that analytic inferences, a priori inferences, conceptually necessary inferences, and the rest arise from relations between complex concepts and their constituents. It is, however, possible to separate these two theses; in particular, to hold that there are many definitions but concede that there is less constituency at the semantic level than the containment account of analyticity had supposed.[11] Enter definitions-in-use. Definitions-in-use are like definitions-tout-court in that both make certain inferences constitutive of the concepts that enter into them. But definitions-in-use are unlike definitions-tout-court in that the former don't suppose that defining inferences typically arise from relations between complex concepts and their constituents.

The canonical definition-in-use of 'and' will serve to give the feel of the thing. The suggestion is that the semantics of 'and' ought

---

[10] I guess Plato thought that philosophers detect apriority by the exercise of a special intellectual faculty of which it is the object, in something like the way that things-in-the-world are the objects of vision. Maybe he was right; there are still philosophers who think so. But it's no help if one's goal is a naturalistic psychology or a naturalistic epistemology.

[11] Indeed, one might try holding that there just isn't a semantic level; that is, that the 'surface' lexical inventory is preserved at every level of grammatical representation. I strongly suspect that's the right view, but I won't try to defend it here.

to explain (for example) why inferences of the form 'P&Q → P' are a priori valid. What's required in order to do so is that there are (presumably analytic) inferential rules that serve to introduce ANDs into some Mentalese expressions and eliminate them from others.[12] The idea is that a formulation of these rules would in effect provide a conceptual analysis of AND by reference to its use in inference.[13] Traditional definitional theories propose to explain conceptual necessity and aprioricity indirectly, by postulating a semantic level at which relations of *conceptual containment* are made explicit. By contrast, definition-in-use theories propose to explain both by a direct appeal to the notion of a *defining inference*. A definition-in-use of AND (and the like) by reference to their defining inferences would yield, at a minimum, a plausible account of the logical constants, and definition-in-use accounts of the logical constants are regularly offered as parade cases for inferential-role semantics at large.[14] The standard formulation of the rule of 'and' introduction is:

P

Q

P and Q

The standard formulation of the rule of 'and' elimination is:

P and Q   P and Q

---   ---

P   Q

There are, in the recent philosophical literature, strikingly many passages that go more or less like this: 'You want to know how

---

[12] Systems of 'natural logic' are the inspiration for this sort of treatment of the logical constants. For discussion see Boghossian (1997).

[13] *Mutatis mutandis*, it would provide a definition of 'and'.

[14] Terminology: 'Inferential-role semantics' (IRS hereafter) claims that the meaning of a word(/the content of a concept) is determined by its role in inferences. *Definitional* semantics is thus the special case of IRS according to which they are determined by their role in *defining* inferences. (Please do not ask what 'determined by' means.)

meaning works? Let me tell you about "and"; the rest is just more of the same'. Since, moreover, the usual suggestion is that the inference rules that define 'and' are what you learn when you learn what 'and' means, definition-in-use purports to exhaust not just the semantics of the logical concepts, but also their 'possession conditions'. It is, in fact, a typical claim of inferential-role semanticists that an account of the individuation of a concept should do double duty as an account of what it is to grasp the concept, and that examples like AND suggest that IRS can meet that condition. All in all, not a bad day's work, one might think.

How plausible is it that definition-in-use will do for semantics what old-style definitions weren't able to? Not very, it seems to me. There are two main sorts of objection, each of which strikes me as adequately fatal. The first purports to show that the definition-in-use story doesn't work even for the logical concepts; the second purports to show that even if it did work for the logical concepts, it doesn't generalize to anything much else. I think both these objections are well taken. I propose to discuss the first of them now and the second in the second part of this chapter.

2.1.3 *The circularity objection*

As I mentioned above, it is a widely advertised advantage of definitions-in-use, indeed of use theories of meaning in general, that they comport with a plausible account of concept possession. But, on second thought, maybe they don't. The relevant point is straightforward: Please have another look at the rules of 'and' introduction and 'and' elimination. Notice that, in these rules, 'and' occurs; not only as the term defined, but also as part of the definitions. There is thus a prima facie case that to claim that knowing its definition-in-use reconstructs knowing what 'and' means is simply circular: if there's a problem about what it is to understand 'and', there's the same problem about what it is to understand its definition-in-use. The corresponding point is glaringly clear if a definition-in-use is offered as an answer to 'What is learned when "and" is learned?'. What's learned can't possibly be a rule in which 'and' occurs, since, if it were, nobody could learn 'and' unless he *already* knows what it means. Prima facie. That is not a desirable outcome. The implication is that there are problems about co-opting definitions in use as theories about what it is to understand a word (*mutatis mutandis*, to grasp the concept that a word expresses).[15]

There is, however, a standard scratch for this itch, and it's one of the places where the connections between definition-in-use theories of concept individuation connect to pragmatist theories of concept possession.

Philosophers who accept the idea that having(/learning) a word(/concept) is knowing its definition-in-use just about invariably also assume that the kind of knowing that's pertinent is 'knowing how' rather than 'knowing that'. The idea is that we should save the identification of concepts with definitions-in-use by refusing to identify having a concept with *knowing* the rules that constitute its definition-in-use. Contrary to the spirit of RTM, one doesn't reconstruct knowing what 'and' means as mentally representing its definition (or, indeed, as mentally representing anything else). Rather, in the sense of 'know' that's relevant to specifying the possession conditions of concepts, knowing what 'and' means consists simply in being disposed to make(/accept) such 'and'-involving inferences as are licensed by its definition-in-use. It isn't further required, for example, that one *consult* this definition in drawing the inferences. The claim that *knows how* precedes *knows that* in order of analysis is, of course, the pragmatist thesis par excellence. So, we have at last arrived at the subject of this chapter.

It's worth pausing to reflect on what's happened thus far. There was a prima facie argument that even if the definition-in-use story captures the content of AND, it doesn't do so in a way that offers an

---

[15] Likewise, it couldn't be that learning AND (the concept of conjunction) requires learning that X AND Y IS TRUE IFF X IS TRUE AND Y IS TRUE.

unvacuous account of what it is for someone to grasp that concept. Enter, however, a pragmatist construal of rule-following: To follow the rule that determines what 'and' means is just to be disposed to reason in accordance with the rule. To suppose that *following* a rule requires *anything more* than reasoning in accordance with the rule is to commit what Ryle (1949) called the 'intellectualist fallacy' of supposing *knowing how* ought to be analyzed in terms of *knowing that* rather than the other way round. So, pragmatism comes to the aid of the notion that concepts have (definitional) analyses and vice versa.

Thus Paul Boghossian (1996): 'surely it isn't compulsory to think of someone's following rule R with respect to an expression as consisting in his explicitly stating that rule in so many words; on the contrary, it seems far more plausible to construe x's following the rule R with respect to e as consisting in some sort of fact about x's behavior with e ... [For example, it might] consist in [x's] being disposed to conform to rule R in [x's] employment of e, under certain circumstances'. The marriage of pragmatist theories about having concepts[16] with inferential-role theories about their content was a defining event in twentieth-century anglophone analytical philosophy of mind. Arguably it was *the* defining event; think not just of Ryle and Wittgenstein, but of Dewey, Sellars, Dummet, Davidson, and many, many other luminaries. But it was, for all that, a misalliance, and it bred monsters.

The first thing to say about such proposals is concessive: the 'knowing how' account of concept possession must be right at least some of the time. The relevant point is the one that Lewis Carroll (a Wittgensteinian *avant la lettre*) makes in his fable about Achilles and the tortoise: Not all of a mind's transitions from premises to conclusions can be mediated by the application of rules; some of

---

[16] Is this really pragmatism, or is it just behaviorism? That depends on whether the 'behavior' that rule-following is supposed to 'consist in' is itself characterized in intentional terms. Neither the philosophical literature nor the psychological literature is often very clear about this, and that is no doubt reprehensible. But I don't think it matters much, since the proposed account of concept possession is surely hopeless on either reading.

them must be 'immediate', on pain of regress. If, in particular, following a rule itself required first reasoning about which rule to follow, or about how to follow it, the process of inference could never get started. Philosophers make this sort of argument all the time, and it's sound as far as it goes.

But it doesn't go far. It isn't, in particular, an argument that concept possession must *always* have a dispositional analysis; only that it must do so for at least some concepts at least some of the time. I take it that this reply to the threatened regress is pretty much common ground in cognitive science (though, oddly enough, not in philosophy). Thus computational models of mental capacities always assume that at least some steps in at least some processes of reasoning are 'built into the cognitive architecture' of the reasoner. Computers *sometimes* follow rules for executing their instructions when they execute their instructions; but they don't *always* do so. A Turing machine instructed to move its tape doesn't have to apply, or even consult, a procedure for moving its tape; it just (as one said in the sixties) *does it*.[17]

Fair enough, then; sometimes having a concept can consist in knowing how to proceed and having a disposition to proceed that way. But it's still wide open, even in the case of the logical constants, whether the knowing-how account of concept possession can save the definition-in-use story about concept individuation. In fact, I think there's a lurking dilemma, of which the quotation from Boghossian affords a perspicuous instance.

Boghossian says it's plausible that 'following rule R may consist in our being disposed to conform to rule R in our employment of [an expression] e, under certain circumstances'. But that can't be right; mere conformity with R just isn't sufficient for following R. That's because following R requires that one's behavior have a certain kind of etiology; roughly, that one's intention that one's

---

[17] Likewise, suppose someone tells me: 'Close your eyes and touch your nose'. Presumably I must then decide on a plan for complying; that is, I plan first to close my eyes and then to touch my nose. But if I'm just told to close my eyes, I don't need a plan for complying; I just do so.

behavior should conform with R explains (or partly explains) why it does conform to R. A fortiori, *you aren't following R unless R is the 'intentional object' of one of your mental states.*

To put it more in the formal mode, 'x follows R' equivocates between an opaque and a transparent reading depending on whether substitution of equivalents is permitted at the R-position. There's one way of reading it that makes 'x follows R' transparent. On this reading you are disposed to follow R if you are disposed to follow any rule that's equivalent to R; for example, you would be disposed to follow the introduction/elimination rules for 'and' if you were disposed to reason in accordance with its truth-table. But the transparent reading of 'following R' is surely too weak for the pragmatist's purpose, which, remember, is to define 'and', not merely to define 'equivalence to "and"'. If, on the other hand, you read 'follow R' opaquely, then you need to provide a construal of 'following R' such that, though it's not transparent, following R doesn't require *grasping* (knowing R; understanding R; whatever). Otherwise we're back to precisely the kind of analysis pragmatists want to avoid; namely, the kind that understands 'knows how' in terms of 'knows that' instead of the other way round. In short, pragmatists have a choice between analyses of rule-following that are too weak and analyses of rule-following that are circular. This is, I think, a bona fide dilemma; there's just no way out. The long and short is that you can't hold both that its definition-in-use has a privileged role in a semantics for 'and' and also that grasping 'and' requires no more than reasoning in a way that accords with its definition-in-use. *Rule-according reasoning isn't sufficient for rule-following reasoning.* I repeat for emphasis: *You aren't following R unless R is the intentional object of one of your mental states.*

But we can't just stop here; an account of rule-following that invokes behavioral intentions needs a story about what's going on when an intention to behave in accordance with R is (part of) what explains behavior that does accord with R. Well, if the working commitment to RTM and CTM still holds, then what distinguishes following R from mere action in accordance with R is that in the former case R is mentally represented ('in the intention box', as one says) and the mental representation of R is implicated in the etiology of the behavior that accords with R. But if *that's* right, then only someone who is *already* able to mentally represent conjunction can intend to follow the rules that constitute the definition-in-use of AND. The moral, I think, is that—ever so many philosophers to the contrary notwithstanding—*adopting a dispositional account of rule-following won't save an inferential-role theory of semantics*[18] *from the charge that it implies a circular account of concept possession*; not even if the account of the semantics is restricted to the logical vocabulary. Perhaps I should say that again, louder: *ADOPTING A DIS-POSITIONAL ACCOUNT OF RULE-FOLLOWING WON'T SAVE AN INFERENTIAL ROLE SEMANTICS FROM THE CHARGE THAT IT IMPLIES A CIRCULAR ACCOUNT OF CONCEPT POSSESSION; not even if the account of the semantics is restricted to the logical vocabulary.* Perhaps I should say that again, louder still. But, on second thought, perhaps not.

In fact, though the two are often held in conjuction these days, inferential theories of content are distinctly in tension with pragmatist theories of the relation between what one knows and how what one knows eventuates in how one acts. That being so, it's unsurprising that attempts to combine pragmatism with use theories of meaning have inspired a lot of bad philosophy. In particular, the definition-in-use story about concept individuation wants certain Gentzen-style rules of inference to be constitutive of AND. But, according to concept pragmatists, what's required for AND possession is just being reliably disposed to make valid conjunctive inferences; which rules you *follow* in making the inferences (indeed, whether there *are* any rules that you follow in making them) isn't relevant to whether you have a grasp of AND. Well, I really don't think you can have it both ways. An account of the semantics of AND that appeals to its definition-in-use (or, indeed, to any other sort of definition of AND; or, indeed to

---

[18] Of which, as remarked above, a definitional semantics is a special case.

any other property of the inferential role of AND) is inherently intellectualist and *must not embrace a dispositional account of AND possession* on pain of engendering circularities.[19]

Well, suppose it's right to claim that the choice between IRS and pragmatist theories of concept possession is exclusive. Still, nothing so far prejudices the question *Which of the two should be abandoned?* I think, in fact, that neither is tenable; the second because it leads to the sort of circularities we've just been exploring; and the first because it can't accommodate the compositionality of conceptual content. If so, then most of what philosophy and cognitive science have had to say about concepts and concept possession over the last fifty years or so simply isn't true; a conclusion that strikes me as independently entirely plausible. Thus the agenda for the second part of this chapter.

2.2 Pragmatism and the compositionality arguments

The first half of this chapter considered a kind of theory that conjoins a definition-in-use account of the individuation of (at least some) concepts with a pragmatist, 'knowing-how' account of concept possession.[20] The former purports to reconstruct the intuitive notion of a concept's 'content' or 'sense' by appealing to the rules that govern its role in inference. The latter purports to avoid the circularities and regresses that are (purported to be) implicit in intellectualist analyses of rule-following. Combining the two (purports to) illustrate how an inferential-role account of

---

[19] In fact, this is just a special case of a very general consideration: if, qua pragmatist, you insist on identifying mental *states* with dispositions, you are then debarred from distinguishing mental *processes* by the computational routes the mind takes to get from one such state to another. Computations don't apply to dispositions, they apply to representations. The Ryle–Wittgenstein program in philosophy of mind foundered on this very rock. It's *why* it provides no account of mental processes.

[20] I can imagine, all too easily, a philosopher who says: 'But you can't have a *theory* of concepts or of concept possession; those aren't the *kinds* of things that one can have theories of'. The way to rebut this complaint is, of course, to provide the theory. We're working on it.

conceptual content and a dispositional analysis of concept possession can be made to take in one another's wash. That amounts to a substantial lot of purporting, but (give or take a bit) it is the current consensus view in much of philosophy and cognitive science.

The main conclusion of Section 2.1, however, was that the two halves of this mainstream view don't really fit together; not even in parade cases like AND. What you get if you conjoin the two is: a circle. The moral is that you can (maybe) individuate concepts by their definitions-in-use; but, if you do, then your story about conceptual content will come unstuck from your story about concept possession, which pragmatists take it as a matter of principle that it must not do.[21] And that's not all that's wrong with pragmatist accounts of concept possession. Not nearly.

I suggested in the Introduction that compositionality is a highly nontrivial constraint on any serious theory of conceptual(/lexical) content; and, by extension, on any serious theory of concept possession. The systematicity, productivity, etc. of thought requires the content of BROWN DOG to be a construction out of the contents of BROWN and DOG. Likewise for the possession conditions of BROWN DOG: They've got to explain why anybody who has BROWN and DOG thereby has all the concepts he needs to grasp BROWN DOG. The productivity of concepts goes hand in hand with the productivity of concept possession; neither is the slightest use without the other, and compositionality is the essence of both. I'm now going to argue that, circularity considerations aside, the pragmatist account of concept possession as know-how can't be right because it's incompatible with the compositionality of a concept's possession conditions.

---

[21] Here's a passage from David Pears that gives the feel of the thing. (Pears is discussing Hume's thesis that a typical concept is some sort of mental image.) 'When a concept manifests itself as a mental image...it cannot be identified with that image...We have to add that it is only the image with its special function. ...Wittgenstein insisted not merely that the image must have a function, but also that the function is the use we make of it' (1990: 25). But though Witttgenstein often gets the blame for this kind of view, it has a history in the American-pragmatist movement including, in particular, Pierce, James, and Dewey.

To begin with, let's suppose that AND is distinguished by its entrance and exit rules. Still, a pragmatist who takes AND as a model for the general case is on risky ground, since it's patently not true of concepts in general that one's having them is constituted by one's use of them *in inference*.[22] Unlike AND, most concepts apply to things in the world. Or, anyhow, that's what they are supposed to do. Accordingly, to have DOG requires knowing how to apply it to dogs;[23] and one's grasp of AND doesn't so much as purport to offer a model for that.

So, what besides grasping its inferential role is required to have concept C? All the formulations of concept pragmatism I've heard of hold that the capacities that constitute concept possession are either or both of: knowing how to use C to draw C-involving inferences, and knowing how to sort things-in-the-world into the Cs and the not-Cs. Presumably it's the second kind of capacity that a pragmatist will appeal to in order to explain how having DOG and the like differs from having AND and the like. So, let's discuss the ability to sort dogs as such.[24] The first thing to say about it is surely that nobody, excepting (possibly) God, has it; not if being able to sort dogs as such means being able to recognize just any old dog under just any old conditions. Of course having DOG isn't sufficient for that. Consider dogs that are very, very small (smaller, say, than an electron); or dogs that are very, very big (bigger, say, than the whole universe); or dogs that are outside one's light cone; or dogs that won't be born till after our species is extinct; or dogs that you encounter on a very dark night; or when you happen to

---

[22] I take this to be just about truistic, but there are those who don't. See e.g. Brandom (2000); for discussion see Fodor and Lepore (2007).

[23] Just what this amounts to is, of course, hotly debated. The standard pragmatist view is that having DOG requires being able to sort things-at-large according to whether they are dogs. In my view that can't be right since sorting dogs requires, *inter alia*, using the concept DOG to think about them. More to come on both these views.

[24] The 'as such' is there to remind us that 'sort' is intensional in this context. Suppose dogs are Granny's favorite animals; even so, the ability to sort animals into *Granny's favorites* and *others* would not *ipso facto* manifest a grasp of the concept DOG. It might just manifest a grasp of the concept GRANNY'S FAVORITE ANIMAL.

have your eyes closed. And so forth. Maybe it is possible to finish this list, but there's no reason to think so. I suppose that this point is uncontentious, indeed trite. It's the sort of thing that was the despair of verificationists.

One way to put the point of the last couple of paragraphs is that what you are able to sort in virtue of having C is enormously context-dependent. And it's dependent, likewise, on the choice of C. The good conditions for sorting dogs as such are quite unlike the good conditions for sorting fish as such; and these are again quite different from the good conditions for sorting sounds made by an oboe as such. Etc.

The moral is correspondingly trite: if there are sorting conditions for C possession, they must specify conditions that are 'good' or 'normal' for the identification of things that C applies to; inability to sort Cs doesn't count against one's having C unless such conditions obtain.[25] I won't bother to argue for this; I take it to be common ground.

There's now a clear path to the conclusion that the capacity to sort Cs can't be a possession condition for C; namely, that 'normalcy' conditions themselves don't compose. The normalcy conditions for sorting As that are Bs need not be determined by the normalcy conditions for sorting As together with the normalcy conditions for sorting Bs. Consider the ornithological concept NIGHT-FLYING BLUEBIRD.[26] Suppose that having

[25] This kind of point has wide application. Consider the claim, frequently encountered in the philosophical literature, that there are forms of argument (perhaps, for example, arguments from P&Q to P) such that it's a priori that nobody rational could fail to accept their instances. Here again, such claims are implausible unless they are hedged around with caveats; in particular, that the form of the argument is perspicuous in the cases in question. One can fail to accept instances of simplification of conjunction compatible with being fully rational and compatible with having the concept AND if, for example, the premise is, say, 10^{10} words long. A criterion for rationality (if there could be such a thing; which I don't believe for a minute) would thus have to be a peculiar mixture of formal and empirical constraints. What do you suppose is the likelihood that such a criterion would be a priori?

[26] This is, of course, *philosophical* ornithology. On the one hand, there aren't, to my knowledge, any night-flying bluebirds; but, on the other hand, it doesn't matter that there aren't.

this concept includes, *inter alia*, being able to recognize instances of that kind (as such). Well, night-fliers are best recognized (as such) at night. But the best time to recognize bluebirds (as such) is in broad daylight. So, one might say, the normalcy conditions for NIGHT-FLYING 'screen' the normalcy conditions for BLUEBIRD: To satisfy the normalcy conditions for one is, de facto, to not satisfy the normalcy conditions for the other. A fortiori, the possession conditions for NIGHT-FLYING BLUEBIRD aren't compositional if ability to sort is among them.

None of that is to deny that there are normalcy conditions for recognizing night-flying bluebirds. Perhaps these birds have a unique song, the singing of which invariably signifies their presence; if so, then they can be sorted by the song they sing. The point, however, is that the normalcy conditions for recognizing night-flying bluebirds can't be constructed from the normalcy conditions for recognizing bluebirds and the normalcy conditions for recognizing things that fly at night: By assumption, the properties that one uses to sort night-flying bluebirds (their song or whatever) aren't either properties that they have in virtue of being night-fliers, or properties that they have in virtue of being bluebirds; they're properties they have in virtue of being night-flying bluebirds. That being so, passing the sorting tests for having NIGHT-FLYING and for having BLUEBIRD doesn't insure passing the sorting test for NIGHT-FLYING BLUEBIRD or vice versa.

The 'vice versa' matters, by the way. I've heard it suggested (about eight million times) that perhaps epistemic constraints (on sorting or whatever) apply to the possession conditions of primitive concepts, and the content of complex concepts is a construction from the extensions of their primitive constituents. To have BROWN is to be able to sort brown things from the rest; to have DOG is to be able to sort dog things from the rest, and BROWN DOG is the concept whose extension is the intersection of the brown things with the dog things.

SNARK [*appears suddenly*]. What if there is more than one
concept whose extension is the intersection of the
brown things and the dog things?

AUTHOR. Shut up!

SNARK [*Disappears suddenly*].

But that can't be right. If it were, it would be possible to have
BROWN DOG without having BROWN, which it isn't (see
below pp. 59–60).

That leaves open a kind of question which (I should have thought) pragmatists are passionately committed to not begging; namely:
If the possession conditions for complex concepts aren't epistemic,
what on earth are they? What is it for a mind to have the concept
of which {brown dog} is the extension?' Surely it can't be anything
like *knowing*, or *believing*, or *being able to figure out* that the extension
of BROWN DOG is the intersection of the brown things with
the dog things; for that's exactly the kind of Cartesian account of
concept possession that pragmatists are set on avoiding. But nor
is it anything epistemic (like being able to recognize things in the
extension BROWN DOG as such), since, as we've been seeing, the
epistemic account of concept possession doesn't hold for complex
concepts; even if it holds for their constituents. So now what?[27]

If being able to sort instances of NIGHT-FLYING BLUEBIRD
is constitutive of having that concept, then the possession conditions of NIGHT-FLYING BLUEBIRD don't compose. But the
possession conditions for concepts must compose;[28] how else could
one explain why our concepts are productive and systematic? So

[27] The situation is still worse than this suggests. Suppose C is a complex concept of
which C′ is a constituent. And suppose that there is some possession condition on C′
(a sorting condition, as it might be) that C doesn't share. Then it is possible for a creature
to have C without having C′; a palpably unsatisfactory consequence. One might, to be
sure, just *stipulate* that nobody has a complex concept unless he has each of its constituents.
But surely one shouldn't need to stipulate that; it should follow from one's account of
compositionality.

[28] Or, at least, they must do so in indefinitely many cases, NIGHT-FLYING BLUEBIRD
surely included. Notice that you didn't require coaching to grasp the concept of a night-flying
bluebird; you grasped it as soon as I mentioned it.

sorting capacities aren't constitutive of concept possession. In fact, there can't be *anything* epistemic that is constitutive of concept possession,[29] since any epistemic condition must have associated normalcy conditions; and, to repeat, normalcy conditions quite generally aren't themselves compositional.[30]

Let's pause to see where we've got to. In Section 2.1 I argued that having concept C can't be identified with knowing that C is governed by R where R is a rule for using C in inferences. That sort of account looks circular at first blush, and it continues to do so on close examination. The indicated moral was that pragmatists have got the relation between concept individuation and concept possession backwards. The analysis of 'has C' presupposes C, not the other way around. Contrary to pragmatists, the individuation of concepts is prior, in the order of explanation, to the specification of their possession conditions. It's entirely characteristic of pragmatists to get things backwards in this sort of way.

I also argued that this situation can't be remedied by saying that having C is being disposed to act *in accordance* with R. The problem was that 'acts in accordance with R' is extensional at the 'R' position, so that behaviors in whose explanation the grasp of R plays no role at all can nonetheless be in accord with R.

Section 2.2 has been devoted to considering the pragmatist suggestion that, in at least some cases, the possession conditions for C include knowing how to sort Cs under 'normal' conditions. The

---

[29] It follows that concepts can't be anything like stereotypes, though the identification of having a concept with knowing the corresponding stereotype is very widely endorsed in the psychological wing of the cognitive-science community. For further discussion see Fodor (1998); for an experimental demonstration see Connolly et al. (2007).

[30] This means, in particular, that one can't use a presumptive internal connection between having C and recognizing Cs (as such) as a stick for beating up skeptics. Paradigm-case arguments are paradigm cases: '*Of course* there are chairs; anybody who has the concept CHAIR(/understands the word "chair") can recognize that this is one of them [points to a chair]; and, contrapositively, anyone who fails to recognize that this is a chair doesn't have the concept CHAIR. Skepticism about chairs is therefore not a coherent option.' That is a dreadfully bad argument; all that's true is that if somebody who does have the concept CHAIR fails to recognize that this is one, that can't be because he doesn't have the concept CHAIR. (Perhaps it's because the normalcy conditions for recognizing chairs aren't satisfied in the case in question.)

objection was that since normalcy conditions do not themselves compose, this account of concept possession can't possibly be true. Pragmatism really is dead.

Pragmatism really is dead (or have I mentioned that?). And, as far as I know (and eliminativism to one side), the only available alternative to pragmatism about concept possession is Cartesianism about concept possession. That is, it's the thesis that having concept C is being able to think about Cs (as such). So, as Henry James likes to say, 'here we are'.

SNARK [*is once again manifest*]. I'm back.

AUTHOR [*with no great show of enthusiasm*]. So it would appear.

SNARK. Can I make a legalistic sort of point?

AUTHOR. Can I stop you?

SNARK. Well, you say that whatever having concept C may amount to, it can't amount to knowing how to use C, since it's inevitable that *using* C will presuppose *having* C. But you yourself hold that having the concept C is constituted by an ability; namely, by the ability to think about Cs. So why doesn't that make you a kind of pragmatist too? And why isn't what distinguishes your kind of pragmatist from the usual kind only that whereas the latter claim the concept-individuating capacities are something like abilities to infer or to sort, you claim that they are something like abilities to think-about or to represent-in-thought?

AUTHOR. Say that if you like; but I do think it's mostly quibble. Suppose being able to think about Cs is itself a case of knowing how to use C. But nothing of metaphysical interest follows, since, according to Cartesians (against whom the issues may not be begged), being able to think about Cs doesn't require the ability to sort Cs or to draw C-involving inferences. As usual, the metaphysically interesting issue is: what's the right order of analysis; and that issue isn't touched by whether we do or don't say that thinking of Cs is itself a use of C. There is, however, a substantive point that shouldn't on any account be overlooked. We've seen that abilities to sort and abilities to infer don't compose; *BY CONTRAST, ABILITIES TO THINK ABOUT DO*. If you can think about dogs (as such) and you can think about brown things (as such) you can thing about brown dogs (as such). The moral of this strikes me as clear and urgent: The basic explanatory category required for a theory of concept possession isn't know-how; it's *thinking about*. Getting this wrong breeds monsters, concept pragmatism among them.

2.3 Concluding rhetoric

I think we're overdue for a counterrevolution both in cognitive science and in the philosophy of mind. It's a Cartesian truism that minds are for thinking, and it's again a Cartesian truism that concepts are for thinking with. For all sorts of bad reasons (but, particularly, for dread of skepticism[31]) the twentieth century came to flout these truisms; indeed, to think that flouting them is a condition for responsible theorizing about the mind. So, by and large, the twentieth century thought that mental states are dispositions, typically the kinds of dispositions that get manifested by behavior.

But the twentieth century was wrong to think that, and the project has come unraveled. That's not surprising. Mental states have causal powers. Indeed, my having and deploying the concept C is itself part of the etiology of my C-sorting behaviors. By

---

[31] Actually, psychologists don't generally care much about skepticism. But they do care about testing things, and it's a lot easier to design an experiment to test whether Ss can sort Cs than it is to design an experiment to test whether Ss can think about Cs. (This is so especially if the Ss are rats or pigeons.) I've more than once been told that if Cartesianism is true, experimental cognitive psychology is impossible. In fact, of course, that's wildly hyperbolical; but suppose it were so. Could it really be a condition on a good theory of the cognitive mind that it provide job insurance for cognitive psychologists?

contrast, *mere dispositions don't make anything happen*. What causes a fragile glass to break isn't its being fragile; a glass that is fragile may sit intact on the mantelpiece forever. What causes a fragile glass to break is *its being dropped*. Likewise what causes my arm to raise is *my deciding to raise it*. From my merely *being disposed to* raise it nothing follows.

3

LOT Meets Frege's Problem (Among Others)

3.1 Introduction

Here are two closely related issues that a theory of intentional mental states and processes might reasonably be expected to address: Frege's problem and the problem of publicity.[1] In this chapter I'd like to convince you of what I sometimes almost believe myself: that a LOT version of RTM has the resources to cope with both of them. I'd like to; but since I'm sure I won't, I'll settle for a survey of the relevant geography as viewed from a LOT/RTM perspective.

If reference were all there is to meaning, then the substitution of co-referring expressions in a linguistic formula should preserve truth. Of course it should: If 'Fa' is true, and if 'a' and 'b' refer to the same thing, how could 'Fb' not also be true? But it's notorious that there are 'opaque' contexts (including, specifically, propositional-attitude (PA) contexts) where the substitution of co-referring expressions doesn't preserve truth. It's old news that John can reasonably wonder whether Cicero is Tully but not whether Tully is; and so forth. I'll call examples where substitution of co-referring expressions isn't valid 'Frege cases'.

That there are Frege cases wouldn't be so bad if substitution *always* failed in PA contexts (as, arguably, it always does inside

---

[1] A concept is 'public' iff (i) more than one mind can have it and (ii) if one time-slice of a given mind can have it, others can too.

quotation marks); we could then just say: 'Well, such contexts are frozen to substitution for some reason or other; I'll worry about why they are tomorrow'. But it's common ground (more or less) that there is some sort of interaction going on, since *synonymous* expressions—expressions with the same content—do substitute *salve veritate*, even in (PA) contexts.[2] So, prima facie, the moral is that reference can't be the same thing as content.

SNARK. Whoever said it was? I thought our topic is the viability (or otherwise) of LOT and CTM. Well, as far as I can see, the identification of content with reference isn't intrinsic to either of those. If you wish to change topics in mid-course, go right ahead. But I charge extra for overtime.

AUTHOR. Yes, but there's been a hidden agenda. We've been talking about LOT and CTM in the context of a *naturalistic* theory of mind; which is to say, in the context of a naturalistic theory of (mental) *content*. The difference between saying that there's no such thing as mental content and saying that yes there is, but it's not a natural phenomenon, strikes me as not worth arguing about. Well, if *that's* the project, then—for reasons I'll try to make clear as we go along—I think that the referential kind of content affords by far the best hope of naturalization. So, here's the plan:

1. Make PA psychology metaphysically respectable by constructing a naturalistic theory of PAs.

2. Make PAs metaphysically respectable by constructing a referential theory of mental content.

---

[2] This leaves the 'Mates cases' (Mates 1951) out of consideration; but perhaps they are special (perhaps they're metalinguistic). It doesn't matter for present purposes, since, in any case, it's plausible that synonymous expressions substitute in non-Mates PA contexts but co-referring expressions do not, and that needs accounting for.

3. Make the referential theory of mental content metaphysically respectable by naturalizing reference.

But you will have noticed that achieving (iii) will achieve (i) only if it's plausible that a theory of reference can do whatever psychology requires a theory of mental content to do. And, prima facie, Frege cases show that it can't; prima facie, Frege cases show that a purely referential theory of content can't account for failures of substitutivity in PA contexts. Or, to put the same issue more in the material mode (which is, I think, how it ought to be put): If content is just reference, what kind of thing could a belief be such that it is possible to believe Fa and not believe Fb when a = b?

So, those of us who are friends both of RTM and of naturalism arrive at a tactical divide. One option is to grant the prima facie implications of Frege cases and look for something (call it the expression's *sense*) that expressions share if and only if substitution of one for the other is valid in PA contexts. The residual (and highly nontrivial) problem would then be to provide a naturalistic account of senses as so construed.[3] The other option is somehow to deflate the Frege cases; to argue that they show less about content (or about propositional attitudes; or about either) than has generally been supposed.

I think that a purely referential theory of content is much to be desired if only one can pull it off. At a minimum, one might reasonably prefer a version of LOT/CTM that's compatible with a referential semantics to one that isn't. Here are some reasons, together with brief comments. This is, to be sure, a digression; but I suppose you're used to those by now.

---

[3] Frege clearly thought that a naturalistic theory of senses is out of the question; and so did Husserl; and so do I. However, they didn't mind a naturalistic theory of senses being out of the question because they weren't naturalists. I am, so I do.

3.2 Digression: meaning or reference or both?

(i) If semantics is to recognize both the sense and the reference of an expression as parameters of its content, it will have to say something about what holds the two together. (It seems pretty clear that they're not independent; I suppose there couldn't be a word that means *bachelor* but refers to doorknobs.) This issue turns out to be intricate. On the one hand, Putnam's well-known argument about water and XYZ has convinced lots of philosophers that meaning doesn't determine reference (or, anyhow, that mental content doesn't). On the other hand, it's clear that reference doesn't determine meaning either, since many senses can have the same extension. So, then, what *is* the relation between the two? If reference is the only semantic property that distinguishes mental contents, we are spared this sort of worry. If not, then we're in for it.

(ii) The standard alternative to identifying meaning with reference is a 'two factor' semantics according to which words-(/concepts) have both referents and senses. These days senses are widely supposed to be something like inferential roles, so the sort of view I have in mind goes under the name 'inferential-role semantics' (see Ch. 2).[4] Since, for better or for worse, IRS is currently far the most popular version of two-factor semantics (more or less explicitly in philosophy, more or less implicitly in cognitive science), it will be the stalking horse in the discussion that follows.

> SNARK. What if I'm the kind of snark who thinks there are senses but doesn't think they are anything like inferential roles?

---

[4] It's possible to find philosophers and (more often) linguists who endorse a reference-free semantics, specifically a version of IRS according to which the content of an expression is *entirely* constituted by its role in inferences. On that sort of account, neither words nor concepts refer to anything. Chomsky and Jakendoff have said things that suggest that they favor some such view (see also Brandom 2000). But I don't understand how a semantics can avoid lapsing into idealistic solipsism unless it recognizes some sort of symbol-world relation. For better or worse, I assume in what follows that we use 'tables' and 'chairs' to talk about tables and chairs (respectively).

AUTHOR. You're on your own. Don't forget to pack an umbrella.

Now, prima facie, the inferential role of an expression is constituted by its inferential relations to every other expression that
belongs to the same language. In consequence, according to IRS,
the individuation of whole languages is metaphysically prior to
the individuation of the expressions that belong to them. Likewise, whole conceptual systems are prior to the concepts by
which they are constituted. On reflection, one might well find
that odd. Surely it ought to be possible to distinguish 'chien'
from other words without first distinguishing French from other
languages? Prima facie, one identifies French with a (presumably
infinite) set of linguistic expressions, 'chien' included, that are in
turn individuated by reference to their phonology, syntax, and
semantics. The right direction of metaphysical analysis is thus from
' "chien" is a noun that is pronounced [she-an] and means *dog*' to
'French is the language that contains (*inter alia*) a word "chien"
that means *dog*'.[5] Even a linguist who is skeptical about whether
there really are such things as languages (as, in fact, many linguists are) can without inconsistency grant the claim that 'chien' is
a word.

So, arguably, positing senses would require some kind of IRS;
and IRS would require some kind of semantic holism; and semantic
holism would require a not-very-plausible account of the metaphysics of words and languages. By contrast it is plausible prima
facie that reference is atomistic; whether the expression 'a' refers
to the individual *a* is prima facie independent of the reference of
any other symbol to any other individual. Indeed, it's plausible
prima facie that 'a' might refer to *a* even if there are *no* other

---

[5] This claim is, to be sure, tendentious; some think that French can be identified
geopolitically. (e.g. as the language that was spoken in a certain spatiotemporal region
and/or by a certain population). We can then identify 'chien' as the word that means *dog* in
French. This proposal isn't, however, strikingly plausible; surely, the modal intuition is that
French might have been spoken at some other time or place. Or, for that matter, not at all.
For discussion see Devitt and Sterelney (1987); Cowie (1999).

symbols. The whole truth about a language might be that its only well-formed expression is 'John' and that 'John' refers to *John*. I do think that uncorrupted intuition supports this sort of view; the fact that 'John' refers to *John* doesn't *seem* to depend on, as it might be, such facts as that 'dog' refers to *dogs*.[6]

(iii) If, as I suppose, IRS is intrinsically inclined to holism, then it's an account of content that psychologists and philosophers of mind might particularly wish to avoid, since it's only insofar as the possession of any given concept is *in*sensitive to the possession of any other that concept possession can be reasonably stable over variations of persons and times. I guess Homer had the concept WATER, and I guess I have it too. But I have many concepts he didn't, and he had many concepts I don't. Likewise, although I've acquired many concepts since I was seven, I still have today many of the concepts I had back then; that would seem to be required if learning is to be cumulative.[7] We'll return to these and related issues when we discuss publicity. Suffice it for now that a holistic semantics makes problems about the individuation of the mental that an atomistic semantics might reasonably hope to avoid.

(iv) Consideration of the productivity and systematicity of languages (and minds)[8] strongly suggests that both the syntax and the

---

[6] The issue here is *not* Quine's worry about ontological relativity. Suppose the ontology of a language recognizes as individuals what we would take to be time slices of individuals. Still, it's not plausible that *this* symbol's referring to *this* time slice depends on *that* symbol's referring to *that* time slice. That's so even if, metaphysically speaking, there being any time slices depends on there being others.

[7] Perhaps you hold (as do many psychologists who believe in 'stages' of cognitive development) that the concepts children have are radically different from the concepts of adults, so that children can't think the same thought that we and grown up Hopi do. If so, so be it. But surely you want such claims to be *empirical*; you don't want to be forced to make them by a priori assumptions about the individuation of mental(/linguistic) representations. A referential semantic leaves such issues open, but IRS appears to shut the door. It's no accident that linguistic relativists just about always assume that the content of terms/concepts supervenes on their inferential roles.

[8] One can imagine a view according to which *only* thought is compositional in the first instance and the apparent productivity, systematicity, etc. of languages is parasitic on that of the thoughts they are used to express. In fact, I'm inclined to think that's the right view (see Fodor 2004); but the present discussion doesn't care one way or the other.

semantics of complex expressions(/thoughts) must be composed from the syntax and the semantics of their constituents.[9] It turns out to be surprisingly difficult to devise a version of IRS that meets this condition.[10] By contrast, the clearest available examples of semantic compositionality concern the relation between the reference of complex phrases and the reference of their constituent parts: 'brown cow' refers to *brown cows* because 'brown' refers to *brown* and 'cow' refers to *cows*. There are, to be sure, lots of problem cases in the way of actually constructing a compositional, referential semantics for any natural language; the best anybody has so far achieved is to manufacture fragments. Still, there is a recognizable research tradition there, and it has made recognizable progress. Nothing of the sort is true of IRS.[11]

I take the moral of all this to be as previously announced: It would be nice to have an analysis of Frege cases that is at least compatible with a referential semantics. But what are the chances of such an analysis? Philosophers in droves have held that Frege cases are convincing arguments that concepts have not just referents but also senses. Well, convincing they may be, but apodictic they are not. I do think Frege cases show that there must be something more to the individuation of concepts than what they refer to. But it doesn't follow that the relevant something more is the concept's sense or even that it is a parameter of the concept's content. That doesn't follow and I doubt that it's true.

End of digression, except for this caveat: As far as I know, *all* there is to support the standard construal of Frege cases is modal intuitions about, for example, whether someone could believe that the evening star is wet while not believing that the morning star is wet. Modal intuitions are fine things; they are not simply to

---

[9] For discussion see Fodor and Pylyshyn (1988). For a review see Aizawa (2003).

[10] For discussion see Fodor and Lepore (2002).

[11] I strongly suspect that problems with compositionality are intrinsic to IRS. The versions I've heard of (mostly variations on the idea that meanings are stereotypes) assume that having a concept(/understanding a word) is to be construed *epistemically*. But, epistemic properties are per se non-compositional. For discussion and some data see Conolly et al. (2007).

be ignored. But, since they are notoriously under pressure from such demands on theory as simplicity, coherence, explanatory power, and the rest, they are the sorts of things that can, in principle, be overridden from time to time; and it's not possible to determine a priori which times those are. It could turn out that the intuitions that generate Frege cases are simply *wrong*.[12] If so, so be it.

End of digression; we return to Frege's problem per se. I propose to try to convince you that it is a less general horror than has often been supposed; in particular, that absolutely untendentious cases where intuition reports that co-referring concepts fail to substitute are, actually, very thin on the ground. I think most of the standard examples are equivocal. My strategy will be to nibble away at them until all that's left is the question whether coextensive *basic* concepts substitute in PA contexts. Then I'll argue that if RTM and CTM are assumed, the Frege problem about basic concepts solves itself. (This is a fresh start; I've suggested other treatments in other publications, but nobody has found them awfully convincing, not even me. 'Clean cup, move down.')

3.3 First nibble: complex concepts

Very early in the *Treatise* (1739/1985) Hume notes a distinction that 'extends itself both to our impressions and ideas. This division is into simple and complex. Simple impressions and ideas are such as admit of no distinction nor separation. The complex... may be distinguished into parts' (p. 50). Hume saw that it is primarily issues about productivity that force this distinction: whereas our simple ideas can't outrun our experience,[13] 'many of our complex ideas never had impressions, that correspond to them... I can imagine to

---

[12] There is, to be sure, a kind of methodological Platonism according to which modal intuitions are, in effect, taken to be infallible. I think that's simply preposterous (and, to my knowledge, nobody has even tried to explain how it could be true).

[13] This ignores the infamous problem about the 'missing shade of blue'. Perhaps, qua empiricist, Hume should have worried about that more than he did; but we're not empiricists, so we don't need to.

myself such a city as the New Jerusalem ... tho I never saw any such' (p. 51). Hume wasn't, of course, a LOT theorist; he thought that typical mental representations are nondiscursive, perhaps something like images. But LOT needs a simple/complex distinction too, and for much the reasons that Hume alleged: The mind is productive and systematic because complex mental representations have simple representations as their (ultimate) parts, and because simple representations can be rearranged (by the 'imagination', Hume says) in indefinitely many ways. That line of argument still stands.[14]

So, how does the simple/complex distinction work if LOT is assumed? I'll be brief, since the relevant points are pretty familiar.

One of the respects in which Mentalese is supposed to be language-like is that its formulas exhibit constituent structure.[15] To a first approximation, the constituents of a discursive[16] representation are its semantically interpretable parts, and it is characteristic of discursive representations that not all of their parts need be semantically interpretable. Consider a complex expression like sentence (1) below. It's constituents consist of: the sentence itself, together with the lexical items[17] 'John', 'loves', and 'Mary' and the two phrases 'John$_{NP}$' and '(loves Mary$_{VP}$)'. By contrast, it has among its 'parts' non-constituents like (e.g.) 'John loves' and (assuming that 'parts' can be discontinuous) 'John ... Mary'. So,

---

[14] Connectionists have frequently tried to undermine it, but with vanishingly little success. For discussion see Fodor and Pylyshyn (1988).

[15] I shall assume that linguistic expressions (whether of English or of Mentalese) have their constituent structure intrinsically. According to this way of talking, there are no constituent-structure ambiguities in fully analyzed linguistic or mental representations. For example, it's not that there is an English sentence 'I shot an elephant in my pajamas' that is ambiguous between the parsing (I (in my pajamas)) (shot (an elephant)) and the parsing ((I) (shot (an elephant in my pajamas)). Rather, there are two English sentences that are identical in their morphophonology but differ in their constituent structures. If the topic is Mentalese, deciding to talk this way isn't gratuitious; it's required in order that mental processes shall have unique domains for their application. More on this sort of issue presently.

[16] I'll generally use 'discursive' as a short way of saying 'language-like', and 'iconic' as a short way of saying 'image-like'. For discussion see Ch. 6.

[17] Lexical items (roughly morphemes in the case of natural languages) and whole sentences are thus limiting cases of constituents according to this way of talking.

then, every constituent of a discursive representation is one of its parts, but not vice versa.

(1) John loves Mary.

I assume that all this holds for mental representations too. As usual, the arguments in the case of Mentalese run parallel to the arguments in the case of English.

We're about to see that this helps, in quite a straightforward way, in coping with Frege cases. Suppose, in the general spirit of compositional semantics, that each constituent of a complex expression contributes its semantic content to determining the semantic content of its hosts.[18] (If the semantics is assumed to be referential, then each constituent of a complex expression contributes its reference to determining the reference of the hosts.) So, in the case of (1), 'John' contributes (the individual) John, 'Mary' contributes Mary, 'loves' contributes the two place relation *x loves y*, and 'loves Mary$_{VP}$' contributes the property of loving Mary, which property the whole sentence says that John has. The question now suggests itself: Is there anything other than their referents that the constituents of complex discursive representations contribute to their hosts? Yes, clearly. In the linguistic cases, for example, each constituent contributes its pronunciation/orthography).[19] Sentence (1) is pronounced the way it is because 'John', 'loves', and 'Mary' are pronounced the way they are. Anything else? Here's a thought: One of the things that a constituent concept(/word) contributes to its hosts is its *possession conditions*.

Consider, for example, the concept BROWN COW. It's just truistic that a condition for having it is having the constituent concepts BROWN and COW; for, constituents are parts (see

---

[18] NB The kind of determining at issue is metaphysical not epistemological; the discussion is about what 'makes it the case' that a complex representation has the content it does, not how one figures out what the content of a complex expression is. I assume that people who insist on not distinguishing metaphysical issues from epistemological issues will have stopped reading some pages back.

[19] Not, of course, in the case of Mentalese, since its formulas have neither phonology nor an orthography.

above) and it's just truisitic that nobody has the whole of X unless he has all of the parts of X. OK so far, surely. Now consider the complex concept THE MORNING STAR, which is, philosophical astronomy assures us, coextensive with the concept THE EVENING STAR.[20] These two are, on the face of them, complex concepts, and they differ in their constituents, *and hence in their possession conditions*. So, in particular, you can have the first (but not the second) even if you lack the concept EVENING, and you can have the second (but not the first) even if you lack the concept MORNING. It follows that one can have the *belief* (or the hope, or the doubt, etc.) that the morning star is wet without having the belief (or the hope, or the doubt, etc.) that the evening star is wet. *Believing* (as everyone and his granny point out) is a lot like *saying*. Someone who hasn't got the word 'morning' can't speak of the morning star as such (not, anyhow, in English); and that is so even if he has got the word 'evening' and therefore can speak of the evening star as such. (Likewise, of course, the other way around.) Correspondingly nobody who lacks the concept of the evening star can believe that the evening star is wet; not even someone who has the concept THE MORNING STAR and is thus able to believe that the morning star is wet.[21] All that is so even though THE MORNING STAR and THE EVENING STAR are famously co-referential, so that the evening star's being wet and the morning star's being wet are the very same state of affairs.

The idea is that, at least some Frege cases trace back to the fact that complex expressions inherit their possession conditions from those of their syntactic constituents;[22] and that co-referring expressions may differ in their syntactic constituents. Well what's sauce for English is likewise sauce for Mentalese if LOT is

---

[20] Likewise, *mutatis mutandis*, the concepts WATER and H_2O.

[21] Please bear in mind that 'say' and 'believe' are both being read *de dicto*.

[22] Though not *solely* from their constituents; having MORNING and STAR is necessary for having MORNING STAR but it's not, of course, sufficient. You also have to know how to put them together.

assumed, since, according to LOT, mental representations have syntactic constituents too, and there's no obvious reason why co-referring but distinct mental representations shouldn't differ in their constituent structure, much like co-referring but distinct expressions of English. In short, somebody who holds to LOT can reasonably claim to have a syntactic solution to the Frege problem for the special case of *complex* concepts. Here (and often elsewhere), *syntax can do what senses were traditionally supposed to do*; that is, it can distinguish coextensive representations. And syntax costs a lot less than senses, metaphysically speaking, since postulating a syntactically structured LOT has independent justification *however* Frege cases turn; as we saw above, constituent structure is required to account for the systematicity/productivity of thought. It's also required by the only remotely plausible theory of mental *processes* (specifically of thinking) that anyone has so far devised; namely, that the causal role of a mental representation in mental processes is determined by its syntax.

A word about the second of these considerations, since it provides both a serious (though only partial) response to Frege's problem and a serious (though only empirical) argument for LOT.

One of the things that a theory of mental states really must do is connect straightforwardly with a corresponding theory of mental processes. I suppose it's common ground that the causes and effects of thinking about a thing depend on how the thing is conceptualized. (The causes and effects of thinking that Venus is wet depend on, as it might be, whether Venus is conceptualized as THE MORNING STAR or as THE EVENING STAR[23].) *Rhetorical Question*: How are we to understand the connection between the identity of a concept and its causal powers if concepts are (or have) senses? *Rhetorical answer*: I haven't a clue; there are, to my knowledge, *no* serious proposals for connecting the story about concepts being individuated by their senses to the story

---

[23] For purists: The expressions in caps are canonical descriptions of concepts, so that the concept MORNING is a proper part of the concept THE MORNING STAR.

about concepts having causal powers.[24] In practice, philosophers who assert either of the conjuncts almost invariably deny the other.[25]

It is, to put it very mildly, hard to see how mental processes could engage *senses*. By contrast, Turing showed us how mental processes might engage the syntax of discursive representations; that is, how they might be computational. So, if token mental representations are individuated by their constituent structures, it's just possible that we can understand (some of; see below) the processes by which mental states succeed one another in thought.[26] Perhaps we can even understand how they can exhibit *rational* succession if, as we may suppose, computational mental processes are generally truth-preserving.

That is the classical argument that leads from CTM to LOT. Supposing the mind to be conversant with senses can, maybe, provide for a theory of the intentionality of mental states; but it seems to shed no light at all on the nature of mental processes (i.e. of mental-state *transitions*).[27] By contrast, assuming that mental representations are individuated by (*inter alia*) their constituent structure serves to connect what we know about concepts with what we know about computation (and, by that route, with what we know about logic). This strikes me as a Very Good Idea. I think it should strike you as a Very Good Idea, too, even if you're a dualist and thus quite content with senses not belonging

---

[24]   SNARK. A rhetorical question isn't an argument. Shame on you.

   AUTHOR. It is when there is a unique candidate for the rhetorical answer. 'Inference to the best explanation', we call it. (Informally we call it 'What else?'.)

[25] Except that there's a way of reading associationism that makes association content-sensitive: take the content of a concept to be the set of associations it elicits. This makes sense of the idea that mental processes are causal, but the notion of content it provides is, of course, preposterous; DOG is not part of the content of CAT. The problem is to get mental processes to be causal *without* adopting a preposterous theory of mental content (see n. 27).

[26] I'm assuming that the sequence of mental states in thought is literally a sequence of causes and effects. It is the towering virtue of CTM that it allows one that assumption.

[27] So Frege, who thought that semantics requires the postulation of sense as well as reference, was vehement that senses aren't mental objects; and that theories about the individuation of concepts are unconnected to theories of mental processes.

to the 'natural realm' (whatever exactly that may mean). The worry about senses isn't really that we can't see how to square them with a materialistic view of thinking; the trouble isn't (*pace* Ryle) that 'ghostly gears' would have to go around; it's that it's unclear how to square them with *any* view of mental processes.[28] Even ghostly gears need ghostly teeth to grip with, I suppose. By contrast, holding LOT together with CRT offers to explain not just how rationality is *mechanically* possible but how it's possible at all.[29]

Returning to Frege problems per se, here's where we've got to so far. If concepts C and C′ differ in their constituent structure, then they can differ in their possession conditions. This is so even if they are co-referential. If C and C′ differ in their possession conditions, then it is possible for a mind to have one but not the other. If a mind has C but not C′, then it can be in a state of which C is a constituent even if it can't be in a state of which C′ is a constituent. So, attributions of the former state can be true of that mind even though attributions of the latter state are not. That, then, is why John can, without incoherence, and despite the familiar astronomical facts, believe in the wetness of the evening star while not believing in the wetness of the morning star. (Another way to· put this is that it doesn't matter whether the beliefs are different so long as the consequences of having the one differ from the consequences of having the other. Say, if you

---

[28] Generally speaking, theorists who have acknowledged a 'psychologically real' notion of sense and are worried about the nature of mental processes have taken the latter to be associative. The virtue of associative theories of thinking is that they don't require thoughts to have syntactic structure. But such theories can't be right, since association doesn't preserve either sense or reference (to say nothing of truth) and thinking typically preserves all three.

[29] The argument between exponents of connectionist and 'classical' cognitive architectures has turned, in very large part, upon this point. Connectionists agree with classicists that concepts are mental particulars and that they have causal powers. But connectionist architectures (including the relatively sophisticated kinds that acknowledge 'distributed' mental representations and/or 'vectors in semantic space') provide no counterpart to the relation between a complex concept and its constituents. So they have, just as Hume would have predicted, hopeless problems about productivity and systematicity. For much discussion see Fodor and McLaughlin (1990).

like, that there are two different beliefs that the evening star is wet. Or say if you like that there is only one such belief but it can be construed either *de re* or *de dicto*. Exactly what difference does it make which of these ways of talking we choose?[30]) By contrast, what really *is* important is that there is no corresponding issue about mental representations. M(the morning star)[31] must be different from M(the evening star) because their tokens differ in their causal powers.

I think that's reasonable as far as it goes; but it's not, of course, anything like a full solution to Frege's problem. Perhaps it explains why co-referential concepts with different constituent structures may fail to substitute in PA contexts, but it says nothing about why basic(/simple/primitive) concepts may fail to do so: By definition, basic concepts have no constituent structure; a fortiori, they can't differ in the constituent structures that they have. So, then, if our general account says that the possession condition for a concept is entirely determined by its content and its structure, it's unclear how, even in principle, co-referring basic concepts could have different possession conditions. We can (maybe) explain why John can believe ... *the morning star* ... without believing ... *the evening star* ..., but how is it that John can believe ... *Cicero* ... but not believe ... *Tully* ...?

3.4 Second nibble: basic concepts

To begin with, even the question which ones the basic concepts are is, putting it mildly, fraught. The empiricists mostly thought that they could be picked out on epistemological grounds: perhaps basic concepts are the ones that you can acquire from experience alone. But that won't do; there is no way of reading 'experience' (or,

---

[30] 'But Frege's problem *just is* which of these ways of talking we ought to choose.' So be it; but then remind me what turns on solving Frege's problem so long as nobody is confused and nobody scares the horses.

[31] Notation: I'll use formulas of the form 'M(X)' to abbreviate the Mentalese expression (or expressions) that corresponds to the English expression 'X'. So, M(John) is, by stipulation, John's name in Mentalese.

for that matter, 'acquiring'; or, for that matter, 'alone') on which it turns out to be true. I shall assume without discussion that, from the epistemological point of view, there is nothing especially interesting about basic concepts per se; they don't constitute a natural kind for the purposes of epistemological explanation.[32]

So, again, which concepts are basic?[33] How about proper names? That depends on whether proper names are to be construed as implicit descriptions. If they are, then supposing that examples of the Cicero/Tully kind are Frege cases would be tendentious. By definition, descriptions have constituents, so substitution of co-referring proper names can be blocked by differences in their 'underlying' constituent structure. Philosophers have been arguing about the semantics of proper names for a millennium or so, and there's no reason to suppose they'll stop soon. I'll assume that at least some proper names aren't descriptions, and that they do raise bona fide Frege problems. If that's wrong, so much the better, since it reduces the kinds of case I have to worry about.

Well then, what about monomorphemic general nouns like 'cow', 'table', or 'nose' (to say nothing about monomorphemic verbs like 'kill' or 'boil')? Are the concepts they express simple or complex? The answer to this question matters for a surprising number of issues in philosophy and psychology (including, notably, issues about how concepts are acquired, how they are applied in perception, and how inference works). But I propose not to worry about that just now. All I care about just now is the logic of the relation between Frege's problem and the problem about how to

---

[32] I could be wrong about that, of course. Much of the anglophone philosophical tradition is to the contrary. That is not, however, keeping me awake at night.

[33] One way to put this issue is: How closely do the distinctions between simple and complex expressions of (say) English preserve the distinctions among their translation in Mentalese? The traditional view, in both linguistics and philosophy, has been that they correspond very badly indeed. Because lots of English words were supposed to be definable, the 'surface' morphology of English was supposed to be *far* richer than the vocabulary of Mentalese. (I've actually heard it claimed that Mentalese has only about twelve verbs; every faith has its fanatics.) If that is so, then the lexicon of English is highly redundant; it contains a lot more items than its expressive power actually requires. I have very strong views on this issue. I think that God did not make the lexicon in vain. I won't discuss that here, but see Fodor and Lepore (1998).

choose basic concepts, and this remains moot if any concepts at all are basic, whichever they may be. So, choose any concept you like as the working example (except, of course, concepts whose expression in English is patently syntactically complex like BROWN COW).[34]

The preceding survey of candidates for basic concepthood is obviously incomplete; but it points towards the interesting possibility that Frege's problem may be considerably less general than has often been supposed. Perfectly clear cases of Frege's problem arise only where there is an identity statement that has monomorphemes on *both* sides of the '='; pairs of expressions that differ in constituent structure are *ipso facto* equivocal. So, for example, philosophers have been known to worry about how John can believe that water is wet and not believe that H_2O is wet, given that water is H_2O (given, indeed, that water is *necessarily* H_2O according to some metaphysical views). Perhaps, however, this and similar cases can be discharged along the lines just suggested. 'Water' has no constituents, but 'H_2O' has several. So, plausibly, their possession conditions are different: you can have the former, but not the latter, even if you lack the concept HYDROGEN (or, for that matter, the concept 2). And, of course, if their possession conditions are different, the concepts must be different too. This is a prime example of what I referred to as nibbling away at Frege's problem, a tactic that I shall continue to pursue.

But, nibble as one may, some concepts must be basic if any concepts are to be complex (and if no concepts are complex, all concepts must be basic). I'll assume that the most plausible candidates for basic concepts are ones that are expressed by monomorphemic names of individuals (hence, I suppose, CICERO and TULLY but not, perhaps, SUPERMAN); and I'll assume that

---

[34] As the previous note remarked, it's much in dispute whether there are more basic concepts than there are lexical primitives. But (unless 'brown cow' is an idiom, which it's not) it's safe to assume that BROWN and COW are constituents of BROWN COW, hence that the concept BROWN COW is complex. Likewise, *mutatis mutandis*, for whatever concepts are expressed by a syntactically complex, non-idiomatic *phrase* in English (or, of course, in any other natural language).

concepts expressed by monomorphemic names of kinds are basic too, including not just natural kinds (STAR, WATER, LEVER) but also everyday kinds of kinds like GRASS, and CARBUR-ETOR. Assuming all that is, of course, concessive. If there are no such examples, then there are quite possibly no clear cases of Frege problems and there is nothing for the rest of this chapter to be about.

So much for some preliminary clearing of the ground. The issue nibbles down to this: there are, by assumption, true formulas of the $N = N$ type where the Ns are monomorphemic, co-referential, and tokens of the same morpheme type ('Cicero = Cicero') and, also by assumption, there are formulas of the $N = N$ type where the Ns are monomorphemic and co-referential but tokens of different morphemic type ('Cicero = Tully'). It is with respect to the latter such cases (and conceivably only with respect to the latter such cases) that a clear Frege problem arises. Here, then, is where the nibbling has to stop. What is to be done? We turn to what is, from the referentialist's perspective, the heart of the matter.

3.5 The heart of the matter

QUESTION. What makes Frege cases problematic for referentialists?

ANSWER. They seem to show that the *identity* of a propositional attitude doesn't determine it's *causal
powers*. Thus, as referentialists count beliefs, there
is nothing to distinguish believing that F(Tully)
from believing that F(Cicero). It follows that the
causal consequences of believing F(Tully) can't,
in principle, be different from those of believing
F(Cicero). But there looks to be something wrong
with that, since, for example, believing that Cicero
was fat may lead to saying 'Cicero was fat' in
circumstances where believing that Tully was fat

does not. So there must be something wrong with the way that referentialists count beliefs. Which is, of course, just what Fregeans have been saying all along.

Well, if that's the problem, then here's a way that one might reasonably hope to wiggle out of it: Provide some independently motivated account of belief individuation that permits beliefs that are identical in content to be distinct beliefs; in particular, one that permits beliefs with the same content to differ in their causal powers. Frege's problem, that's to say, is problematic only if you work on the assumption that the *content* of a belief exhausts its contribution to the causal consequences of having it. Suppose, on the other hand, that the causal consequences of having one kind of belief-with-the-content-F(Cicero) can differ from the causal consequences of having some other kind of belief-with-the-content-F(Cicero). Then Frege cases cease to be problematic, and all us referentialists can take a well-deserved vacation.[35] My point will be that combining what RTM says about the nature of propositional attitudes with what CTM says about the nature of mental processes does in fact provide the required independent justification for distinguishing the identity of beliefs from the identity of belief contents.

According to RTM, each instance of believing that F(Cicero) is the tokening of a Mentalese formula; and CTM says that the causal powers of a Mentalese formula are sensitive to (not its content but) its syntax. Suppose that CTM is right to say this. Well then, even if F(Cicero) is the same belief content as F(Tully), it doesn't follow that the causal powers of tokens of the Mentalese

---

[35] Suppose someone thought that utterance types are individuated by their contents alone. Then it would seem that an utterance of 'John is a bachelor' must have the same causal powers as an utterance 'John is an unmarried man'. Nobody worries about that because everybody agrees that utterances are typed not just by what they mean but also by their form. You can generate the appearance of a Frege problem by pretending that the content of an utterance is its only type-individuating property. But who cares, since that assumption is patently false. I'm suggesting, in effect, that putative Frege cases of basic concepts might be dismissed in much the same way.

formula 'F(CICERO)' are the same as those of tokens of the Mentalese formula 'F(TULLY)'; it doesn't follow that the causal consequences of tokening one kind of belief-that-Cicero-is-tall must be the same as the causal consequences of tokening the other kind of belief-that-Cicero-is-tall. That being so, adding CTM to RTM shows us how instances of (what referentialists count as) the same belief can differ in their causal powers. Indeed, given CTM, one would predict that there might be such differences even if the Frege problems didn't exist.[36] If we didn't have Frege problems, we would have to invent them. No doubt, philosophers committed to absolute methodological apriority may take exception to this way of proceeding, since, in effect, the resolution of a philosophical problem is being made to turn on a batch of empirical assumptions. So be it; chastity isn't my favorite virtue.[37]

LOT says that propositional attitudes are relations between minds and mental representations that express the contents of the attitudes. The motto is something like: 'For Peter to believe that *lead sinks* is for him to have a Mentalese expression that means *lead sinks* in his "belief box"'. Now, propositional-attitude types can have as many tokens as you like. I can think *lead sinks* today, and I can think that very thought again tomorrow. LOT requires that tokens of a Mentalese expression that mean *lead sinks* are in my belief box both times. Notice, however, that though LOT requires the *semantic* equivalence of these tokens, it doesn't care whether they are tokens of the same Mentalese formula-type. If M1 and M2 are distinct but synonymous Mentalese expressions, it's OK with LOT that my thinking *lead sinks* today is constituted by my tokening M1 in my belief box and my thinking *lead sinks* tomorrow is constituted by my tokening M2 in my belief box. All

---

[36] There was, even in 1975, nothing particularly original about this sort of treatment of Frege problems; it goes back at least as far as Carnap (1956) and Sellars (1956). All *LOT 1* added was the suggestion that the Carnap/Sellars sort of proposal might be literally true; a possibility that Sellars, at least, seems to have viewed with loathing.

[37] If you're independently committed to postulating such and suches, you might as well get as much advantage as you can out of postulating such and suches. If you have a lemon, make lemonade.

LOT requires is that the two tokens express (as one says) the same proposition.[38]

But the situation changes with the adoption of a computational theory of mental processes (CTM). *CTM slices mental states thinner* than mere PA psychology does. That's because CTM distinguishes the causal powers of mental states *whenever* they are tokenings of type-distinct mental representations, *even if the semantic contents of the representations tokened are the same.*[39] Computations are operations defined over the *syntax* of mental representations; it is the syntax, rather than the content, of a mental state that determines its causal powers. To be sure, in the untendentious cases—the ones that *don't* raise Frege problems—token mental states share *both* their content *and* their syntax; whereas in Frege cases they share only the former. From CTM's perspective, the existence of Frege's problems shows *at most* that reference isn't sufficient for the individuation of concepts; something further is required. But Frege's problem *doesn't* show that the 'something' else is a parameter of content; for example, that it is something like a sense.

So far, so good, so it seems to me. We have on the table a theory that permits one to have either a token of CICERO = TULLY or a token of CICERO = CICERO in the belief box when one thinks the thought *Cicero = Tully* (i.e. when one thinks the proposition that Cicero = Cicero). All else equal, this explains how it's possible that although CICERO = CICERO and CICERO = TULLY express the same proposition, the necessity of the proposition expressed may be self-evident in the second case but not in the first. We can even say, if we're in the mood to, that the second belief is analytic; i.e. that its truth follows from

---

[38] Likewise, LOT leaves open that whereas all the occasions of your believing F(Cicero) are tokenings of M1, all the occasions of my believing F(Cicero) are tokenings of M2.

[39] The claim is, in effect, that its propositional content and its causal powers are orthogonal parameters of a mental representation; and the present treatment of the Frege cases won't work unless that claim is true. This means that 'inferential role' semanticists, who think that propositional content is somehow a construction out of causal powers, are prohibited from resolving the Frege problems in the way I propose to. Every night, as I slip between the sheets, I thank God for making me a conceptual atomist.

its linguistics. You may think that it's odd for a self-proclaimed referential semanticist to say that some or other representation is analytic; but it's not. There are plenty of analyticities that referential semantics can perfectly well acknowledge without a blush, so long as analyticity is taken to be a property of (e.g. Mentalese) formulas rather than of the propositions they express; CICERO = CICERO is among them, likewise BROWN COWS ARE BROWN.[40]

SNARK [*in a snit*]. You've forgotten Paderewski; deep shame on you. PADEREWSKI IS PADEREWSKI is of the form a = a (likewise 'Paderewski = Paderewski'); so, by your reckoning, it should be analytic as well as necessary. But, it is possible for John to wonder whether Paderewski the pianist was Paderewski the politican. (*How could one man have done so much*, John wonders?) Surely, a story that takes CICERO = CICERO to be indubitable-because-analytic ought also to take 'Paderewski is Paderewski' to be indubitable-because-analytic. But 'Paderewski is Paderewski' *isn't* indubitable, so presumably it's *not* analytic. So there must be something wrong with the referentialist thesis that Paderewski is the semantic value of PADEREWSKI (or of 'Paderewski').

AUTHOR. God forbid I should forget Paderewski. I am going to tell you a story that copes with him in a way that I think is true, convincing, and fully compatible with—indeed, patently dependent on—RTM/CTM.

SNARK. I doubt that I shall think any of those things.

AUTHOR. So do I.

---

[40] 'But my intuitions *insist* that "analytic"/"synthetic" is a distinction of *content*, not of form.' So much the worse for your intuitions. You should have them seen to.

I commence with a recap: The problem is that we're assuming that John is a rational chap and does not, in typical cases, go about wondering whether obviously analytic truths are obviously analytic and true. Yet John *does* wonder whether Paderewski = Paderewski, and that *is* to doubt what is, on the face of it, analytically true. So, it appears we can't, after all, say both that 'Paderewski' is a pure referring expression and that John is a rational chap. One of the two must go. Let's, for the sake of the argument, suppose that John's rationality is stipulated. Then what's left is that 'Paderewski' isn't a pure referring expression; it must contribute something more (or other) than its referent to its host expressions. What more (or other) could that be? The traditional suggestion is that it contributes its meaning, or its sense; something like that.[41] If so, the claim that the content of 'Paderewski' is its referent fails. So, a fortiori, referentialism fails, which would not please me.

Here's a (slightly) different way to put the case: If reference is content, then if John believes both that Paderewski was a pianist and that Paderewski was a politican, he ought to be prepared to infer that Paderewski was both a politician and a pianist.[42] But he doesn't. Indeed, he explicitly denies this inference. Our problem is to explain how, on referentialist assumptions, this could be true.

Well, that's not so hard if RTM is among our background assumptions. The idea would be that there are two Mentalese names corresponding to the English 'Paderewski'; call them $PADEREWSKI_1$ and '$PADEREWSKI_2$'[43]. Accordingly, the belief that John uses the form of words 'By God, Paderewski was

[41] If sense determines reference, then a term that delivers its sense to its hosts *thereby* delivers its referent to its hosts. If sense doesn't determine reference, then either reference isn't properly a semantic parameter, or if it is, there's more than one kind of semantic parameter. I won't consider these options because, for reasons the text will now discuss, I don't think that Paderewski cases force us to choose between them.

[42] Likewise, since it's untendentious that Lois Lane believes that Superman flies and that Clark Kent walks, why doesn't she infer that Clark Kent flies and Superman walks? And so on through the litany of familiar examples.

[43] Allowing that Mentalese 'Paderewski's have subscripts (and are hence *syntactically* complex symbols) is, by the way, perfectly compatible with supposing that they are *semantic* primitives. In fact, 'full' English proper names ('John Smith') are themselves plausibly construed as complex syntactically but not semantically.

Paderewski' to express when the light finally dawns is that *Paderewski₁ was Paderewski₂*; and that, of course, *isn't* analytic even if it is a logical truth (i.e. even if both names rigidly designate Paderewski). Well, since it isn't analytic, then even a rational chap like John may be surprised to hear of it. I think that what the Paderewski case shows is only that Paderewski, like Cicero, must have two, formally distinct, names in whatever language you think in (from which, by the way, it follows that you don't think in (surface) English; Paderewski has only one name in (surface) English, namely 'Paderewski').[44] Because he thinks in Mentalese, not English, John can't think the thought that Paderewski is tall. That's just as well because, arguably, there is no such thought; all there are is the thoughts *Paderewski₁ is tall* and *Paderewski₂ is tall*.

But perhaps you insist that John must be saying *something* when he says (in English) 'Paderewski is tall'? So be it; but then you put John in the peculiar position of being able to say something that he can't think. Since I prefer not to be burdened with any such paradox, I suppose I'm required to say that, strictly speaking, English doesn't have a semantics; a fortiori English words don't have referents and *mutatis mutandis* English sentences don't express propositions or have truth-conditions. What does have a semantics is Mentalese, in which, by assumption, Paderewski has two names and PADEREWSKI IS PADEREWSKI is ill-formed. (For some further reasons why one might hold this arguably Quixotic view see Fodor 2004.) Accordingly, John can't think *Paderewski is tall* without choosing between PADEREWSKI₁ and PADEREWSKI₂; no more than he can think *Marx was tall* without choosing between Karl and Groucho; no more than he can think *everybody loves somebody* without choosing between the scopes of the quantifiers. That there are ambiguities in English is, indeed, the classic reason for claiming that we don't think in English. But that's

---

[44]   SNARK. But this claim is revisionist, and everybody knows that natural language is 'all right as it stands'.

AUTHOR. In fact, it's not all right as it stands, and one of the ways in which it's not is that different lexical items may both be proper names of the same guy.

all fine: by the present referentialist lights, since PADEREWSKI$_1$ and PADEREWSKI$_2$ are co-referential, PADEREWSKI$_1$ WAS TALL and PADEREWSKI$_2$ WAS TALL (unlike GROUCHO MARX WAS TALL and KARL MARX WAS TALL) have the same content.

SNARK. Maybe so, but I don't really see how the sort of thing you're suggesting could even *purport* to be a solution of Frege cases?

AUTHOR. No?

SNARK. No! For, as I read it, Frege's problem is how the very same proposition can be the object of different thoughts. Well, suppose *F(Paderewski$_1$)* and *F(Paderewski$_2$)* are the same proposition; then the question remains unanswered 'How could the belief that *F(Paderewski$_1$)* fail to be the belief that *F(Paderewski$_2$)*?'. Alternatively, suppose that *F(Paderewski$_1$)* and *F(Paderewski$_2$)* are different propositions. Then the question remains unanswered 'How could the belief that *F(Paderewski$_1$)* and the belief that *F(Paderewski$_2$)* fail to be different beliefs? This would appear to be a dilemma; if so, please pick a horn.[45]

AUTHOR. Neither of the above. You're forgetting that 'the belief that ...' is ambiguous; it can be read either as transparent or as opaque at the ' ... ' position. Read it the first way, then 'the belief that F(Paderewski$_1$)' *is* 'the belief that F(Paderewski$_2$)'; read the second way, it's not. There is, of course, no fact of the matter about which is 'the right' way of reading it; that depends on the task at hand. By and large, however, psychologists are likely to have the second in mind, epistemologists the first.

---

[45] I'm indebted to an anonymous reader (probably Brian Maclaughlin) for this way of putting the issue. Here and elsewhere his comments on my MS were invariably helpful.

In passing: the present line of thought suggests that assessments of rationality are themselves sensitive to the syntactic form of (e.g. mental) representations, not just to their content. It is, I suppose, mad to doubt the truth of 'PADEREWSKI$_1$ is PADEREWSKI$_1$'. But there is nothing mad about the thought that PADEREWSKI$_1$ isn't PADEREWSKI$_2$; not even on the assumption that the terms are, in fact, co-referential. I think that this is perfectly intuitive. It's mad to deny Q if you accept P $\rightarrow$ Q and P; unless, however, the argument is couched in a way that makes the premises too long, or otherwise too complicated, to grasp. What's rational depends (*inter alia*) on what's perspicuous; and what's perspicuous depends (*inter alia*) on both content and form. In the good old days they taught logic and rhetoric together. They were right to do so.

As far as I can see, then, once it's conceded that Mentalese must be distinct from surface English, the dialectical situation is as follows:

There is no Frege problem for concepts that are expressed by complex Mentalese formulas (i.e. Mentalese formulas that have constituent structure). Since complex concepts can differ in their constituency, they can differ in their possession conditions.[46] That is so whether or not the concepts are coextensive; or even *necessarily* coextensive. If there is a Frege problem, it must be about how to draw the type/token relation for (syntactically) *primitive* concepts. But if there is a Frege problem about primitive concepts, then it is resolved by appeal to their form, not by reference to their content.

Some Snarkish questions and objections (not necessarily in order of their importance) before we proceed.

> SNARK. That's not what I call philosophy. That's what I call
> an empirical speculation. Real philosophy assumes
> only what is a priori. It is, in my view, *not* a priori

---

[46] And, of course, in lots of other ways too. Suppose (what's far from obvious: see Ch. 5) that there is such a process as concept acquisition. Then, since PADEREWSKI$_1$ and PADEREWSKI$_2$ are different concepts, their acquisition may perfectly well have different ontogenetic courses.

that there are two, formally distinct, Mentalese counterparts of the English word 'Paderewski'.[47]

AUTHOR. OK, so I'll settle for its just being true. Come to think of it, all I really care about is whether it *might* be true since, if it might, then it's at least possible that we can reconcile our intuitions about John with the sort of referential semantics that I would otherwise wish to endorse. By contrast, a lot of the cognitive-science community (many philosophers included) think that Frege arguments show, knockdown, that a referential semantics isn't an option for LOT (or for English either).

By the way, who cares what gets *called* philosophy? It's my impression that most of what happened in philosophy before 1950 wouldn't qualify according to the present usage.

SNARK. Isn't the proposal ad hoc? I mean, is there any *other* reason for insisting on Paderewski having two names in thought? I mean, is there any reason other than one's deep desire to make (the Paderewski version of) the Frege problem go away?'

AUTHOR. Sure, lots. LOT is supposed to be an explanatory hypothesis about how minds represent things. (At least that's what I suppose it to be.) And theories

---

[47] Snark isn't the only one who is offended. In the course of Kripke's discussion of the London/*Londres* puzzle about Pierre (1979) he offers a methodological comment that strikes me as thoroughly ill-considered. Having noted that one way out of the conundrum would be to say that Pierre believes that the city he calls '*Londres*' is pretty, but that the city he calls 'London' is not (a suggestion that's recognizably in the spirit of subscripting 'Paderewski'), Kripke goes on to remark that 'no doubt other straightforward descriptions are possible. No doubt some of these are, in a certain sense, *complete* [*sic*] descriptions of the situation ... But none of this answers the original question. Does Pierre or does he not, believe that London is pretty?' (p. 259). But why on earth should we suppose that the question *has* a definite right answer when it's phrased that way? And, once one sees *why* it doesn't, *why does it matter* that it doesn't? ('Yes or no: Is the Pope a bachelor or is he not?' 'Well ... '.) It appears that Kripke reads 'Does Pierre, or does he not, believe that London is pretty?' as a short-answer question; but what warrants this fixation on the bottom line? Given a defensible account of the situation that Pierre is in, the usual rule applies: 'Say whatever you like so long as you're not confused and you don't frighten the horses'.

about how minds represent things ought to be sensitive to data about which inferences one does (or doesn't) accept. Plausibly, there has to be something that explains why John isn't prepared to infer from his thoughts that *Paderewski was a politician* and that *Paderewski was a pianist* that someone was both a politician and a pianist.[48] I can't think of anything compatible with CTM that will do so that isn't itself equivalent to the idea that Paderewski has two names in Mentalese. If you can, please do call me collect at your earliest convenience.

SNARK. Remind me why the two Mentalese names of Paderewski have to be *formally* distinct. Why isn't it good enough to say that John supposes (wrongly) that 'Paderewski' is referentially ambiguous?

AUTHOR. I repeat: It's because CTM says that only *formal* differences among Mentalese expressions can affect mental processes. That means that computations, in the intended senses of that term, can 'see' only the formal properties of the representations in their domains. There's a lot to be said for cognitive science co-opting for this 'classical', Turing-style understanding of computation; but it doesn't get to do so for free. (For more on this see Ch. 4.) I very much like the idea—which, after all, many philosophers have endorsed ever since Aristotle—that surface sentences aren't, in general, explicit about

---

[48] Declining to infer a phrasal conjunction from the corresponding sentential conjunction often indicates a referential ambiguity at some level of representation. You can't conjunction reduce 'Paderewski ran and Paderewski swam' if there are two Paderewskis in the premise. Likewise, before John cottons on, he will be unwilling to take 'Paderewski shaved himself' as a paraphrase of 'Paderewski shaved Paderewski'. If, as is generally assumed, reflexivization is a formal operation, then there must be two 'Paderewski's to block its application here. (For elaboration see Fodor 1994: ch. 3.)

   This sort of point turns up in all sorts of places. I suppose that John, who thinks there are two Paderewski's, can think to himself: *Paderewski was a pianist and Paderewski wasn't a pianist.* How does he do that if he doesn't have two names for Paderewski?

their logical form, hence that they don't provide a formal domain for inferential processes.[49] CTM is in large part about the psychology of our inferential processes. So, CTM requires a way of drawing the distinction between surface English and Mentalese that makes the latter perspicuous in ways that the former is not. It seems to me that this is just the way that our theories of mental processes ought to shape our theories of mental representation and vice versa. If it turns out that 'classical' assumptions about the architecture of cognitive processes solve Frege's problem as a by-product, that's a *very* strong reason to suppose that the classical assumptions must be true.

SNARK. The most you've shown is that LOT isn't *surface* English. If, as many linguists think, 'LF' is a level of the grammatical description of natural languages, then perhaps there's a sense in which we do think in English after all.

AUTHOR. True. So, a lot that's interesting turns on whether LF is a level of description of natural languages rather than a level of description of thoughts. But, fortunately, solving the Frege problem doesn't.[50]

SNARK. I do believe I have uncovered a dilemma: What, according to you, does the difference between tokens of 'PADEREWSKI$_1$' and 'PADEREWSKI$_2$' actually consist in? They can't really differ in

---

[49] It's often said that English sentences only *have* logical form 'under regimentation'. I have no idea what that means. If a sentence doesn't have a logical form before it's been regimented, how could that *very same* sentence have a logical form thereafter?

[50] I think that LF is a level of description not of English, but of Mentalese (though practically nobody agrees with me except, perhaps, my erstwhile Rutgers colleague Steven Neal). If that's right, then LF can't be identified as (for example) a level of English grammar at which 'Padwereski = Padwerski' is represented as an instance of the logical truth $a = a$ (or, *mutatis mutandis*, at which 'John killed Mary' is represented as a token of the type 'John caused (Mary die))'. Quite possibly there isn't any such level of English grammar.

their subscripts, since you tell us that they are both *primitive* expressions of Mentalese, whereas 'PADEREWSKI$_1$'; 'PADEREWSKI$_2$', are both complex; both consist of a PADEREWSKI followed by a subscript. And they can't differ in their orthography (or phonology) because Mentalese isn't the sort of language that can be spelled (or pronounced). So, then, what *does* make a certain brain event (or whatever) a 'PADEREWSKI$_1$' token rather than a 'PADEREWSKI$_2$' token?[51]

AUTHOR.   I don't care. Type distinctions between tokens of primitive mental representations can be distinguished by *anything at all*, so long as the difference between them is of a kind to which mental processes are responsive. Since, by definition, basic representations don't have structures, type identities and differences among primitive Mentalese tokens are bedrock from the computational point of view. Tokens of primitive Mentalese formulas are of different types when they differ in the (presumably physical) properties to which mental processes are sensitive. Perhaps it's how long it lasts that determines whether a brain event is a tokening of 'PADEREWSKI$_1$' rather than of 'PADEREWSKI$_2$'. (I doubt that it is; but given the utter lack of a neuroscience of Mentalese, that guess seems about as good as any.)[52]

Sort of analogously, it's a familiar point that you can't distinguish the types of letter tokens in

---

[51] I assume, for the sake of the argument, that tokenings of Mentalese formulas are brain events. But it wouldn't matter, for present purposes, if dualists are right and minds are made of something *sui generis*.

[52] I've heard it offered, as an argument against LOT, that no one so far has ever seen a neural token of an expression in Mentalese. But given that we have no idea how Mentalese (or anything much else) is implemented in the brain, how would one know if one did?

the way that you distinguish the types of word tokens; namely, by their constituent structure. We distinguish 'dog' tokens from 'cat' tokens by their spelling, but we don't distinguish 'a' tokens from 'b' tokens that way, since 'a'and 'b' don't, of course, *have* spellings. What they have is *shapes;* and their shapes are different in ways to which our visual system is responsive; if they weren't, we wouldn't be able to read. Likewise *mutatis mutandis* for the way that minds draw type distinctions between tokens of basic mental representations.

All that being so, there's a certain kind of mistake that a mind that computes in Mentalese can't make: It can't systematically mistake the type/token relation for a primitive expression of Mentalese.[53] There can be the odd mechanical failure, of course; but what mental processes can't be is mistaken *across the board* about what type a basic Mentalese token belongs to. *That* kind of mistake is possible only in a *public* language. So, for example, I might get things confused and assign tokens of the (English) expression 'big' to the word type 'pig'. This would be wrong of me because 'big' tokens are typed by their spelling (*inter alia*), and how they're spelled is fixed by the conventions of English. The possibility thus arises of a mismatch between the way I type English tokens and the way that the rest of the language community does; and, since there are more of them than there are of me, it's my mistake, not theirs. But that sort of thing can't happen with basic concepts in a private language like Mentalese. If my cognitive mechanisms systematically identify tokens

---

[53] 'Systematic' is doing all the work here. It means something like 'including counterfactual cases'.

of a certain kind of brain event as tokens of a certain primitive concept type, then they *are* tokens of that primitive concept type. There is, to repeat, nothing that would count as *systematic* mistranscription in such a case. Wittgenstein saw this sort of point, but, for some reason or other, he found it upsetting. I wonder why.[54]

SNARK. Everybody has to sleep with his own conscience. I do not wish to sleep with yours. In fact, I find what you've been saying not satisfactory; it lacks, one might say, nutritional value. I mean: it may be that, with a sufficient lot of judicious nibbling, you can make a case that Frege's sorts of examples aren't really knockdown arguments that semantics has to recognize senses as well as references. But, like, let's face it, Frege has a pretty plausible story about what the Frege examples are examples of; namely, that substitution in opaque contexts depends on identity of *senses* rather than identities of *referents*. Whereas, the very most you can claim to have is a batch of tricks, all more or less ad hoc, for staving them off piecemeal. What you need, and what you don't have, is a plausible story about what the Frege cases have in common—where the Frege intuitions

---

[54] Rush Rhees, in a rather oracular paper about why there can't be a private language (1963), subscribed to this line of thought: 'If one spoke of the independent existence of a tree, this might mean partly that I could think there was no tree there and be wrong. But the meanings of words are not quite comparable with that. Since you have learned the meanings of the expressions you use, it may happen that you do not mean what you say ... You can describe [this sort of mistake] only by taking into account the speaker's relation to other people. There must be something more like an organization, in which different people are, as we may put it, playing different roles ... That belongs to the use of language. Without it there would not be words and there would not be meaning'. Perhaps that's true of English, but none of it transfers to Mentalese (not, anyhow, without further argument). Mentalese isn't learned and we don't use it to communicate. No doubt Rhees thinks it's somehow a conceptual truth that a language is *essentially* a vehicle of communication, essentially learned, and essentially public. But no reason for thinking that is offered and I doubt that there is any.

spring from, as it were—if it's not that they exhibit various ways in which semantics requires a richer notion of content than referentialism has on offer.

AUTHOR. Fair enough, I guess; so here's a sketch of such a story. In effect, it's an account of why there are Frege cases; but it's one that doesn't depend on supposing that there are senses. None of it is particularly surprising or even particularly new, but maybe that's a virtue in such troubled times.

The received view is something like this: The sentence 'Lois thinks Clark has a drinking problem (= L1)' is ambiguous. What shows that it is, is the strong intuition that the hypothetical 'if L1 & if Clark is Superman, then Lois believes Superman has a drinking problem (= L2)' is valid on one reading of the antecedent but not on the other. There are, to be sure, various proposals for squaring this intuition with a referential semantics (including, notably, Frege's own suggestion that the referent of a term in an opaque context is systematically different from the referent of the same term when it occurs in a transparent context). But, deep down, everybody knows that none of the standard suggestions is very persuasive. The fact is, so it seems to me, that if L1 really is ambiguous with respect to its truth-conditions, that's a pretty good reason to doubt that a purely referential semantics is tenable.

SNARK. So you give up?

AUTHOR. So L1 isn't ambiguous with respect to its truth-conditions. If LL1 is true, and Clark is identical to Superman, then Lois believes that Superman has a drinking problem. End of story.

SNARK. You're not seriously proposing to just stop there?

AUTHOR. Why exactly should I not?

SNARK. [*aside*]. Thank God Granny isn't here; I do believe this would break her heart. [*Aloud*] What about the aforesaid strong intuition that L2 is valid on one reading but not on the other?

AUTHOR. Intuitions are made to be flouted. I flout three or four before breakfast every morning, just to keep in practice.

SNARK. [*with a show of methodological indignation*]. Intuitions are *not* made to be flouted. What is perhaps allowed (from time to time; but only infrequently; and with great discretion; and with a due sense of the solemnity of the occasion) is to explain them away. If you think that L2 is valid, sheer decency requires that you tell some story or other about why everybody else thinks that it isn't.

AUTHOR. Oh, very well. Here's a thing that a committed referentialist might claim is running the Frege intuitions, consonant with his holding out for the validity of L2. I think it's a not unattractive story since, though it denies that the standard intuitions are responsive to the *semantics* of PA attributions, it does allow that they reveal some important truths.

There are at least two quite different sorts of consideration that might account for one's being interested in what somebody says or thinks. (Perhaps, indeed, the reason intuitions about the truth-values of PA attributions are so sensitive to context is that they respond to an unsystematic mix of the two concerns.) One might be interested in what what someone says(/thinks) tells you about the world; or one might be interested in what what someone says(/thinks) tells you about the speaker(/thinker). Both sorts of case are thoroughly familiar. Smith says 'It's raining again' and, all else equal, that's a pretty good reason for you to think that it is, indeed, raining again. For, why should Smith say that it is unless he believes that it is? And what's a more likely cause of his believing that it is raining again than that it is raining again? There are various ways of thinking about how, exactly, testimony can ground rational beliefs; but *that* it often does is surely epistemological common ground. Because the things people say(/think) are responsive to how things are in the world, we can justifiably infer how things are in the world from what people say(/think).

SNARK. [*yawns*].

AUTHOR. OK, but I'm not finished. A quite different kind of reason that you might be interested in what someone says is that you want to know what psychological state he's in. What he believes, of course; but also, often enough, whether he's pleased or bored or sincere, or duplicitous or angry, or out of his mind, or whatever. For these purposes, what is said may be less informative than how what is said is said.[55]

SNARK. [*yawns again*].

AUTHOR. I'm still not finished. My point is that when you want to make inferences from what is said to how the world is, a *referential* semantics will generally be exactly what you need. If John says it's raining again in the biggest city in Minnesota; then you can justifiably infer that it's raining in the biggest city in Minnesota. What's more, if you happen to know that the referent of 'the biggest city in Minnesota' is Minneapolis, then you can justifiably infer, given what John said, that it is raining again in

---

[55] 'Mightn't one also be interested in the *truth* of what John said?' Sure; but it comports with referentialism to hold that an interest in the truth of a saying is just an interest in the satisfaction of its truth-conditions.

Minneapolis. Indeed, it may be that you can infer that even if John himself can't because he *doesn't* know that 'the biggest city in Minnesota' refers to Minneapolis. Likewise in cases about Lois, Clark, and Superman; the morning star and the evening star; and so forth. [Author *yawns*.]

By contrast, if you're interested in what John says because you want to know how things are (psychologically speaking) with John, what the words he uses refer to *isn't* primarily what you want to know about.

SNARK. I'll bite: What is it that you primarily want to know about what John says if you want to infer from what he says to how things are (psychologically speaking) with John? If it isn't the kind of thing that a referential semantics tells you about, what kind of thing is it?

AUTHOR. You mean, assuming RTM?

SNARK. Oh, very well; assuming RTM.

AUTHOR. Then, roughly, it's *how John represents things*; in particular, what mental representation prompted his utterance. (Of course, that's likely to be what you want to know if you're interested in how things are with John *cognitively*. You might, however, want to know *how John felt* about its raining again in Minneapolis (bored, angry, indifferent, distraught, outraged, whatever). In that case, it might well matter that he referred to Minneapolis as 'that bloody wet city' rather than as 'Minneapolis' or as 'the largest city in Minnesota'.) In short, when you are interested in how things are with John psychologically, you quite likely want to know not, or not just, what he referred to when he said what he did, but what mental representation of things prompted his saying it.

Sum and substance: all you need for inferring from John's utterance to the world is the sort of thing that a semantics (i.e. *referential* semantics) provides. But if you want to infer from John's utterance to (e.g.) his state of mind, or to his subsequent behavior, you need something rather like his mode of representation of whatever it is that he is talking about; which is to say, you need something that can slice things thinner than reference does.

Lois rather fancies Superman but Clark leaves her cold. Your referential semantics can't, all by itself, make sense of that. You also need to know that Lois has two, co-referential representations of Clark Kent(/Superman), and that each representation is connected with its own, distinct, set of inferences and attitudes. And, if you want to predict Lois's behavior, predilections, inferences, etc. from the mental state that she is in you have to know which of these representations is activated. So be it; why, after all, should semantics per se have to make sense of all that *all by itself?*

SNARK.   Then you do have a two-factor theory of content after all. I knew it, I knew it, I knew it. Stand still while I bite you.

AUTHOR.   Not in the least. I don't think that the beliefs, feelings, etc. that cluster around a mode of presentation of a concept have anything to do with the content[56]

---

[56]   SNARK. I knew you'd have to cheat sooner or later. Haven't you now implicitly given up claiming that psychological laws are intentional? Didn't you say in the Introduction that (I quote) 'relations among the *contents* of mental states are in play in typical propositional attitude explanations [emphasis Snark's]'?

AUTHOR. I did indeed; but there's room to wiggle between signing on for psychological laws expressing the content of mental states and signing on for mental representations having senses. If an intentional explanation is one that appeals to laws that subsume mental representations in virtue of their senses, then I am indeed committed to saying that there are no such things; after all,

of the concept. But then, on *any* reasonable story, you don't predict behavior (just) from the content of concepts (i.e. from their semantics; i.e. from what composes). You predict behavior from the galaxy of beliefs, desires, hopes, despairs, whatever, in which the concepts are engaged. *EVERYBODY* agrees with that, referentialists very much included. The question at issue is which, if any, of the beliefs, desires, etc. in which a concept is engaged is constitutive of its identity. Referentialists say: 'None of them; all that matters is the extension'. People who aren't referentialists must draw this distinction some other way. But everybody has to draw it (excepting content holists, which nobody ought to be on account of their being beyond the pale).

So, the long and short is that you can see why someone might come to think that concepts have both referents and senses. Thinking that, though erroneous, would be responsive to something real; namely, that concepts have both referents and a congeries of beliefs (etc.) in which they are embedded. It's just that, whereas the former has to do with the content of the concept, the latter has to do with its (e.g. inferential) role in mental

---

a main point of CTM is to define mental processes over syntactic properties of mental representations, thereby avoiding a psychology that's committed to meanings; with respect to senses, CTM is a program of *eliminative* reduction. On the other hand, if what you mean by an intentional law is one that cuts things finer than reference does (for example, by distinguishing Clark Kent thoughts from Superman thoughts), then psychological laws are characteristically intentional after all. It's OK with me whichever way you talk. In the long run, computational psychology is a sort of trick that Turing invented to make it seem that there are senses and that they cause things (even though, strictly speaking, there aren't and (therefore) they don't). The rule of thumb: If there's something that it seems that you need senses to do, either do it with syntax or don't do it at all. (*LOT 1* goes on about this at length.)

processes. The distinction between these is independently motivated; *content is what composes*, and
inferential roles and the like do not.

It is a very bad idea to confuse psychology
with semantics: psychology is about what goes on
in heads. Semantics is about constitutive relations
between representations and the world (between
representations and what they represent). *THERE
IS, AS A MATTER OF PRINCIPLE, NO SUCH
THING AS A PSYCHOLOGICAL THEORY OF
MEANING* (just as there is, as a matter of principle, no such thing as an epistemological theory of
meaning; and for reasons that are not dissimilar).[57]

SNARK. I suppose you think that the inferential roles that
thoughts have (unlike their semantic contents) are
more or less idiosyncratic to each thinker? That, for
example, whether John packs an umbrella when he
goes to Minneapolis depends (in the case imagined)
on whether he knows that it's the biggest city in
Minnesota?

AUTHOR. Precisely so.

SNARK. But then: *WHAT ABOUT PUBLICITY?* In particular, what about the publicity of primitive concepts?

AUTHOR. So? What about it? Two people have the same
primitive concept iff they have coextensive primitive concepts. Cf. me, Aristotle, and WATER.

---

[57] I remark, in passing, that the story I've just been telling about how PA attributions work
fits rather comfortably with one I've told elsewhere about how a theory of language should
understand phenomena like 'deference' to 'experts'; namely, that they belong neither to
semantics nor to (cognitive) psychology, but to the pragmatics of linguistic communication
(see Fodor 1994). One of the reasons it pays to be a speaker of (as it might be) English is
that you are thereby enabled to use other members of the English-speaking community as
instruments of observation. If you want to know whether that's an elm tree or a birch tree,
hire an English-speaking botanist, point him at the tree, and take note of which he says:
'birch' or 'elm'; chances are he'll say 'elm' iff it's an elm and 'birch' iff it's a birch. If he
fails in either of these respects, demand your money back. (Another reason it pays to be a
speaker of English is, of course, that you get to read Shakespeare in the original.)

SNARK. Ah, but how can primitive concepts themselves be public? How can your concept WATER be the same one as Aristotle's concept WATER?

AUTHOR. Good question; therefore let us turn to:

3.6 Publicity

CTM relies on the empirical assumption of a certain stability in whatever language a mind thinks in. Tokens of the same concept type must be recognizable as such by whatever computations are defined over them. And tokens of different concept types must also be recognizable as such *even if the concepts are coextensive.* If the concept is complex, it is identifiable by its lexical inventory and its (constituent) structure. If the concept is primitive, it is identifiable by some or other (possibly neurological) property to which mental processes are sensitive. I think that's all a referentialist requires in order to explain why it seemed so clear to Frege that a thinker can believe Fa and not believe Fb even though a = b. (And why so many other philosophers followed after Frege to the same dead end.) *But what becomes of the identity conditions for concepts when more than one mind is involved?*

In particular, what becomes of the identity conditions for *primitive* concepts when more than one mind is involved? Perhaps it belongs to the architecture of my mind that all my tokens of a given basic concept are tokens of the same (e.g.) neurological property (I suppose minds generally don't change brains in midstream). But it surely can't be taken for granted that a certain basic concept is realized by the very same neurological property in *different* minds. What about Martians? Or infants? Or dogs and cats? Or, for all I know, you and me?

In short, it seems entirely likely that distinct minds should turn out to *be more similar under PA description than they are under neurological description.* Indeed, the more broadly a propositional-attitude psychology applies across different kinds of creatures, the *less* the likelihood that it is implemented in the same way in all the creatures it applies to. That won't much worry anyone who thinks that the domain of a PA psychology is likely to be very narrow; for example, that it could apply only to fluent speakers of the same public language.[58] But the transcendental arguments that are supposed to show that never were plausible and they are growing less so as they age. It ought to be an empirical issue which kinds of creatures have our kinds of minds; which is to say that it ought not be a priori that only creatures with our kinds of brains do. Generality is *ipso facto* an epistemic virtue, so it's a truism that, all else equal, the more widely the laws of PA psychology apply, the more empirical reason we have for believing that PA psychology is true.

Hence what I'm calling the 'publicity problem': typing tokens of primitive mental representation can't be done by appeal to their constituent structure. Primitive concepts don't have any constituent structure; that's what makes them primitive. And they can't be typed by their neurology; that would make it a priori that silicon Martians don't think. So, how is it possible to reconcile referentialism with concepts being public? Or, to put the same puzzle slightly otherwise: We can't take for granted that computationally homogeneous primitive Mentalese expressions *ipso facto* have neurologically homogeneous implementations; indeed, we had better take for granted that they often don't. So, then, how do we get a type/token criterion for basic concepts that holds across different minds?

Answer: *endorse functionalism not just about the relation between intentional psychology and its various computational implementations, but also about the relation between computational psychology and its various physical implementations.*

It's more or less common ground these days that, in principle at least, the computational implementations of a PA may

---

[58] That is, of course, a main thesis of much twentieth-century philosophy of mind. Wittgenstein, Quine, and Davidson all accepted it in one version or another. I find that consensus unconvincing.

For a different way of arguing that PA psychology generalizes only over very narrow domains see Kim (1992). For (largely unsympathetic) comments see Fodor (1998: ch. 2).

differ from mind to mind, consonant with the usual functionalist strictures: your believing that P may have different computational consequences than my believing that P does in any case where the computational consequences of having the belief aren't constitutive of its content. 'In principle, you can make a mind of practically anything' has been, for years, the functionalist mantra in philosophical psychology. But there is likewise the possibility-in-principle that *computational* states also may be multiply realized across minds or across times. In particular, tokens of the same primitive mental representation may be realized by different *sub*computational properties in minds that are type-identical under their computational descriptions. That's just to say that it's no more likely that neurological explanations will provide *reductions* of computational explanations than that computational explanations will provide reductions of intentional explanations.

What's common to minds that have the same psychology is the intentional laws that subsume them, not either the computational or the neurological mechanisms that implement the intentional laws. Intentional states and processes are multiply realized by computational states; computational states and processes are multiply realized by neurological states (or whatever), and, for all I know, neurological states are multiply realized by biochemical states; and so on down to (but not including) basic physics.[59] For all I know, it can be multiply realized implementations all the way down so long as each of the multiple realizations implements the same intentional laws.

It is a great mystery, and not just in psychology, why so many different kinds of lower-level phenomenon converge to sustain the same high-level generalizations. If they didn't, there would be no high-level generalizations to capture and we wouldn't need special sciences at all; we could get along quite nicely with just basic physics (or, to put it less in the material mode, we

---

[59] Functional taxonomy allows things that are type identical at a certain level of description to be heterogeneous at the next level down. That's what functional taxonomy is *for*. But there is no next level down from basic physics; basic physics is where the buck stops.

could get along without any functional analyses and make do with just reductions). That is a metaphysical puzzle, the key to which I have not got. But, as far as I can see, this puzzle isn't specific either to the relation between intentional psychology and its various computational implementations or to the relation between computational psychology and its various physiological representations. So, it's all right, for present purposes (though not in the metaphysical long run), to just pretend that it isn't there.

Appendix: a note on Frege's problem and the utility of files

Philosophers have generally discussed Frege cases in the context of a rather restricted set of questions about validity and semantic equivalence. In particular: What semantical properties must expressions share such that the substitution of one for the other is valid in the scope of verbs of PA? If, however, the approach to such cases that I've been recommending is accepted, the Frege issues are seen to connect with a galaxy of broadly empirical topics in cognitive science. This should hardly be surprising, since that treatment is motivated largely by a desire to comply with the chief demand that a computational account of mental processes imposes on a theory of mental representation: that if mental representations differ in their roles in mental processes, they must be formally distinct in ways that mental processes can distinguish. So, for example, tokenings of a mental representation that refers to Paderewski can have quite different mental/computational consequences depending on whether it's the pianist or the politician one has in mind. That, basically, is why Paderewski needs two different Mentalese names even though there is only one of him. I think this is typical of the way RTM and CTM can, and ought to, interact with familiar issues in the philosophy of language and the philosophy of mind. I want to expand that a little before this chapter limps to an end.

If the sort of story I've been telling you is right, then the nonlogical vocabulary of Mentalese is the pivot that cognitive mind/world relations turn on. On the one hand, according to RTM, Mentalese singular terms, predicates, and the like refer to things in the world and, on the other hand, expressions of Mentalese are the representations over which mental processes are defined. Any credible version of the LOT story will have to explain how formulas of Mentalese can play both these roles; how its formulas can both apply to things in the world and causally interact with one another in the course of mental processes. If a version of the LOT story can't do that, it should opt for early retirement.

Many philosophers, even of the RTM persuasion, have tried to dodge this issue. No wonder, after all; since RTM and CTM are supposed to be at best *empirical* theses, it's at best contingent that there is anything that's both semantically evaluable and a domain for mental processes. From the epistemologist's point of view, this may seem a catastrophe. If contingent connections are plausibly what empirical knowledge rests on, there isn't likely to be a sound a priori argument against skepticism about empirical knowledge. A sound a priori argument against skepticism about empirical knowledge is to epistemologists much what the Holy Grail was to the Knights of the Round Table. (I gather they didn't have much luck either.)

So, we find two perennial streams of philosophical thought, both of which seek to avoid the mind-world-connection problem: idealists (like Hume and, I think, Kant) in effect deny that there is anything on the world end; and behaviorists (like Ryle and, I think, Wittgenstein) in effect deny that there is anything on the mind end. According to the former everything there is is mind-dependent. According to the latter there are no minds, there are only (as it might be) behavioral dispositions. In either case there's no problem about how there could be things in the head that both interact with each other causally and have semantic values depending on how the world is. There's no such problem because there are no such things.

Psychologists, by contrast, are often content to take realism about the mind, the world, and the connections between them for granted, letting the epistemological chips fall where they may. (Behaviorism was in this respect an aberration.) What follows is a sketch of a theory fragment that such cognitive psychologists have of late been taking seriously. I think it's inherently interesting and that it's worth noticing in the present context because of its connections to Frege's problem. In a nutshell: Tokens of M(JOHN) can function both to refer to John in our thinking and to interact causally with tokens of other mental representations in the course of mental processes. That's because mental representations can serve both as names for things in the world *and as names for files in the memory.* I want to pursue this file metaphor.[60]

Think of your head as containing (*inter alia*) an arbitrarily large filing cabinet, which can in turn contain an arbitrarily large set of files, which can in turn contain an arbitrarily large number of memos.[61] We can think of these files, and of the memos that they contain, as quite like real files that contain real memos in the real world (except, of course, that mental memos are written in Mentalese; and, since there has to be room for them in people's heads, mental filing cabinets can't occupy much space).[62] The basic idea is this: When you are introduced to John (or otherwise become apprised of him), you assign him a Mentalese name and you open a mental file,[63] and the same Mentalese expression (M(John)) *serves*

---

[60] As far as I know, the file metaphor was first suggested in Treisman and Schmidt (1982). For discussion see Pylyshyn (2003).

[61] It's an interesting question whether 'arbitrarily large' means potentially infinite; and, if it does, what 'potentially' means. Familiar worries about how to apply the performance/competence distinction arise here. I propose, for present purposes, simply to beg them.

[62] How big they have to be is anybody's guess; maybe as large as neural nets, maybe as small as sub-neuronal molecules. Nobody knows, though many pretend to.

[63] Which, if any, memos are in the file at birth? Nativists will say 'lots', empiricists will say 'very few or none'. Either view is compatible with the general structure of the file story; but notice that both presuppose a cognitive endowment that includes an inventory of (possibly empty) files; and both presuppose the availability of Mentalese (i.e. of the language in which memos are written). It's really built into RTM that the least amount of innateness

both as John's Mentalese name and as the name of the file that contains your information about John; just as, in the ontologically untendentious files that one comes across in ontologically untendentious filing cabinets, the file labeled 'John' is likely to be the one where you'll find stuff pertaining to John.

Tokens of M(John) are what you use to represent John in your thoughts. Names in thought (in contrast to, say, descriptions in thought) afford a *primitive* way of bringing John before the mind. Thinking about John is thus not unlike speaking about John; in the simple cases, both are achieved by using a representation token (i.e. his name); and, as RT assures us, representation tokens have both causal powers and conditions of semantic evaluation. But, also, according to the present suggestion, M(John) is the name of the file you 'go to' when you want to get at John's phone number (or at his cat's name; or his mental image (if, indeed, there are such things), or whatever). In effect, according to this story, *we think in file names*; tokens of file names serve both as the constituents of our thoughts and as the Mentalese expressions that we use to refer to the things we think about. If you are given John's name in Mentalese, you are *thereby* given the Mentalese name of a file where you keep (some of; see below) what you believe about John.[64] That one thinks in file names is the best short summary I'm able to formulate of the version of RTM that I'm currently inclined to endorse.

We see, once again, why Paderewski has to have two names in Mentalese. If you think that there are two Paderewskis, it's important that the file that you get when you want to retrieve what you know(/believe) about the pianist is different from the file that you get when you want to retrieve what you know(/believe)

you can get away with is actually quite a lot; as, indeed, many sensible empiricists have noticed.

[64] Jesse Prinz has raised the question why one shouldn't use the whole 'John' file (rather than just its label) to represent John in thought. The short answer is that, in the typical case, you don't think everything you believe about John when you think M(john). More on this presently.

about the politician.[65] If, however, you should come to believe that the pianist was the politician (i.e. that $Paderewski_1 = Paderewski_2$) you simply merge the corresponding files.[66]

I really do think this file story helps (a bit) with empirical theorizing about the cognitive mind. For example, on any version of CTM that I can imagine there is sure to be a problem about what (i.e. what *else*) comes to mind when you think about X (or Xs) by tokening the representation M(X). To get this problem in perspective, one should bear in mind a puzzle that has always plagued associationist accounts of cognitive architecture. Associationists hold that associative bonds cause regular co-tokenings of mental representations. But then, since everybody knows that typical houses have doors and windows, why doesn't everybody think *door* or *window* when he thinks *house*? Mill (in the *Logic*) is in some perplexity about this.[67]

In fact, of course, tokening M(X) pretty generally *doesn't* cause one to think its associates; a good thing too, since, if it did, one's thinking would be forever getting derailed by one's associations. I've heard it suggested that this is what actually does go wrong

---

[65] 'It's important' means something like: It's an empirically necessary condition for your thoughts to be largely true and your mental processes to be largely truth-preserving.

[66] Except, of course, that no 'you' is required to do the merging. In the simplest cases the files merge themselves as a straightforward causal consequence of there being a token of $PADEREWSKI_1 = PADEREWSKI_2$ lodged in your belief box. There are, to be sure, intellectualized processes in which you actually think the thing through: You say to yourself (presumably in Mentalese) 'Paderewski$_1$ was a politician, Paderewski$_2$ was a pianist, Paderewski$_1$ = Paderewski$_2$, therefore Paderewski$_2$ was a politician and Paderewski$_1$ was a pianist'. But, as previously remarked, these can't be the bedrock cases of file-merging on pain of tortoise/Achilles problems.

Much advertising to the contrary notwithstanding, LOT doesn't need a ghost in your machine; it doesn't even need *your* ghost.

[67] It likewise shows up in the issue, raised explicitly by the 'Wurzburg School' of psychologists, about the 'directedness' of thought. What else one thinks when one thinks *house* depends a lot on which of one's projects the thinking is in aid of. The strong intuition is that one's awareness of one's project somehow guides the flow of one's thought; but this intuition must be anathema to associationists, since they hold that the flow of thought is determined entirely by the strength of the associations among ideas. We still haven't seen the last of this; *vide* the argument between connectionist and classical CTMs about whether mental processes need an 'executive' to run them. It simply isn't true that to someone with a hammer everything looks like a nail. *Why* isn't it?

with schizophrenics; thinking *house* causes them to think *chimney* which causes them to think *smoke* which causes them to think *fire* which causes them to think *water*, and so on and on; with the consequence that they never manage to think (as it might be) *I live in the third house on the left*. I have no idea whether that's right about schizophrenics; but the problem it points to is perfectly real. If, as associationists suppose, your cognitive lexicon is a causal network in which there is a low-resistance connection between the node HOUSE and the node WINDOW, how do you reliably have thoughts about the one that don't cause thoughts about the other?

Answer: your cognitive lexicon *isn't* a network of associations, it's a system of files. There are at least two possibilities that the file story suggests in the present sort of case. Maybe M(window) isn't in your M(house) file at all; maybe your belief that houses have windows isn't something you keep stored in your memory; rather it's inferred 'on line' from whatever you have in your files together with whatever inferential rules you accept. Surely there are cases like this; the belief that Shakespeare didn't have a telephone is a classic example: It's not something you keep in your head but something that you infer when and if the occasion arises.

Or maybe M(window) is in your file M(house) after all. But remember that it's only *the name* of the M(house) file (not the file itself) that serves as a constituent of one's thoughts when one thinks about houses.[68] By contrast, in order to get to M(window) from a token of M(house), you have to look *inside* the M(house) file; which is something that you do or don't do depending (not upon your associative dispositions but) on your estimates of task demands. Since a file architecture makes the distinction between a file and the memos it contains principled (i.e. not merely associative), it allows for a correspondingly principled distinction between entertaining the concept HOUSE and entertaining one or other of one's beliefs about houses. Quite plausibly, that's just

---

[68] i.e. when one thinks about houses 'as such'. Here as elsewhere in the discussion PA contents are specified *de dicto* unless there's explicit notice to the contrary.

what respecting the directedness of thought requires (see n. 62). Associationism took the thinking out of thinking; CTM, together with the file story, puts it back in.

A further small twist. Getting from one file to another is normally a process of inference, not a process of association. But it's perfectly reasonable to suggest that there are associations *among file names*, and that (all else equal) it's easier to access a given file name if you have already accessed an associated file name. I suppose that's what explains the phenomenon of 'semantic priming'. You say to the experimental subjects: 'I am about to show you two stimuli in succession; the first will be a word, the second may be a word, but also it may not. Your task is just to decide, quick as you can, whether it is'. You then divide your subjects in half; one half sees the sequence (as it might be) 'house' followed by 'window', the other half sees the sequence (as it might be) 'house' followed by 'fish'. You control for frequency, word length, word complexity, and other nuisance variables. What you then discover is that, in this sort of situation, thought is *not* directed; here it *is* the strength of the association that matters: Ss do better on 'house' … 'window' than they do on 'house' … 'fish'.[69] This comports very nicely with the file story: When you see 'house' the file M(house) becomes available for being searched. Since M(window) is a high associate of M(house), accessing the latter facilitates access to the former. So you can get from M(house) to M(window) faster than you get from M(house) to M(fish). That is plausibly A Good Thing since, quite likely, you will want to get from M(house) to M(window) more often than you will want to get from M(house) to M(fish). It's not possible to take seriously the theory that fixed associations control the flow of thought in the general case; but they might be useful now and then when there's nothing else to go on. I mention this not just because the empirical results are interesting, but also because, once you've seen that file-to-file transitions can't

---

[69] The empirical status of this result is, however, less than certain; if there is semantic priming, it's a pretty subtle effect. For a review see Forster (1998).

be associative in the *general* case (that association can't be what guides thinking), you might well begin to wonder what on earth association could be *for*. A good question, to which the present considerations might conceivably be part of the answer.

I've been telling you a story about some ways that postulating a file architecture might contribute to explaining the normal directedness of thought. The notion of a named file, together with the suggestion that files are accessed via their names, is at the heart of that story. Clearly, this is just a variant of the suggestion I appealed to in trying to construct an account of Frege cases for basic concepts: It was because the file named 'PADEREWSKI$_1$' is distinguished from the file named 'PADEREWSKI$_2$' that John can coherently wonder if Paderewski = Paderewski. So, the Frege problem and the directedness–of–thought problem turn out to be parts of the same problem if LOT is true; which is itself a reason for believing that LOT is true. Each turtle stands on another turtle's back, all the way down.

Notice, finally, that there are two ways of telling the story about files and file names, both of which are compatible with both LOT and CTM. One might hold that file names are constrained by the contents of the files that they name; or one might hold that they aren't. (The latter is to say, approximately, that somebody who thinks that Plato was a prime number can nevertheless have thoughts about Plato; all he requires is a Mentalese expression M(PLATO) which denotes Plato and a file whose name is M(PLATO) which contains whatever is the Mentalese for *is a prime number*). If, like me, you're a referential atomist, then you are committed to this latter option; not, however, because RTM or CTM per se requires it, but because referential atomism does. If you opt the other way, holding that the semantics of a file name is somehow constrained by the contents of the file it names, you will have to say that Mentalese names are *ipso facto* required to have some descriptive content, and that for each file name there is some descriptive content that the corresponding file is *ipso facto* required to have. But *either* way you have a reasonable answer to the question 'How is it possible for us to think about the world?'.[70] Namely, that we think in file names and file names are Janus-faced: one face turned towards thinking and the other face turned towards what is thought about. I do think that's rather satisfactory. Maybe everything is going to be all right after all.

SNARK. Or, on the other hand, maybe not.

---

[70] It goes without saying that this answer won't satisfy a skeptic who doubts (or, anyhow, says he does) that we *can* think about the world. Psychology operates within the assumptions of normal science; skeptics, by definition, don't.

4

Locality

I suppose this book might have been called: 'Notes on a Certain Program'. The goal throughout is to say what's become of the idea of building a psychology of cognition by conjoining the thesis that (at least some) mental representations are language-like with the thesis that (at least some) mental processes are syntactic transformations of mental representations. I admit that an occasional outbreak of optimism has been perceptible in the text so far; it does seem to me that we know more about cognition now than we did fifty years ago. But not all that much more; not nearly so much more as cognitive science propaganda often likes to make out. In fact, I think the really hard problems about cognition have just recently begun to dawn on us in something like their full awfulness. In particular, I think there are increasingly good reasons to doubt that the 'classical' RTM LOT CTM model is anything like a general account of how the cognitive mind works; and the magnitude of our current bewilderment about certain aspects of cognitive processes is the measure of the failure.[1] This is not, of course, a cause for lamentation. A lot of our best science has been learned from the falsification of prima facie interesting ideas: It's a matter of figuring out where you are by finding out where you aren't. Just as Holmes says: 'When you've eliminated all the impossibles, what's left must be the truth'. Assuming, of course, that there *is* anything left, and assuming that there is only one of them. This chapter, anyhow, is about what seems to have gone wrong.

[1] I warned in *LOT 1* that things were likely to turn out this way; see its last chapter.

Every schoolchild knows that cognitive science started back in 1959 with Chomsky's epoch-making review of B. F. Skinner's *Verbal Behavior*. Chomsky's deconstruction of the Skinnerian paradigm (though of course we didn't call it that back then. In those days 'paradigm' still meant *paradigm* and could be uttered, even by the fastidious; 'deconstruction' had yet to be invented and, with luck, wouldn't be) set the agenda for modern representational theories of mind that we've all been working on ever since. Thus the standard story about what's been going on in cognitive science for the last fifty years or so. There is, of course, much to be said for reading the history that way. Chomsky's Skinner review, together with his *Syntactic Structures*, fundamentally (and, one might still hope, permanently) altered the way that psychologists think about language in particular and cognition in general. That said, it's also striking that a main topic of cognitive-science discussions over the last several decades is one that Chomsky hardly touches on, least of all in his early work; namely, the nature of mental representation in general and of concepts in particular.[2] These are, of course, the main preoccupations both in *LOT 1* and here.

It bears emphasis that Chomsky's critique of Skinner was woven from several different strands, of which his assault on behaviorism was much the most influential at the time. Chomsky charged that Skinner had left the mind out of cognitive psychology and suggested that the proper course was to put it back in. I take it that Chomsky was entirely right about this[3] and

---

[2] It's a question of some exegetical interest why Chomsky so regularly avoids this issue. I suspect it's because he takes some sort of 'theory theory' of concepts more or less for granted. (So, for example, a speaker/hearer's concept of his language is constituted by his (internally represented) grammar of the language; his concept of a noun phrase is constituted by the rules of the grammar that determine the behavior of 'NP'; and so forth.) This is a point at which several important aspects of Chomsky's thinking converge, including, notably, his discussions of semantics and of the 'psychological reality' of linguistic constructs. It's tempting to try and run this down, but I'm not going to.

[3] Or, anyhow, so near right as makes no matter. It might be argued that what Skinner intended was not an eliminative but a reductive behaviorism. According to that sort of view, there are, after all, mental states like believing, intending, desiring, and such, but they

that the issue is no longer seriously moot. Behaviorism now survives mostly as a horrible example of what can happen when psychologists believe what philosophers tell them about 'the scientific method'.

In any case, behaviorism was an anomaly. The mainline of anglophone psychology, at least since Locke, was a mentalistic assocationism; Skinner diverged from that in respect of his mentalism, but not in respect of its associationism. Whereas the empiricist tradition thought of association as a relation between 'ideas', Skinner took it to be a relation between stimuli and responses. But associationism itself was seriously doubted by neither. Indeed, this associationist consensus remains intact in much current theorizing in neuropsychology (see, for example, Ledoux 2002) and, of course, in connectionism. It's not difficult to find that pretty depressing. Correspondingly, what now seems most important about Chomsky's critique is the dilemma that he posed for associationists; namely, that you can have *associative* mental processes or you can have *productive* mental processes, but you can't have both.

The heart of the matter is that association is supposed to be a *contiguity-sensitive* relation. Thus Hume held that ideas became associated as a function of the temporal contiguity of their tokenings. (Other determinants of associative strength were said to be 'frequency' and, on some accounts, 'similarity'.) Likewise, according to Skinnerian theory, responses become conditioned to stimuli as a function of their temporal contiguity to reinforcers. By contrast, Chomsky argued that the mind is sensitive to relations among interdependent elements of mental or linguistic representations that may be arbitrarily far apart.[4] Since association is *contiguity*-sensitive such relations can't be associations. The connection with issues

---

somehow reduce to what Dennett calls 'real patterns' in behavior. Reading Skinner that way would make him more like (e.g.) Ryle or Wittgenstein and less like (e.g.) Watson than he's generally taken to have been.

[4] Consider, for a trivial example: '(John) (is...likely to loose) (his suspenders)', where the reference of 'his' depends on the reference of 'John' and the possible intervening sequence includes 'is very likely', 'is very, very likely', 'is very, very, very likely', and so on indefinitely.

about productivity is straightforward: To say that a relation can hold among *arbitrarily* discontinuous parts of a representation is to say that there can be arbitrarily many such representations; so the same considerations that argue for the productivity of complex (mental or linguistic) representations thereby argue against an associative account of the structure of the representations. You can have associationism or you can have productivity but you can't have both, as previously remarked.

That will all be familiar to old hands, and I won't bother to recount the dialectics that ensued. Details aside, it seems pretty clear that the productivity argument against associationism had its heart in the right place. Associative networks are systems with *intrinsically* finite capacities. The best they can do is therefore to *approximate* productivity, in effect by listing finite subsets of the infinite outputs that bona fide recursive capacities can produce.[5] Since it appears that human cognition routinely exhibits such infinite capacities (notoriously, the set of well-formed English sentences is infinite) our minds can't be networks of associations.

Moreover, the main argument *for* associationism had always been the lack of serious competitors. The laws of a naturalistic psychology would presumably posit causal relations among the objects in their domains; and what could these be if not associations? But the computer changed all that. On the one hand, there is no reason why computational relations need to be contiguity-sensitive, so if mental processes are computational they can be sensitive to 'long distance' dependencies between the mental(/linguistic) objects over which they are defined. On the other hand, we know that computations can be implemented by causal mechanisms; that's what computers do for a living.[6] So, the thesis that mental

---

[5] Some are suspicious of proceeding on the assumption of infinite cognitive capacities, but it turns out that much the same sorts of points can be made without doing so, since our minds(/languages) are not just productive but also 'systematic'. For discussion see Fodor and Pylyshyn 1988.

[6] In this respect computational psychology is arguably in a better condition than Newtonian physics ever achieved; they both require action at a distance among the objects they apply to, but only the former has a mechanical explanation of how there could be such

processes are computations was not committed to the dualist metaphysics for which earlier versions of mentalism had frequently been chastised. In short, a serious cognitive science requires a theory of mental processes that is compatible with the productivity of mental representations, and CTM obliges by providing such a theory. So, then, is that all there is? Is CTM the whole story about where associationism went wrong?

Pretty clearly not. In fact, productivity is embarrassingly cheap; all it requires is computational procedures that can apply to their own outputs, so computational systems that can do recursion needn't be able to do anything much else that's interesting.[7] (I guess everybody knows about the computer scientist who was found dead in his bathtub holding a bottle of shampoo with the instruction: 'Soap, Rinse, Repeat'.) True enough, associationism didn't notice the importance of recursion in mental processes; but it also didn't notice what's equally essential; namely, that the recursions in question are defined over the *constituent structure* of mental representations.

It seems clear in retrospect that associationists failed to distinguish two irreducibly different (indeed, orthogonal) kinds of relations that mental representations can enter into: on the one hand, there's *association*, which is a causal relation of the kind that holds between, say, the idea SALT and the idea PEPPER; on the other hand, there's *constituency*, which is a mereological relation that

---

a thing. (A friendly amendment to Chomsky's thesis that it's bodies, not minds, that make the mind/body problem.)

[7] Strictly speaking, the target of Chomsky's early polemics was often not associationism per se but rather 'finite state' models of mental processes. Unlike associative systems strictly so called, finite-state generators can exhibit a limited sort of recursion. For example, if they contain 'loops' they can generate the infinitely many sequences of 'very's that can fill the blank in 'John is … likely to forget his suspenders' (see n. 4). It seemed, early on, that it was important to determine the position of various kinds of psychological models in the 'Chomsky hierarchy' of recursive functions. In that context, getting clear on (e.g.) the exact relation between associative networks and finite-state generators was essential. It seems less so now. Why should it matter, in evaluating an empirical theory, what *other* such theories *could* be formulated using the same logico-syntactic apparatus? Does anybody care whether theories in (e.g.) geology could be formalized as a finite-state generator? But these are complicated issues and I propose to ignore them for the purposes at hand.

holds between a complex representation and the constituents out of which it's constructed.[8] This matters a lot if CTM is the model for mental processes, since computations apply to representations in virtue of their constituent structure (not of their associative structure). *Since CTM is being assumed, mental processes are computations; it follows that they are defined over the constituent structure of mental representations.* That is, I think, among the most central claims that CTM imposes on cognitive science. It can hardly be overemphasized enough.

So, then, is *that* all there is? I mean: do the constituent structure of mental representations and the recursive character of mental processes exhaust the plausible demands that CTM imposes on the 'architecture' of cognition?[9] There are certainly cognitive scientists who think so. When they offer to tell you 'how the mind works', productive processes defined over the constituent structure of mental representations is the crux of what they have for sale. On that view, the task that we're now faced with (the admittedly *enormous* task that we're now faced with) is to fill in this architectural sketch by making explicit the rules of mental computation and the constituent structure of the mental representations on which the computations operate. This sense of the state of the art is pervasive in cognitive science, so I'll call it 'the received view'.[10]

The received view may after all be right. In particular, the evidence that mental representations typically have constituent structure is very persuasive, since it turns out that not just the productivity but also the compositionality[11] of mental representations

---

[8] Some hoped, for a while, that constituency might somehow reduce to *strength* of association (see e.g. Osgood and Tzeng 1990), and it's true that association is often relatively weak across the major constituent boundaries; for example, across the major constituent boundaries of sentences. But there's clearly no hope of a general reduction of constituency to association. 'Dogs bark' and 'dogs sing' have the same constituent structures even though the association (the 'transition probability') from 'dogs' to 'bark' is no doubt much stronger than the association from 'dogs' to 'sing'.

[9] For this useful notion see Pylyshyn (2003).   [10] See Fodor (1998: ch. 17).

[11] Reminder: a system of representations is 'compositional' if the syntactic/semantic properties of the complex representation are fully determined by their structural descriptions together with the syntax/semantics of their primitive parts.

is intimately dependent on their constituency.[12] Still, I'm strongly inclined to doubt that CTM is the last word about mental processes. The rest of this chapter will argue that given what CTM understands computations to be, it is constrained by the intrinsic *locality* of the mental processes that it postulates; and that, because it is, there are pervasive features of cognition that it is unable to explain. I don't begin to suppose that the considerations I'll have on offer are anything like a refutation of the received view; but I do think there are lots of straws in the wind, and that they're all blowing in much the same direction.

Here, by way of prolepsis, is the general form of the argument I'll propose:

(1) Computation, as our current cognitive science understands it, is an intrinsically local process; when a computation 'looks at' a representation in its domain, what it is able to 'see', or to operate upon, is the identity and arrangement of its constituents. Nothing else.[13]

(2) But constituent structure is *ipso facto* a local property of representations.

(3) So, according to CTM, mental processes are themselves *ipso facto* local, and their locality imposes substantial constraints on what models of the mind CTM can allow.

(4) But broadly empirical considerations suggest that these constraints can't be met.

I'll start on that presently. First, however, a few digressions, beginning with one about what 'locality' means.

4.1 First digression: what 'locality' means

I won't try to give a general account of what makes a property local, but the rough intuition is that local properties of X are *ipso facto*

---

[12] For extensive discussion see Fodor and Pylyshyn (1988).

[13] This isn't, of course, to deny that a computational process can *compare* representations; only that, if it does, it must compare them in respect of their constituent structures.

independent of the properties of anything except X. The paradigm is the part/whole relation. Consider the left hind leg of a cow. It bears the relation *part of* to the whole cow; and that it does so is independent of how the things in the rest of the world are; the left hind leg of this cow is a part of this cow even in a world that contains *only* this cow. Now, by assumption: Computational processes are defined over the syntactic structure of mental representations; and the syntactic structure of mental representations is their constituent structure; and constituent structure is a species of the part/whole relation.[14] So, it follows that computational processes are local in the intended sense: Whether a certain mental representation is in the domain of a certain mental process depends solely on the relation between that representation and its parts[15]. So, the received view implies the locality of cognitive processes. As it turns out, however, the thesis that cognitive processes are local has consequences that are highly substantive and, quite possibly, not true. So the main line of argument will go. End of digression on what 'locality' means.

4.2 Second digression: the metaphysics of constituent structure

I've said that constituent structure is a species of the part/whole relation. Accordingly, the fact that 'brown' is a constituent of 'brown cow' is independent of facts about any other English expressions; indeed, it's independent of whether there *are* any

---

[14] It's convenient to read 'part' as 'improper part', so that every mental representation is a constituent of itself. The requirement that computations apply to representations in virtue of their constituent structure thus holds for primitive representations *inter alia*.

[15] This isn't much more than a gesture in the direction of making clear the sense in which computations, as CTM understands them, are local. For example, it leaves out computational relations between constituents of different thoughts that belong to the same stream of thought, as in '*John* kissed Mary. Then *he* kissed Sally'. (These would be analoguous to what grammarians call 'discourse relations' in natural languages.) It's apparent, however, that this sort of liberalization would still make computational relations very local as compared, for example, with ones that depend on the configurations of whole belief systems. That's all we require for present purposes.

other English expressions. It's, as it were, an atomistic fact that the form of words 'brown cow' is composed of the constituent form of words 'brown' and 'cow'. On the view of the metaphysics of constituency that I'm inclined towards, that the constituents of 'brown cow' are 'brown' and 'cow' could be all there is to say about the structure of the symbols in English. (*Mutatis mutandis*, of course, for the concepts BROWN COW, BROWN, and COW.)

Now, that view is not widely received. The widely received view is that constituent structure is an emergent from substitution relations among representations. So, the fact that 'brown' and 'cow' are constituents of 'brown cow' supervenes on such other facts as that English also contains such expressions as 'green cow', 'brown pig', 'dark green cow', 'Farmer Jones's largest dark green cow', 'Farmer Jones's brown pig', and so forth. To a first approximation, the idea is that the constituents of an expression are the ones for which other expressions can substitute salve well-formedness. If that's true, it would follow that the relation between a form of words and its constituents isn't local after all;[16] it's metaphysically dependent on what other forms of words belong to the same language. Likewise, *mutatis mutandis*, for concepts, as usual.[17]

But I don't believe it. One reason I don't is that no uncircular formulation of the thesis would seem to be available; the constituents of an expression aren't the *parts* of the expression for which you can substitute; they're the *constituents* of an expression for which you can substitute; a not very helpful truism. Consider

[16] There's no paradox implied. Constituents aren't just *any* parts of a representation, they're it's *canonical* parts; and it's perfectly coherent to claim that, whereas the relation between a whole and its parts is local, the metaphysical facts that make a part canonical depend on its relations to other representations. It could be that *just* being a part of an expression depends solely on the identity of the expression, but that being one of its *constituent* parts does not. But though I take this claim to be coherent, I also take it not to be true.

[17] This substitutional kind of account of constituent structure has a long history in 'taxonomic' linguistics (Harris 1988 is a classic text), and it's been known to pop up in philosophy too (see e.g. Brandom 2000). It comports naturally with the doctrine that languages are inherently *systems* of representations; that is, with a metaphysics according to which there couldn't be a 'punctate' language (see Fodor and Lepore 1992). If I'm right about constituent structure being atomistic, then that doctrine isn't true.

(3) (in which 'chopped down the' is not a constituent) and (4) (in which 'plants' substitutes for 'chopped down the').[18]

(3) Farmer Jones chopped down the trees.

(4) Farmer Jones plants trees.

I think the constituents of a representation are not those of its parts that you can substitute for, but those of its parts that are semantically evaluable; and, prima facie, what parts of a representation are semantically evaluable doesn't depend on facts about other representations.[19] (Prima facie, the fact that 'dog' refers to *dogs* doesn't depend on what other English words refer to. Nor, *prima facie*, does the fact that 'dog' means *dog*.) I'll assume, in what follows, that this is so. If I'm right, then the locality of mental processes follows from their being defined over the constituent structure of mental representations. If I'm not right, however, so be it. It remains open that there are mental processes that aren't local. If there are, then there are mental process that aren't computations in CTM's proprietary sense of that term. End of digression on the metaphysics of the constituency relation.

4.3 Third digression: locality considered as a virtue

I want to describe a case in which the assumption that a mental process is local does some serious and useful explanatory work. I don't at all doubt that some cognitive processes are local. What worries me is that some apparently aren't.

---

[18] In face of this, one might try for a recursive definition of 'constituent' along the lines: 'a is a constituent; Y is a constituent iff Y substitutes for a constituent'. But now everything turns on 'a' being chosen by some criterion that *isn't* itself substitutional. It remains to be explained, that is, why 'chopped down the' can't be a value of X in 3. (Recursive definitions can often be a useful way to specify extensions; but they're unlikely to help you much if your problems are metaphysical, since it's of their nature to contain the metaphysically worrying term in their starting premises.)

[19] Though, to be sure, *what the semantic evaluation of a part of an expression is* can depend on relations that aren't local; as in discourse anaphora. Consider the value of 'him' in 'Bill has many friends. But John doesn't like him'.

The locality of a cognitive process can be a Very Good Thing. Here's a case: Suppose you're working with a kind of computational architecture that allows you to 'fetch' a symbol S from some location in memory. Suppose, also, that C is a constituent of S. Then (barring malfunction) if the 'fetch' operation delivers S, it is guaranteed also to deliver C. That's because, by assumption, the fetch operation is defined over the constituent structure of the representations it applies to, and constituents are parts; and it's just a truism that if you fetch all of a thing, you thereby fetch all of its parts. This is an agreeably trivial example of an interaction between the kind of computational operation that 'fetch' is and the kind of structural relation that constituency is.

But now suppose your favorite cognitive architecture recognizes association but not constituency as a relation among mental representations. Well, association comes in strengths from, say, very strong to very weak. Consider, then, a very strong association like DOG/CAT. Presumably even if the probability that thinking CAT causes you to think DOG is very high (compared, say, to the probability that thinking CAT will cause you to think KANGAROO), still it's surely less than 1: there are sure to be at least some occasions on which thinking DOG doesn't cause you to think CAT. At a minimum, it's always *possible* (statistically, logically, nomologically, conceptually, and metaphysically)[20] that a mind of our kind should think DOG but not think CAT.

So, sometimes fetching DOG retrieves CAT and sometimes it doesn't. By contrast, you can't think BROWN DOG unless you think BROWN; you can't however hard you try.[21] What, then, is the difference between *fetching DOG fetches CAT*, which appears to be probabilistic, and *fetching BROWN DOG fetches BROWN*, which appears not to be? The answer is obvious if your

[20] That's all the kinds of possibility that there are this week, as far as I know. But do feel free to add any others that I may have inadvertently omitted.

[21] Likewise, you can, at least in principle, have acquired the concept DOG and not have the concept CAT; but you can't, even in principle, have acquired the concept BROWN DOG unless you have acquired the concept BROWN. Associations, however strong, don't *individuate* the concepts that have them.

architecture postulates not just association but also constituency as a parameter of representations: Fetching retrieves associates of an idea in proportion to the strength of the association; but (short of malfunction) it *always* retrieves their constituents. The point of all this is that the locality of computations does some serious explanatory work in the theory of cognition. It explains why you can think BROWN DOG without thinking CAT, but you can't think BROWN DOG without thinking BROWN and DOG. More generally, it explains why a mental operation can always 'see' the constituents of the representations it applies to, though it can't always see their associates. There are, in short, cases where the locality of computations is a thing that we can't conveniently do without.

On the other hand, I'm reasonably convinced that the locality of computational processes also has some very disagreeable consequences, since it appears that some of the computations the mind performs simply aren't local; which is to say that they aren't computations in the sense of the term that CTM endorses. Just as there are no free lunches, so there are no unmixed blessings.

The main point is, I think, quite straightforward: Computational processes are (by definition) syntactic, hence local. CTM says that mental processes are *ipso facto* computations. But it's very plausible, as a matter of fact, that at least some of what goes on in cognition depends on the mind's sensitivity to nonlocal relations among mental representations. So, it's very plausible that at least some mental processes aren't computations. So it's very plausible that CTM isn't true of the general case.

If there's anything wrong with this line of argument, it must be the claim that much of cognition depends on the sensitivity of mental processes to nonlocal properties of mental representations; RTM being assumed, the rest is just logic.[22] So, what's the

---

[22] SNARK. [who, in this chapter, is confined to footnotes; I've got quite enough trouble in the text without him]. So much the worse, then, for RTM.

argument for that? Well, typical cognitive processes (perception, learning, thinking[23]) are species of the nondemonstrative fixation of belief. In consequence of the operation of such processes, one acquires beliefs that one didn't have before (or one abandons beliefs to which one was previously committed); and, typically, the beliefs that are so acquired (or expunged) are logically independent of one's prior cognitive commitments. In short, the psychological fixation of empirical beliefs is closely analogous to the scientific confirmation of empirical hypotheses (individual psychology = science writ small). I suppose, for example, that the fixation of perceptual beliefs is initiated by the (subdoxastic) registration of sensory information, from which beliefs about the distal percept are (subdoxastically, nondemonstratively) inferred; roughly, the inference runs from sensory states to their distal causes. Since the relation between a distal object and the sensations it causes a perceiver to have are (typically; maybe always) contingent in both directions, the inferences that mediate the fixation of perceptual beliefs are (typically, maybe always) contingent too.

I propose in what follows to rely on the analogy between the psychology of cognition and the epistemology of confirmation. This ought to be common ground, but it isn't. Consider, for example: 'Granted that several millennia of Western science have given us nonobvious truths involving circuitous connections among ideas; why should theories of a single human mind be held to the same standard?' (Pinker, 2005). The answer is, of course, that although science is a social phenomenon, scientific reasoning

AUTHOR. That's easy to say, but what's the alternative? RTM *really is* the only game in town. Even connectionists think so, though they don't often 'fess up to it. Notice that even connections *label* their nodes, which are thus taken to have semantical properties as well as causal ones. (The deep trouble with connectionism isn't that it wants to do without mental representations but that it wants to do without mental representations that have constituent structure. I may well have said this before. I may well say it again.)

[23] But presumably not memory, unless you hold that remembering is a radically reconstructive process.

goes on in, and only in, the heads of individual scientists; and, as far as anybody knows, scientists mostly reason in much the same way other people do. (Dewey is good on this; he suggests that scientific thinking is continuous with what goes on in the refinement of craft skills. See 2002). If you suppose otherwise, you are in debt for an explanation of how the one kind of thinking could have arisen from the other; and the greater the postulated difference between them, the more the explanation would have to account for. Perhaps Pinker (or somebody) will some day offer at least the outlines of such a theory; but I am not holding my breath, nor do I advise you to hold yours. (For a recent discussion of analogies between individual cognition and the projection and evaluation of scientific theories see Murphy 2006.)

The claim that cognition exhibits the typical properties of nondemonstrative inference bears special emphasis in the present context. Here's why: It's the main burden of this chapter that some cognitive processes aren't local, hence that they can't be computations in the proprietary sense of 'computation' that CTM endorses; also that, as things stand, cognitive science hasn't the foggiest idea what to do about them. This view is eccentric, so I'd like to have an argument for embracing it. Well, I do: Since cognition is a species of nondemonstrative inference (as per above), we have good reason to expect it to exhibit the typical properties of such inferences. Since nonlocality is pretty clearly among them, we have every reason to expect cognitive process often not to be local.

There are, I think, two pervasive characteristics of nondemonstrative empirical inference that strongly suggest that it isn't local in the general case;[24] hence, that the evaluation of inductive inferences isn't, in the general case, a computational process. We'll now take a look at them, one at a time.

---

[24] The caveat is because I don't, of course, claim that processes of nondemonstrative inference are *never* local. To the contrary, devising and confirming theories of local inferential cognitive processes is exactly what cognitive science has proved to be a success at.

4.4 Relevance

Typical nondemonstrative inference is (to stick with the term that I've used before; Fodor 2000) *isotropic*. That's to say that, in principle, *any* of one's cognitive commitments (including, of course, the available experiential data) is relevant to the (dis)confirmation of any new belief.[25] There is, in particular, no way to determine a priori what might turn out be germane to accepting or rejecting an empirical hypothesis.[26] It is one of the differences between a theory of scientific *confirmation* (say, an inductive logic) and what positivists used to call a 'theory of scientific *discovery*' that the former simply takes for granted that both the hypotheses to be assessed and the data relevant to their assessment are specified *prior to* the computation of confirmation levels. It is then left to the theory of discovery to explain how the relevance of the data is to be estimated (and, for that matter, where the candidate hypotheses come from).

It's just as well that we can divide the issues by isolating the problem of evaluating confirmation levels from the problem of deciding what is relevant to what, since, as it turns out, the question how cognition estimates relevance is very hard to answer if much generality is required. There is always an infinite corpus of previous cognitive commitments any of which might, in principle, be germane to estimating the level of confirmation of any new belief (see n. 18), and only some relatively small finite subset of them can actually be surveyed in, as one says, 'real time'; life is short but belief fixation is shorter still. Something must somehow 'filter' what actually gets thought about when one considers what next to believe or, *mutatis mutandis*, what next to do.

[25] Indeed, any *consequence* of one's cognitive commitments is, in principle, relevant to the (dis)confirmation of any new belief; for these purposes, one's cognitive commitments are to be viewed as closed under the reliable-consequence relations (including, of course, entailment).

[26] This is, I take it, exactly what 'criteriological' accounts of the individuation of concepts wanted to deny. I shall, however, spare the reader a repetition of the arguments against criteriology. Let the dead bury the dead.

Hence the infamous 'frame problem' in AI: How does one decide what to consider to be relevant (and what to consider not to be) when one is (dis)confirming a hypothesis that is up for empirical evaluation? Since nondemonstrative belief fixation is isotropic, any substantive criterion of relevance is at risk of eliminating something that is in fact germane; that is, something that if it *were* attended to *would* affect the estimated subjective probability of the belief. This sort of risk can't be completely avoided in evaluating inductive inferences; that's part of what makes inductive inferences nondemonstrative. But, all else equal, one wants one's inferences to minimize the risk. And there's some indirect evidence that we're pretty good at doing that; witness our not all being dead. How, then, *do* we do it?[27]

The frame problem arises when we try to use intrinsically local operations (computations as CTM understands that notion) to calculate an intrinsically nonlocal relation (namely, inductive relevance). Or so I'm much inclined to suppose. But I don't (you'll be glad to hear) propose now to discuss the frame problem per se. Suffice it to remark on one nonsolution that is frequently found in the literature; I mention it because it's among the most characteristic ways that cognitive scientists have of not recognizing how serious the issues are that the isotropy of relevance raises for a theory of the cognitive mind. Not recognizing that is something that cognitive science has gotten pretty good at over the years.

The thought is that the frame problem might be (not so much solved as) circumvented by a resort to heuristic procedures. In and of itself this suggestion is, of course, entirely empty, since the notion of a heuristic procedure is entirely negatively defined; a heuristic is just a procedure that doesn't always work; if a problem has a computational solution at all, it *ipso facto* has as

---

[27] In fact, this formulation underestimates the complexity of the problems that the isotropy of relevance brings in train: Criteria of relevance are themselves sensitive to changes in cognitive commitments. If I come to believe that As are (or probably are) Bs, then beliefs about Bs become, to that extent, germane to assessing the hypothesis that something is an A. If one's cognitive commitments constitute a field of beliefs, then proximity relations within the field are constantly in flux. More on this later.

many heuristic solutions as you like. So, whether there is any interest to the suggestion that there's a heuristic solution of the frame problem depends on the specifics of the heuristics on offer. To my knowledge, the heuristic procedure that is, pretty much invariably, proposed for coping with issues of relevance that arise when deciding which action to perform (/which belief to adopt) is some version of the 'sleeping dog' strategy: *If things went all right last time, do the same again this time.* I don't know how many cognitive scientists think that the sleeping-dog strategy defangs the problems that relevance poses to CTM—in particular, the frame problem—but I suspect that their numbers are legion. I have on offer a few quotations (in, roughly, increasing order of opacity) that I believe to be entirely representative.

Peter Carruthers: "choices [among heuristics] could be made by higher-order heuristics, such as 'use the one that worked last time' (2001: 30)."

Eric Lormand: "a system should assume *by default*, that a fact persists, unless there is an axiom specifying that it is changed by an occurring event... [G]iven that an event E occurs in situation S, the system can use axioms to infer new facts existing in S + 1, and then simply 'copy' the remainder of its beliefs about S over to S' (Lormand, p. 66 in Pylyshyn 1987). That's to say: 'The last time this situation arose, I tiptoed by the sleeping dog and I didn't get bitten. So if I tiptoe by the sleeping dog again now, I probably won't get bitten this time either'."

Henry Kyburg (p. 51 of Pylyshyn 2003) [The issue is whether the current position of Jupiter should be considered when I decide which way to move my hand when I wish to pick up a glass of beer.]: "what is the difference between worrying about the position of my hand relative to the beer glass and worrying about the position of my hand relative to Jupiter? Baldly stated, it is that the former has what we know to be immediate consequences for our plan of drinking some beer, and the latter, *so far as we know* [*sic*], does not". But Kyburg doesn't say how we figure out what part of what we know has 'immediate consequences for our plan'.

Since that *is* the frame problem, his suggestion doesn't seem to make much progress.

In fact, it's characteristic of sleeping-dog solutions of the frame problem that they beg the question they are supposed to answer; they all presuppose the availability of a (feasible) procedure for estimating relevance, which is precisely what we haven't got. Kyburg says that he *just knows* that the position of one's hand has immediate consequences for one's plan to grasp a glass of beer and the position of Jupiter does not. What could be more reasonable? What could be less problematic? Except that the frame problem is precisely: *How* does one know that none of one's beliefs about Jupiter are germane without having to recall and search one's beliefs about Jupiter? It's no good saying that when I decide to move my hand in this sort of situation I just *automatically* don't worry about where Jupiter is, and automatically do worry about where my hand is. 'How do you get to Carnegie Hall?' 'No problem; it's automatic.'[28]

What makes this dialectical situation hard to recognize is that, very often, the relevance problem is begged by taking for granted some principle for individuating *situations*; one that itself presupposes an entirely unexplicated notion of relevance. Thus Carruthers suggests that the rule of thumb is: Use the heuristic that worked last time this (sort of) situation arose.[29] That's good advice on the face of it; but it does require that we know how to decide when

---

[28] There is, of course, a sense in which Kyburg is quite right to insist that the choice of a heuristic must be 'automatic'; otherwise circularities threaten. If the problem of deciding which heurisitic to activate is itself to be solved by a computational process, then the question arises how one decides which heuristic is relevant to performing *that* computation. And so forth. The trouble is, this doesn't say how the frame problem is solved; only how it isn't. It's the practice in AI to assume that this kind of regress is blocked (not computationally but) in the 'cognitive architecture'. This too is fine as far as it goes; but it leaves untouched the question 'What kind of architecture is required to do the blocking?' That's to say that it too recapitulates the frame problem without solving it.

[29] Carruthers also suggests that heuristics '[could] be cued automatically by particular subject matters'; but he says nothing about how 'subject matters' might be individuated, which is, very plausibly, itself a problem about relevance. How does one decide (i.e. what's relevant to deciding) to which 'subject matter' the problem about getting past the sleeping dog belongs? Is the subject matter 'getting past a sleeping dog' or 'getting past this sleeping dog' or 'getting past a sleeping dog of Farmer Jones', etc.?

two situation tokens are both instances of the same situation type; and, since this is itself a relevance problem, there would seem to be no yardage gained overall. What I'm to do when I'm *doing again the same thing that I did before* depends on what I'm to take as a recurrence of *the same situation I was in before*, either in general or for the case in hand. But that, in turn, depends on what I'm to take to be the *relevant* description of my previous situation; the description under which the kind of action I performed explains the success of my action. So, lacking an account of relevant sameness, the advice 'it worked last time, so just do the same again' is empty. You might as well say: 'Well, what you did last time was: you got past the sleeping dog. So do that again this time, and all will be well'.[30] 'Buy low, sell high', my stockbroker always advises. Fat lot of help that is.

'Just do what you did last time.' But what *did* I do last time? Was it that I tiptoed past a sleeping dog? Or was it that I tiptoed past a sleeping brown dog? Or that I tiptoed past a sleeping canine pet of Farmer Jones's? Or that I tiptoed past *this* sleeping canine pet of Farmer Jones's? Or that I tiptoed past a creature that Farmer Jones had thoughtfully sedated in order to enable me to tiptoe safely past it? It could well be that these are all descriptions that I think are true of what happened last time. So, the question I'm faced with is: Which of these descriptions is relevant to deciding what I ought to do *this* time? It seems I'm back where I started: I want to figure out what course the success of my previous action suggests that I should follow now.[31,32] What I need, in order to do that, is to figure out which description of my past experience

---

[30] To repeat the moral of the previous note: It mustn't be assumed the agent of a successful action generally knows what it was about the action that made it successful. ('It worked, but I'll be damned if I know why.') If he doesn't, the advice to 'do the same thing again' isn't a solution of his problem; it's just a way of saying what his problem is.

[31] Kant says (something like) 'Act so that you could rationally will that others act likewise'. But, notoriously, this advice is useless unless one knows *what is to count* as acting likewise. Everybody agrees that terrorism is wrong. The trouble is that one man's terrorist is another man's freedom fighter.

[32] For yet another example of what I take to be a vacuous solution of the frame problem there's a recent paper by Daniel Sperber that undertakes to defend the thesis that cognitive processes are massively modular against the charge that, prima facie, it makes a mystery of the

was relevant to the success of my prior action. But relevance is a nonlocal relation, and I have, by assumption, only local operations at hand. So now what?

It really is striking how often otherwise perfectly sophisticated philosophers make this sort of mistake. Thus Laudan is worried about what considerations might vindicate the rational choice of a scientific methodology. He thinks (quite reasonably) that neither the philosophical analysis of intuitions of rationality nor a historical analysis of the methods of past 'scientific elites' is likely to do the job. He advises instead an inductive appeal to practices that have previously reliably led to scientific progress. 'If actions of a particular sort, *m*, have consistently promoted cognitive ends *e*, in the past, and rival actions *n*, have failed to do so, then [with appropriate caveats] assume that... the rule "If your aim is *e*, you ought to do *m*" is more likely to promote those ends than actions based on the rule "if your aim is *e*, you ought to do *n*."' The trouble is that lacking an independent notion of 'same sort of action as *m*' the advice is entirely empty. By and large, *we don't know* what it is about the way we do science that makes the science we do work so well. That, indeed, is what arguments about scientific methodology are typically arguments about.

I do seem to be going on about this. That's because it strikes me as remarkable, and more than a bit depressing, how regularly what gets offered as a solution of the frame problem proves to be just one of its formulations. The rule of thumb for reading the literature is: If someone thinks that he has solved the frame problem, he doesn't understand it; and if someone thinks that he does understand the frame problem, he doesn't; and if someone thinks that he doesn't

sensitivity of belief fixation to nonlocal properties of belief systems (simplicity, coherence, and the like). Sperber suggests that such considerations can be accommodated 'in a variety of ways without compromising the computational character of the devices. Saliency is an obvious possible factor' (2002). But 'saliency' is as obscure as relevance and in the same way and for the same reasons. Sperber is exactly right: that what we need to make massive modularity plausible is a local way of insuring that global properties of belief systems that are *relevant* to the problem at hand will be psychologically *salient* when one is trying to solve that problem. Likewise: all we need to solve the perpetual motion problem is for someone to invent a perfectly frictionless bearing.

understand the frame problem, he's right. But it does seem clear that whatever the solution of the frame problem turns out to be (if it is just one problem; and if it has a solution), it's not going to be computationally local. You usually can't tell from the local (e.g. compositional) structure of a thought what is relevant to its (dis)confirmation. Clearly, you have to look at a lot else too; the frame problem is how you tell which else you have to look at. I wish I knew.

4.5 Globality

The frame problem concerns the size of the field of cognitive commitments that has to be searched in the course of belief fixation. But there are also cases where it's the shape of the field that's the problem. Many parameters of systems of one's prior beliefs that are germane to the choice of new ones are (what I've elsewhere called) 'global'; that is, they are defined over more or less the whole system of background beliefs, so computations that are sensitive to such parameters are nonlocal, on the face of it.

Suppose I have a set of beliefs that I'm considering altering in some way or other under (e.g.) the pressure of experience. Clearly, I would prefer that the alteration I settle on is the simplest of the available ways to accommodate the recalcitrant data. The globality problem is that I can't evaluate the overall simplicity of a belief system by summing the intrinsic simplicities of each of the beliefs that belongs to it. In fact, there is no such thing as the 'intrinsic' simplicity of a belief (just as there is no such thing as the intrinsic relevance of a datum). Nothing local about a representation—in particular, nothing about the formal relations between the representation and its constituent parts—determines how much I would complicate (or simplify) my current cognitive commitments if I were to endorse it.[33]

---

[33] One shouldn't find this surprising; there are lots of precedents. For example, the *truth* of P and Q is (roughly) a function of the truth of P and the truth of Q; but the *consistency* of P&Q isn't a function of the consistency of P and the consistency of Q.

Notice that, unlike the problems about relevance, this sort of worry about locality holds even for very small systems of belief. It holds even for punctate systems of belief (if, indeed, there can be such things). Suppose that my sole belief is that P, but that I am now considering also endorsing either the belief that Q or the belief that R. What I therefore want to evaluate, if I'm to maximize simplicity overall, is whether P&Q is simpler that P&R. But I can't do that by considering P, Q, and R severally; the complexity of P&Q isn't a function of the simplicity of P and the simplicity of Q. So the operations whereby I compute the simplicity of P&Q can't be local.

Likewise, *mutatis mutandis*, for other parameters of belief systems that one would like to maximize all else equal; for example, the relative conservatism of such commitments. Nobody wants to change his mind unless he has to; and if one has to, one prefers to opt for the bare minimum of change. The trouble is, once again, that conservatism is a global property of belief systems. On the face of it, you can't estimate how much adding P would alter the set of commitments C by considering P and C severally; on the face of it, conservatism isn't a property of beliefs that they have taken severally.

In short, it appears that many of the principles that control the nondemonstrative fixation of beliefs have to be sensitive to parameters of whole systems of cognitive commitments. So, computational applications of these principles have to be nonlocal. So, they can't be computations in the sense of CTM. If you suppose (as I'm inclined to) that nondemonstrative inference is just about always a species of argument to the best available explanation, the present considerations will be seen to apply very broadly indeed. For example, what's the best of the available explanations depends on what *alternative* explanations are available; and, by definition, the presence or absence of alternatives to a hypothesis isn't a local property of that hypothesis. There may be heuristic computational procedures that would make this sort of problem go away. But, to my knowledge, no examples have thus far been proposed that are even remotely plausible.

I should, however, add a caveat. Suppose that something you want to measure (simplicity, as it might be) is a property of complex beliefs but not of their parts; and suppose, for example, that you want to assess the relative simplicity of P&Q as compared to the relative simplicity of P&R. My point has been that, prima facie, the computations you have to perform aren't local; they must be sensitive to properties that P&Q has as such. One could, however, make the computations local by brute force. True, the complexity of the representation 'P&Q' isn't determined by local properties of 'P' together with local properties of 'Q'; but perhaps it's determined by local properties of the representation 'P&Q'. Perhaps, indeed, you can *always* preserve the *locality* of computations by inflating the size of the *units* of computation. The distance between Washington and Texas is a nonlocal property of those states; but it's a local property of the Northern hemisphere.

That brute-force reduction of global problems to local problems is, however, a kind of cheating, since it offers no clue about how to solve the local problems that the global ones reduce to. You might suppose, indeed, that it's a kind of cheating that nobody sensible would even consider. To the contrary: Recent discussions of confirmation (from, say, Duhem forward) have increasingly emphasized the holism of nondemonstrative inferences by claiming, in the limiting case, that whole theories are the proper units for the evaluation of such inferences (likewise; that whole languages are the units of translation and/or of meaning). This saves the locality of the required computations by fiat; but only at the cost of making them wildly intractable. More to the point: Even if we could, somehow, take whole theories as the units in computations involving inductive confirmation, the patent fact is that we don't. If it's true that we don't alter our cognitive commitments one by one, it's conspicuously false that our options in the evaluation of theories are 'take it or leave it'. Prima facie, there is also the option of fixing it.[34]

---

[34] Hard-nosed cognitive scientists may feel that worries about the problems that relevance are just a philosopher's neuroses. In fact, however, such issues are ubiquitous.

The long and short is: It appears that the processes by which we evaluate nondemonstrative inferences for simplicity, coherence, conservatism, and the like are *both* sensitive to global properties of our cognitive commitments, and *tractable*. What cognitive psychology would like to understand, but doesn't, is how on earth that could be so. I take the moral to be that there is quite possibly something deeply wrong with the cognitive psychology that we have currently available; just as there was something deeply wrong with a cognitive psychology that couldn't acknowledge recursion; just as there was something deeply wrong with a cognitive psychology that couldn't acknowledge the constituency and compositionality of mental representations. In fact, the argument that leads to this dire conclusion can be stated quite succinctly: Computation is, by stipulation, a process that's sensitive to the syntax of representations and to nothing else. But there are parameters of beliefs (and hence, RTM being assumed, of the mental representations that express them) that determine their role in nondemonstrative inference but are, on the face of them, not syntactic: relevance, conservatism, simplicity are extremely plausible examples. So, either learning, perception, belief fixation, and the like aren't processes of nondemonstrative inference (but what on earth else *could* they be?) or they aren't computations. The upshot is that the more a mental process is plausibly not local, the less we understand it.

Consider, for example, the notion of a memory file mentioned above as plausibly useful in accounts of cognitive architecture. The provenance of the file idea is irreproachably unphilosophical, so it may be worth noting that postulating files almost certainly violates the locality of computations. There's no use to having files unless you can figure out what in which.

But figuring out which file a memo is likely to be in is itself the kind of problem that you'd expect to be sensitive to issues of globablity, relevance, and the like. Which file the memo is likely to be in depends on which files the cabinet contains; and that is not, of course, a local property of any of the files. Likewise, you don't want to search *all* the files in the cabinet in order to find the memo; at most you want to search only the *relevant* ones. It's, by the way, a complicating factor (in case you feel in need of yet another one) that memos get moved around. If you have come to believe that Napoleon was a Bulgarian, you may well have moved his data from the FRANCE file to the BULGARIA file. Or maybe not. Whether you did depends, I suppose, on whether you think that what you know about Napoleon's place of birth is likely to be relevant to other things that you're likely to want to know about him.

Conventional cognitive science has been trying for decades now to wiggle out of this, but with, I think, not the slightest indication of success. Sooner or later, we shall have to face up to the bind we're in. Now might be as good a time as any.

What, then, is to be done?

Actually, I don't know. One possibility is to continue to try for an unvacuous heuristic account of how relevance and globality and the like might be computationally approximated. I haven't heard of any such unvacuous proposals, but it's perfectly possible that there are some somewhere. Or that there will be tomorrow; or the day after that. Hope is notorious for springing eternal. Alternatively, what our cognitive psychology needs may be a new notion of computation; one that doesn't have locality built into it. That is, of course, a lot easier to say than to provide. Turing's proposal for a nonassociative account of mental processes is surely the most important thing that has happened in cognitive science so far; arguably, the rest of it is just a footnote. Discarding, or seriously amending, that proposal would be a scientific achievement of the first importance; the failure of connectionist models of cognition to do so bears graphic witness to how hard it is likely to be.

The theory that thinking, perceiving, and the like are computations is what connects our account of mental representations to our account of mental processes; it does for us what the laws of association promised (but failed) to do for empiricists. As of this writing, however, we have no account of computation that isn't local; and we have good reasons to think that there are fundamental aspects of mental processes that a local account of computation can't capture. That being so, perhaps the best we can do, for now, is try to understand the intrinsic limitations of psychological explanations that rest on a local notion of computation. In the long run, that could lead to revising CTM, perhaps to replacing it by some theory that transcends its limitations. A consummation devoutly to be wished. In any case, as things stand the representational theory of mind is useless without a theory of mental processes; and the computational theory of mind (reading 'computation' as Turing taught us to) very possibly isn't true. Plato said 'Hard is the good'; and Plato was right.[35]

---

[35] Some years ago gestalt field theory was proposed as an account of mental processes that was both nonlocal and (unlike connectionism) nonassociative. I'm no expert, but my impression was that it too was a sort of cheat. The globality of mental processes was inferred from the (presumed) globality of their neural implementations according to what gestalt psychologists called 'the isomorphism principle'; namely, that the properties of 'consciousness' are isomorphic to the processes of its neural implementation. Thus Koffka (1935: 109): 'We can ... select psychological organizations which occur under simple conditions and can then predict that they must possess regularity, symmetry, simplicity. This conclusion is based on the principle of isomorphism ... according to which characteristic aspects of the physiological processes are also characteristic aspects of the corresponding conscious processes.

The isomorphism principle isn't, however, one that functionalists about psychological explanation can accept (and, by the way, there isn't the slightest reason to suppose that it's true).

PART II
Minds

PART II

Minds

5

Nativism

5.1 Introduction

The philosophical community greeted *LOT 1* with various degrees
of unenthusiasm. Some said that Wittgenstein (or Ryle (or somebody)) had already shown why there can't be a mentalism of
the kind that *LOT 1* commended. (Dire forecasts of impending
regress.) Others said that postulating a language of thought is harm-
less because all it comes down to *really* is the truism that beliefs and
the like are representational states; and all *that* comes down to is
the truism that beliefs and the like are *about* things. Instrumentalists
said *LOT 1* was naively realistic about the mental. A few said that
there might be something to it, but that further research would, of
course, be required.

There was, however, a striking consensus about chapter 2 of
LOT 1, which argued (*circa* p. 80) that primitive (i.e. undefined)
concepts must *ipso facto* be unlearned; and that since most quotidian concepts (TREE, CHAIR, CARBURETOR, HORSE,
UMBRELLA, and the like) are primitive, it follows that most
quotidian concepts must be unlearned. This conclusion, according to the consensus, was downright loopy; and a fair number
of critics, having noted the putative loopiness, chose simply to
ignore the argument. Their thought, apparently, was that it's all
right to ignore an argument if you dislike its conclusion *very
much*. (I remember being told, by some guy in computer science,
that he 'could not permit' concepts like HORSE to be innate;
hence, presumably, that they aren't.) More reasonably, some critics
remarked that since the premise that quotidian concepts are mostly

primitive is empirical, the conclusion that most concepts are unlearned isn't apodictic (or, anyhow, it isn't a priori). That's surely right; though the implied inference from 'empirical' and 'not apodictic' to 'probably untrue' struck me as dubious then and still does.

Anyhow, it seemed to me that the argument in *LOT 1* was prima facie sound. Hence that, barring some convincing refutation, one might wish to reflect on what it does (and what it doesn't) imply for the traditional dispute between nativists and empiricists. I subsequently revisited these issues several times (see Fodor 1981: ch 10, 1998: chs. 6, 7). Part of the project in the present chapter is to summarize, sharpen, and extend aspects of those discussions. But also I must confess that I have come to agree with my critics that there *is* something wrong with the argument as *LOT 1* presented it; namely, that its conclusion is too weak and the offending empirical assumption—that quotidian concepts are mostly primitive—is superfluous. What I should have said is that it's true and a priori that the whole notion of concept learning is per se confused. *Punkt.*

So, then, here's the present agenda: first, I'll briefly review the *LOT 1* argument, and amend it along the lines just suggested. Then I'll consider what it shows about the status of nativism. Prolepsis: It does, I think, show that there is something radically incoherent about the thesis that concepts can be learned. But, for two reasons, it doesn't quite follow that any concepts are innate: First, 'learned' and 'innate' don't exhaust the options; God only knows how many ways a creature's genetic endowment may interact with its experience to affect the inventory of concepts at the creature's disposal, but surely there are lots. Second, as Chapter 6 will argue, mental content needn't be conceptual and, plausibly, that applies to innate mental content *inter alia*. Making these points requires some delicate splitting of hairs, to be sure. But there are also matters of substance at issue; so, at least, I shall try to convince you.

5.2 The gospel according to *LOT 1* (with emendations)

Here are some principles which I take to be common ground; not seriously controversial:

(CG1) *Minds like ours start out with an innate inventory of concepts, of which there are more than none but not more than finitely many.*

If you are going to run a belief/desire psychology, you must have beliefs in your ontology; if you are going to have beliefs in your ontology, you are also going to have concepts, since the latter are the constituents of the former. But not all concepts can be learned; some must be there at the start to mediate the acquisition of the others. Even hard-core empiricists (like Hume) held that sensory concepts are innate.[1] Blank slates learn nothing; likewise rocks 'Out of nothing, nothing comes' is truistic.

But there are also respects in which (CG1) is thoroughly substantive. For example, something needs to be said about what 'at the start' means. At conception? At birth? Before one's thirty-fifth birthday? Some time after the mylenization of one's neurons? Prior to the acquisition of one's first language? And to what extent, if at all, may one's grasp of the putative starting concepts be analyzed as merely dispositional? Still, it seems likely that some or other version of (CG1) is true. I propose that we assume so.

(CG2) (also relatively untendentious) *There are all sorts of mind/ world interactions that can alter a conceptual repertoire. Concept learning* (if there is such a thing) *is one, but it's certainly not the only one.*

Other candidates conceivably include: sensory experience, motor feedback, diet, instruction, first-language acquisition, being hit on the head by a brick, contracting senile dementia, arriving at puberty,

---

[1] 'Innate' rather than 'unlearned', since Hume didn't consider the possibility that there is a variety of kinds of unlearnedness. It was, strictly speaking, only the unlearnedness of primitive concepts to which his arguments entitled him (see n. 2).

moving to California, learning physics, learning Sanskrit, and so forth indefinitely. Since nobody actually knows what 'exogenous' variables may affect a creature's capacity for conceptualization, it's a wide-open empirical issue what belongs on this list. For terminological convenience, call any process that adds to a conceptual repertoire *concept acquisition*. Our question is thus: 'What distinguishes the concept-learning kind of concept acquisition from other kinds?'.[2]

(CG3) There is, I think, a pretty general consensus in the cognitive science literature about what makes a kind of concept acquisition a kind of concept learning. Roughly, it's that *concept learning is a process of inductive inference*; in particular, that it's a process of projecting and confirming hypotheses about what the things that the concept applies to have in common. (I'll call this the 'HF' model of concept learning hereinafter.) But though this consensus is pretty general, it's much more often than not inexplicit. There are very, very many theorists who accept HF without fully realizing that it's HF that they accept. I imagine, indeed, that's the usual case. Some exposition is therefore required.

Over the years, a truly remarkable number of cognitive scientists who think that concept learning is a kind of inductive inference have assured me that they do not think that concept learning is a kind of inductive inference. (As I write this, I'm just back from a large cognitive science conference where *almost everybody* thought that concept learning is a kind of inductive inference and almost everybody denied that they did. My nerves are in terrible shape.)

---

[2] Much of the traditional nativist/empiricist debate was framed as a controversy between the thesis that some (many/most/all) concepts are *innate* (if you're a nativist) and the thesis that all concepts are *learned* (if you're an empiricist). On any reasonable account, however, these are too few options, since it mustn't be taken for granted that learning is the only way that a concept might be acquired. I use *concept acquisition* for any process that eventuates in the attainment of a concept. I use concept *learning* for a species of concept acquisition (see text just below). I take 'innate' to mean 'not acquired'. This is, of course, not a theory but just a way of talking. Presumably providing a substantive account of innateness (e.g. a genetic or 'evo-devo' account) would be the way to break into the circle. You will be unsurprised to hear that I haven't got one.

I think this unhappy state of affairs results from a pretty general failure to recognize that if concept acquisition is a learning process, then (assuming RTM) it requires the mental representation of the conditions under which the concept applies (as in: 'It's the *green* things that GREEN applies to'[3]). Here's a little dialectic to reinforce this point. (It's excerpted from an as yet undiscovered Platonic dialogue.)

Q. Do you think that two concepts could be intentionally distinct but coextensive?

A. Yes, Socrates.

Q. Such that someone might learn one of the concepts without learning the other?

A. Yes, Socrates.

Q. And such that the concepts in question might both be learned from their instances?

A. Yes, Socrates.

Q. Very well. Now consider the coextensive but distinct concepts C and C*. Do you not agree that, since these concepts are coextensive, everything that's an instance of C is likewise an instance of C*?

A. Yes, Socrates.

Q. And vice versa?

A. Yes, Socrates.

Q. Now tell me: if everything that is C is C* and vice versa, what determines whether it is C or C* that one learns from one's experience?

A. Yes, Socrates.

Q. What's that?

A. I mean: I suppose it's a matter of how one mentally represents the experiences; whether one represents them as C-experiences or as C*-experiences.

Q. And if one represents them as C-experiences then the concept one learns is C?

[3] Notice that the concept GREEN is used (not just mentioned) in 'it's the *green* things ...'.

A. Yes, Socrates.

Q. And if one represents them as C*-experiences then the concept one learns is C*?

A. Yes, Socrates.

Q. So, the difference between learning C and learning C* depends on this: in one case the learner represents his experiences as experiences of Cs

A. Yes, Socrates.

Q. (Not yet, stupid!) and in the other case the learner represents his experiences as experiences of C*s?[4]

A. Yes, Socrates. Can I go home now?

Q. Presently. But first tell me this: *Why is it* that learners who represent the things they encounter as Cs learn the concept C, but learners who represent the things they encounter as C*s learn the concept C*?

A. Huh?

Q. I mean, mustn't it be something like this: in consequence of their respective experiences, one learner comes to think to himself 'All those things are Cs' but the other comes to think to himself 'all those things are C*s'?

A. Yes, Socrates.

Q. And is not inductive inference the process par excellence by which one proceeds from representing some things as Cs to representing all such things as Cs?

A. Yes, Socrates.

Q. And can you think of any other mental process by which one might proceed from representing some things as Cs to representing all such things as Cs?

A. Not at the moment, Socrates.

Q. And is not the formation and confirmation of hypotheses the very essence of inductive inference.

A. Yes, Socrates; certainly, Socrates; by all means, Socrates.

---

[4] Socrates fails to raise the question how anyone who doesn't have the concept C *could* represent his experiences as C-experiences. That question will recur, in one form or other, through the rest of this chapter.

Q. So, does not the fact that it is possible to learn one but not the other of two distinct but coextensive concepts show that concept learning is indeed some kind of hypothesis formation/confirmation?

A. I see no alternative, Socrates.

Q. Good. Go away.

A. Yes, Socrates.

The long and short is:

First, the learning processes that distinguish between coextensive concepts require representing the same experiences in different ways. (This is a consequence of assuming that RTM is true of concept learning; that is, that experience affects concept learning only as it is mentally represented.)[5] If an experience can affect concept learning in a number of different ways, there must be a number of different ways in which the mind can represent the experiences.

Second, the experience from which a concept is learned must provide (inductive) evidence about what the concept applies to. Perhaps COW is learned from experience with cows? If so, then experiences with cows must somehow witness that it's cows that COW applies to. This internal connection between concept learning and epistemic notions like *evidence* is the source of the strong intuition that concept learning is some sort of rational process. It contrasts sharply with kinds of concept acquisition where, for example, a concept is acquired by surgical implantation; or by swallowing a pill; or by hitting one's head against a hard surface, etc. Intuitively, none of these is concept *learning*; but any or all of them might eventuate in concept attainment.[6]

---

[5] As usual, it's crucially important to observe the distinction concept *learning* and concept *acquisition*. All sorts of things can affect concept acquisition *without* being mentally represented; insomnia and intoxication are plausible examples.

[6] It's sometimes supposed that concepts are learned 'by abstraction' from experience with their instances. On this sort of model, experiences of the instances provide evidence about which of the shared properties of things in a concept's extension are 'criterial' for being in the concept's extension. Accordingly, concept learning involves inducing the criteria from samples of the extension. Here, as elsewhere, superficial differences in vocabulary mask

So, what happens in concept learning is exactly as though some (subpersonal) kind of inference goes on in the subject's head; in effect, he says to himself: 'In my experience, some of these kinds of things are C and none of these kinds of things are not-C; so *it's compatible with my experience that all of these kind of things are C*'. Correspondingly, as in any routine case of induction from empirical data, confidence that all things of this kind are C is proportional (all else equal) to the degree to which this inference is justified.[7] This HF model is, I think, the standard cognitive science view of concept learning; though, as previously remarked, it is widely unrecognized as such.

SNARK. Maybe there is such a consensus, but a consensus is not an argument. What's the evidence that children (for example) actually do learn concepts by some sort of induction?

AUTHOR. Fair question. The answer is that, as far as anybody knows, there is simply no alternative. The only reliable way to infer from a batch of singular beliefs (*this instance of EMERALD is green; that instance of EMERALD is green; that other instance of EMERALD is green;* etc.) to general conclusions (EMERALD applies to *green things*) is to take the truth of the former as evidence for the truth of the latter. So, either concept learning is what HF says it is or there isn't any such thing. I am opting for the second alternative.

SNARK. Who says concept learning *is* an *inferential* process at all? Perhaps it's just some kind of brain tickle.

AUTHOR. Right. But I'm assuming at this point that concept learning is in the domain of cognitive psychology,

---

deep similarities between versions of the same inductivist accounts of concept learning. The consequent confusions are ubiquitous in the literature.

[7] I'm not, of course, the first to have noticed the close similarity between concept learning and inductive inference; see, for example, Glymour (1996).

hence (according to CTM) that it's some sort of *computational* process; a process in which computations take a mind from premises to conclusions preserving such semantic properties as content and/or truth. It really is a *very* interesting question what happens if this assumption is abandoned and concept acquisition is treated as *not* a computational process. We'll return to this in due course.

Having got this far, *LOT 1* proceeded as follows: Consider any concept that you're prepared to accept as primitive, the concept GREEN as it might be. Then ask '*What is* the hypothesis the inductive confirmation of which constitutes the learning of that concept?' Well, to acquire a concept is at least to know what it's the concept *of*; that is, what's required of things that the concept applies to.[8] So, maybe learning the concept GREEN is coming to believe that GREEN applies to (all and only) green things; it's surely plausible that coming to believe that is at least a *necessary* condition for acquiring GREEN. Notice, however, that (assuming RTM) a token of the concept GREEN is a constituent of the belief that the concept GREEN applies to all and only *green* things. A fortiori, nobody who lacked the concept GREEN could believe this; nobody who lacked the concept GREEN could so much as *contemplate* believing this. A fortiori, on pain of circularity, coming to believe this *can't* be the process by which GREEN is acquired.[9] Likewise *mutatis mutandis* for any other primitive concept; so, *LOT 1* concluded quite correctly that no primitive concept can be learned. If one then throws in

[8] It's essential to bear in mind that this is different from saying that learning C requires learning that (or knowing how to find out whether) C applies to such and suches. That I do not know (and do not know how to find out) whether paramecia are green does not impugn my claim to have GREEN. This is the very point at which it is easiest to confuse semantics with epistemology, and thereby contract pragmatism, verificationism, operationalism, 'computational' semantics, and the like. Beware; here there be monsters.

[9] Please note the difference between this and the claim that learning (the word) 'green' requires having the concept GREEN. This latter strikes me as patently uncircular and true.

the (empirical; see above) assumption that most of the concepts one has *are* primitive (which is to say, not definable) you get the consequence that most of the concepts one has can't have been learned.[10] QED.

That's where *LOT 1* left things. I must have had a failure of nerve, however, since a much stronger conclusion is warranted; namely, that *no* concept can be learned, primitive or complex. And arriving at this much stronger conclusion doesn't, actually, require the empirical assumption that most concepts are primitive. In point of fact, it requires no empirical assumptions at all.

Consider the *complex* concept GREEN OR TRIANGULAR (= C). Unlike GREEN, C has a definition; namely, 'x is C iff x is green or triangular'. So, you might think that, even if you can't learn GREEN, you can learn C; that is, by learning its definition. That is, in effect, what *LOT 1* thought.

But that won't do. Here's the rub:

5.3 The rub

I take the following truth to be self-evident: A sufficient condition for having the concept C is: being able to think about something *as* (a) C (being able to bring the property C before the mind as such, as I'll sometimes put it).[11] If a creature can think of something as green or triangular, then that creature has the concept GREEN OR TRIANGULAR. Further research is not required.

---

[10] By contrast, consider a concept like BACHELOR. On the usual view, the concept BACHELOR is (something like) the concept HUMAN AND MALE AND UNMARRIED. So, arguably, learning BACHELOR presupposes only the availability of the concepts HUMAN, MALE, and UNMARRIED, from which BACHELOR can be constructed by conjunction. If that's right, then the argument in the text shows that primitive concepts can't be learned but leaves it open whether BACHELOR might be.

[11] Why isn't this necessary as well as sufficient? Maybe it is. But I can imagine holding, for example, that some encapsulated mental process might have access to a concept that is not available to *thought*. (Something of the sort might be the case when a concept that isn't inferentially promiscuous is nevertheless available for domain-specific computations. The question would then arise whether the mind in question should be said to 'have' the concept in question. Such possibilities are well worth exploring; but we don't need to decide them for present purposes.)

Now, according to HF, the process by which one learns C must include the inductive evaluation of some such hypothesis as 'The C things are the ones that are green or triangular'. But the inductive evaluation of that hypothesis itself requires (*inter alia*) bringing the property *green or triangular* before the mind as such. You can't represent something as green or triangular *unless you have the concepts GREEN, OR, and TRIANGULAR*. Quite generally, you can't represent anything as *such and such* unless you already have the concept *such and such*. All that being so, it follows, on pain of circularity, that 'concept learning' as HF understands it *can't* be a way of acquiring concept C. For, the one thing that a process whereby C is acquired *can't be* is a process that presupposes having C. Conclusion: *If concept learning is as HF understands it, there can be no such thing.* This conclusion is entirely general; it doesn't matter whether the target concept is primitive (like GREEN) or complex (like GREEN OR TRIANGULAR). And (as I may have mentioned) if we're given the assumption that concept learning is some sort of cognitive process, HF is de facto the only candidate account of what process it might be. But HF is circular when applied to the learning of concepts. So there can't be any such thing as concept learning.

There is, I think, a deep moral to be learned from this. HF is most naturally construed as a theory about what goes on in acquiring *beliefs*. It applies to learning *concepts* only via the (very tendentious) assumption that concept learning is itself a species of belief acquisition. In effect, HF assumes that learning C is coming to believe that *C applies to cs*. But *beliefs are constructs out of concepts, not the other way around*; in particular the belief that all the Cs are green or triangular is a construct out of (*inter alia*) the concepts GREEN, OR, and TRIANGULAR. But if that's so, then, on pain of circularity, *that Cs are green or triangular* can't be learned unless the concepts GREEN and TRIANGULAR and OR are previously available. In short: HF, when construed as a model for *concept* learning, reverses the proper order of explanation as between models of concept learning and models of belief acquisition. The resultant circularity is the special punishment that a beneficent providence meets out to philosophers (and others) who persist in getting the order of their explanations back to front.[12]

In the interest of full disclosure, however, I should emphasize that none of this changes for the better if you assume, as I am strongly inclined to do, that concept individuation is referential and atomistic; nor is any of it offered as an argument in aid of that assumption. It's easy to get confused about this, so I hereby declare a (reasonably brief) digression that may serve to underscore it.

5.4 (Reasonably brief) digression

For a galaxy of reasons that circle around facts about composition-ality, and which I hope previous chapters have made clear, I'm much inclined to think that the semantics of Mentalese (and hence the content of concepts) is purely referential. I would therefore be delighted to announce that adopting a referentialist stance towards the content of concepts somehow avoids the kind of argument against the possibility of concept learning that we have just been exploring. But it doesn't. The referential view of concepts is in the same boat with (for example) definitional views of concepts, stereotype views of concepts, imagist views of concepts, and so forth: Barring the sudden emergence of an alternative to the HF model of concept learning (which is, I promise you, not going

---

[12] Notice, by the way, that nothing changes if one assumes that concepts are some-thing like Ramsey sentences (see e.g. Lewis 1972); not, anyway, if you think of Ramsey sentences as *definitions* of theoretical terms. To the contrary, as we've been seeing, you can't learn a definition unless you can already think the definiens; and that applies, *inter alia*, to definitions like 'x is an electron = df [followed by the Ramsey sentence for "electron"]'. The salient difference between the Ramsey sentence for C and a mere common-or-garden-variety definition of C is that the former tells you *everything* that a theory says about the (putative) referents of C; which is, I should have supposed, rather more than you want for purposes of the semantic analysis of C. What Ramsification gives you that traditional definitions don't is just a particularly vicious case of holism. (In fact, it's sort of misleading to think of the Ramsey sentence for 'electron' as defining it at all. For thoroughly familiar reasons, the concept of an electron has to be transtheoret-ic, which is exactly what Ramsified definitions aren't. What the Ramsey sentence for 'electron' provides is a normal form for expressing what a theory says about electrons. *Punkt.*)

to happen), they all imply that all concepts are unlearned. This shouldn't be surprising. What led to concept nativism wasn't any *particular* proposal about the nature of concepts. Rather, it was the thought that learning a concept involves acquiring a belief about its identity; and that assumption is entirely neutral with respect to the question whether or not the semantics of mental representations is referential. It is, however, very easy to get muddled about this and then to overstate the case for semantic referentialism. Eric Margolis (1999) has recently offered an account of how concepts might be learned that I think makes that mistake. I'm now going to turn to this. The interest, for present purposes, is that Margolis situates his account of concept learning in the context of a number of referentialist/atomist assumptions about the content and possession conditions of concepts that, as the reader will have gathered, I more or less share. To wit:

(1) Conceptual content is entirely referential. In particular, concepts don't have senses.

(2) The metaphysics of concept possession is atomistic. In principle, one might have any one concept without having any of the others (except that having a complex concept requires having its constituent concepts).

(3) From the point of view of the metaphysics of content, the fundamental symbol/world relation is the *locking* of a mental representation (type) to a property. If M is a mental representation locked to property P, then 'tokens of P cause tokens of M' is counterfactual-supporting.[13] (*Which* counterfactuals it is required to support is, of course, the Mother of All Questions.)

(4) The extension of a concept is the set of (actual or possible) instances of the property to which the concept is locked. The concept DOG is locked to the property of *being a dog* and its extension is thus the set of (actual or possible) dogs.

---

[13] It is, I assume, no accident that counterfactual-supporting correlations are what generate 'information' in at least one important sense of that notion (see Dretske 1981).

(5) A naturalistic account of the reference relation would be a naturalistic theory of the locking relation. As such, it would articulate causally/nomologically sufficient conditions for an object to be the referent of a mental representation.

You are not, actually, required to believe any or all of that, though it would be nice of you to do so. But it's the background from which Margolis's discussion proceeds. Our question is: Does it help with the question whether concept learning is possible? And, if so, how?

Margolis notes (rightly, I think) that the thesis that concept possession is atomistic does *not* preclude the possibility that beliefs, hypotheses, theories, and the like may mediate the causal/nomic relation between a mental representation and the property it's locked to. The stress here, however, is on the contrast between *mediation* and *constitution*. It may be that tokenings of beliefs about dogs are (sometimes? always?) links in the reference-making causal chain that connects token dogs to DOG tokens. (Hears bark; thinks: *Where there's a bark, there's a dog; therefore, there's a dog.*) It wouldn't follow that having that belief is *constitutive* of having that concept. It likewise wouldn't follow that 'dog' means *barks*, or that barks are (what Wittgensteinians call) 'criterial' for doghood, or that it's metaphysically necessary that you can't have DOG unless you have BARKS, or that the 'use' of 'dog' is to refer to barkers ... and so forth through the woeful collection of misapprehensions of which twentieth-century accounts of the metaphysics of reference have largely consisted. None of that follows and none of it is true. So says Margolis, and so say I.

Quite generally: Operationalism isn't true, and what psychologists call 'cue validity' (which is an epistemic notion) has approximately nothing to do with concept individuation (which isn't). (If Wittgenstein got this wrong, so too did Brunner.) In fact, all sorts of things can mediate causal linkages between concepts and their referents without being in any sense constitutive of the identity of the concept: Consider stars. The link between token stars and token STARs might depend on: visual contacts (which may themselves be mediated by telescopes or eyeglasses), beliefs, theories; tokenings of English sentences (*a* writes *b* a note about stars); consultations with experts; and so forth, effectively without end. It doesn't follow, and it isn't true, that people who look at stars through telescopes *ipso facto* have a different STAR-concept than people who don't.[14]

OK so far. But then one gets passages like the following: 'It is one thing to think that a file's contents are inessential to how it is labeled, and another to think that they are entirely irrelevant.[15] No one, not even Fodor [!], thinks they are irrelevant. The reason he doesn't suppose this … is that the mind-world relation that he thinks does determine conceptual content must be sustained by a mechanism, and generally the only available mechanism is the inferential apparatus that is associated with the concept' (1999: 553).

I guess the intended argument is something like this: 'Some or other mind–world relation [metaphysically] determine[s] conceptual content; and such mind-world relations are often sustained by some or other "inferential apparatus"; but an inferential apparatus is just the sort of thing that can be learned (not just acquired);[16] so

---

[14] In effect, I espouse a *functionalist* view of the metaphysics of reference, and so in effect does Margolis. Reference wants reliable correlations between things in the world and symbols in the head, but it doesn't care (much?) what causal mechanisms sustain such relations; in principle, the mechanisms that correlate tokens of instances of the mental representation 'C' with things in the extension of C may perfectly well differ from token to token. The trick, in naturalizing reference, is to hold onto the mind-world correlations while quantifying over whatever it is that sustains them. (I've made quite a point of this elsewhere; see Fodor 1988, 1990).

[15] For the file analogy see Chapter 3. Roughly, concepts correspond to the labels of files; beliefs, theories, and the like correspond to what's in the files; so one's beliefs about Cs (insofar as they are explicitly so represented) are stored in the file whose label is 'C'. *Very roughly:* one thinks in file names.

[16] Here, as elsewhere, it's important not to confuse the question whether *concepts* can be learned with the question whether theories, beliefs, and the like can be learned *given the prior availability of the concepts they deploy.* Given AUTOMOBILE and CARBURETOR, I assume one could acquire the belief that *automobiles have carburetors* by mere induction. (To be sure, if you suppose that concepts are 'defined' internal to the theories that deploy them, you will be unable to respect the distinction between learning concepts and acquiring beliefs. Therefore, do not suppose that.)

concepts too can be learned (not just acquired)'. But that's a sleight of hand: The trouble is that 'You can learn (not just acquire) A' and 'Learning A is sufficient for acquiring B' just doesn't imply 'You can learn B'. For, the following would seem to be a live option: If you acquire a concept by learning a theory, then something is learned (namely, the theory) and something is (merely) acquired (namely, the concept); but what is learned isn't (merely) acquired and what is (merely) acquired isn't learned. To acquire the concept C is to lock to the property that Cs have in common; and such lockings may be mediated by theories. The theory that mediates the locking between the concept and the property that the concept is locked to may be, but needn't be, rational, or coherent, or well evidenced, to say nothing of true. That's why Ancient Greeks, who thought stars were holes in the fabric of the heavens, could nevertheless think about stars.

If the sort of referentialist/atomist story about conceptual content that Margolis and I like is true, and if pragmatism, operationalism, and the like aren't true, then learning a theory can be (causally) sufficient for acquiring a concept. But it doesn't follow that you can learn a concept.[17] So, here we are, back where we started; we still don't have a clue what it might be to learn a concept. End of digression.

So, now what? First of all, let's take stock. Suppose that some or other version of the revised *LOT 1* argument is actually sound, and that it shows that concepts can't be learned. What happens next? Well (to repeat a point) you can't infer from a concept's not being learned to its being innate; not, at least, if 'innate' means something like 'not acquired in consequence of experience'. There would appear to be plenty of ethological precedents—from 'imprinting' to 'parameter setting' inclusive—where it's implausible that the

---

[17] For that matter, you can acquire a concept by *acquiring* a theory (i.e. by acquiring but not learning it). I'm dropped on my head and thereby acquire the geocentric theory of planetary motion, and thereby become linked to, say, the property of being a planet. In such cases, neither the theory I've acquired nor the concept I've acquired has been learned.

acquisition of a concept is mediated by a rational process like inductive inference, but where concept acquisition is nevertheless highly sensitive to the character of the creature's experience. So, neither the *LOT 1* argument nor the present revision shows that concepts can't be acquired from experience. The most they show is that acquiring a concept from experience must be distinguished from learning it.

This is all rather unsatisfactory, or so it seems to me. In particular, according to the present account, nativism appears to reduce to the negative thesis that HF was wrong about concept acquisition, and/or to the methodological thesis that theories of concept acquisition belong to neuroscience rather than psychology. A paradox: it looks as though once empiricism is seen to be false, nativism is seen not to be interesting.[18]

I do think that if HF is no longer in the running, then a general reformulation of the issues about concept innateness is mandatory. The central issue isn't *which concepts are learned*, since, if the (emended) *LOT 1* argument is right, none of them are. Nor, however, is it *which concepts are innate*, if an innate concept is one the acquisition of which is independent of experience. Quite likely, there are none of those either. Rather, the problem is to explain how a creature's innate endowment (whether it is described in neurological or in intentional terms) contributes to the acquisition of its conceptual repertoire; that is, how innate endowments contribute to the processes that start with experience and end in concept possession. Denying that GREEN TRIANGLE or CARBURETOR are learned doesn't answer this question. Having once gotten the empiricist theory of concept acquisition off the table—having once overcome the illusion that HF might offer a theory of concept learning—it's time to think about what a nativist theory of concept acquisition might be like.

I'm about to offer a proposal that strikes me as promising, though I'm aware that it couldn't amount to more than a sketch of the

---

[18] For a philosopher who argues this way see Cowie (1999). For a review see Fodor (2001).

relevant geography. I don't know how concepts are acquired. Nor do you. Nor does anybody else. And I do agree that if they aren't acquired by induction, some explanation is required of how experience contributes to their acquisition. So, as Henry James liked to say, there we are.

How could concepts be acquired if concepts aren't learned?

Start again: Why shouldn't a nativist be a flat-out preformationist about concepts? Why shouldn't a nativist say something like this: 'Concepts aren't learned but they aren't acquired either. Concepts are, as it were, there from the beginning. We have the concepts we do because we have the neurology we do; we have the neurology we do because we have the phenotype we do; and we have the phenotype we do because we have the genotype we do. We have CARBURETOR for the same sort of reason that we have ten fingers. The buck stops here'?

SNARK. Preposterous!

AUTHOR. Ethology isn't an a priori inquiry. What strikes you (or me) as preposterous is of no scientific interest. If conceptual preformationism is the only coherent option, then conceptual preformationism is the only coherent option. God gets to choose how the world is; you don't (neither do I).

SNARK. Fiddlesticks. The trouble with preformationism is that it simply doesn't take sufficiently seriously the role of experience in concept acquisition. Maybe the role of experience in concept acquisition isn't what HF takes it to be; maybe it doesn't provide the data for an inductive inference. But you aren't denying, I suppose, that it has *some* role to play?

AUTHOR. Well, no. But maybe what it does is *trigger* concept acquisition. For concepts to be genotypically specified is one thing; but for the genotypically specified information to be phenotypically expressed—for it actually to be accessible to a creature's mental processes— is perhaps quite another. Maybe experience is what bridges the gap between a genetic endowment and its phenotypic expression. Maybe, even, there are quite specific constraints on *which kind* of experience is required if a certain genotypically specified concept is to become phenotyically accessible. There are quite respectable ethological precedents for that sort of arrangement.

SNARK. I'm sorry; I really am; but that just won't do. In the untendentious ethological cases triggers can be quite arbitrarily related to the processes they trigger. Triggers can even be—indeed, often are—entirely hormonal. At a certain (genotypically specified) point in development the neurochemistry alters and a perfectly charming child turns into a perfectly insufferable adolescent. ('Nasty, brutish, and tall', as Alison Laurie put it.) But if *that's* what triggering is like, it's not a plausible model for how experience makes concepts accessible.

In short (Snark continues) there's a dilemma lurking here; and if nativists can't resolve it, they are going to have as much trouble saying how concepts might be acquired as empiricists have in saying how they might be learned. On one side there's Descartes's sort of argument that you can't possibly acquire TRIANGLE from experience of triangles, (to say nothing of *learning* TRIANGLE from experience of triangles) because there aren't any triangles to have experiences of; the best one ever encounters are rough, approximations. So there is a prima facie argument that TRIANGLE is innate if an innate concept is one that's not acquired from experience of things in its extension. On the other side there's what I'll call the doorknob/DOOKNOB problem:[19] Maybe there aren't any triangles, but there are lots of doorknobs; and surely acquiring DOORKNOB is a process that typically involves interacting with some of them; indeed, it typically involves interacting with *good examples* of doorknobs, where this means something like *stereotypic* examples of doorknobs. A viable nativism must have a story to tell about why that is so.

In the typical case one gets DOORKNOB from doorknobs and not from (as it might be) teapots; it's TEAPOT that one gets from teapots. Likewise, one typically achieves the ostensive definition of 'doorknob' by exhibiting not teapots but (good examples of) doorknobs. But why should that all be so unless one's experience with doorknobs provides some sort of inductive evidence about what sorts of things DOORKNOB applies to? Likewise, if concept acquisition isn't a kind of induction, why does it so often go hand in hand with the acquisition of stereotypes? Roughly, the stereotypic instances of a concept are the ones that most resemble most other instances of the concept. So, if concept acquisition uses some sort of induction (perhaps some sort of statistical inference) it's perfectly understandable why it should lead to stereotype formation in the normal course. Well, what explains why it does if, as the triggering story claims, concept learning *isn't* a kind of induction?

And (Snark continues, relentlessly) there's another thought that should worry nativists or, indeed, anybody else who proposes to abandon the HF account of concept learning; it's a philosophical thought, if you please. How is it that so many

---

[19] Snark is plagiarizing shamelessly; see Fodor (1998).

of our concepts fit the world? How is it that so many of them have non-null extensions? We have, as it might be, the concept DOORKNOB and, lo and behold, there actually are things (namely, doorknobs) to which that concept applies. Nor is DOORKNOB the only such case; it happens all the time.[20] The theory that concepts are acquired by learning does explain why concepts very often fit the world: it's because they are very often learned *from* the world by a generally reliable inferential procedure. But if HF is false, then we *don't* learn our concepts from the world by a generally reliable inferential process; in fact, though the world may contribute (e.g. causally) to their acquisition, we don't learn them *from* the world at all. So, then, why do so many of our concepts have instances? A nativist with any sort of conscience must confront this question. *That means you!*

AUTHOR. Can I go home now?

SNARK. Not on your Nelly; not while I'm ahead.

AUTHOR. What of my white hairs?

SNARK. Pull them out!

AUTHOR. Oh, very well. Let's, to start with, think some more about stereotypes. Snark and Descartes agree that there aren't any triangles; so, even if HF were otherwise plausible, learning TRIANGLE couldn't require inductions over encounters with its instances. But there is, nonetheless, a triangle

---

[20] A skeptic might deny that our concepts do fit the world; but I'm not interested in skepticism. A Kantian might say that it's synthetic a priori that our concepts fit the world; but I don't know what that means. A Darwinian might say that our concepts fit the world because that's what they were selected for; but that would offer a historical explanation where a synchronic, mechanistic explanation is called for (and, anyhow, the notion of 'selection for' is probably incoherent, much like the notion of concept learning (see Fodor 2008 and Fodor and Piatelli (forthcoming)). In Snark's view (and in mine) it's a plain, contingent fact that lots of our concepts have actual extensions; it's part and parcel of the fact that lots of our beliefs are true. Such facts require explanations.

stereotype. Even if nothing is, strictly speaking, an instance of the property *being a triangle*, some things are better instances of the concept TRIANGLE than others, just as some things are better instances of DOORKNOB than others. In short, there can be an X stereotype *whether or not* there are any Xs. (There are no unicorns, but stereotypic unicorns are white and have one horn.) So, then, if concepts were stereotypes, some kinds of concept acquisition could be inductive inferences after all; roughly, statistical inductive inferences. Roughly, we might think of stereotypic properties as central tendencies of (actual or possible) populations; and, of course, a property can be the central tendency of a population even if nothing in the population has it (as in 'The average family has two and a half children').[21] But concepts can't be stereotypes since concepts compose and stereotypes don't.

This suggests a working hypothesis about stereotypes that I take to be independently plausible: Although it's quite true that acquiring a concept can't be the same thing as learning its stereotype, it needn't follow that learning a stereotype is just a *by-product* of acquiring the concept; it could rather be a *stage* in concept acquisition. Or, to put the suggestion the other way around, concept acquisition might proceed from stereotype formation to concept attainment.[22] Now, for better or worse, we're still committed to the metaphysical

---

[21] There's convincing experimental evidence that something like the estimation of central tendencies does go on in stereotype formation, and that it can do so even in the absence of stimuli that instance the stereotype. For a review of the relevant literature see Smith and Medin (1981).

[22] At a minimum, there is quite a lot of empirical evidence that stereotype formation often happens *very early* in concept acquisition; young children's judgments about what concepts apply to what things are typically most reliable for paradigm instances. They're

assumption that acquiring a concept is, fundamentally, locking to the property that the concept expresses. Put that all together, and you get a picture that looks like this:

Initial state → (P1) → stereotype formation → (P2) → locking (= concept attainment).

The thought might well be that P1 is a process of statistical inference and P2 is some reliable but not intentional (and hence, a fortiori, not inferential) neurological process. Since, as we've been seeing, forming an X stereotype doesn't require that there be actual Xs, it's so far possible that this picture might apply both to the acquisition of TRIANGLE and to the acquisition of DOORKNOB. That would resolve Snark's worry that no version of nativism could provide a uniform treatment of the role of experience in concept acquisition; that is, one that applies both to concepts that have actual instances (DOORKNOB) and to concepts that don't (TRIANGLE; UNICORN).

SNARK. I notice that you've been uncharacteristically silent about P2. Suppose stereotype formation is a stage in concept acquisition. What, then, is the *next* stage? How do you get from learning the stereotype for C to acquiring the concept C. What sort of inference effects this transition?[23]

AUTHOR. I do not think that this will make you happy.

---

good at whether dogs are animals long before they've got the extension of ANIMAL under control.

[23] If you are a referentialist in semantics, you will take this to be the question how one gets from (a representation of) the extension of the stereotype to (a representation of) the extension of the corresponding concept. The extension of the stereotype of C would be something like the set of those individuals who have the typical properties of Cs. The extension of the concept C is the set of Cs (or perhaps, the set of actual-or-possible Cs).

SNARK.   I'm used to that; *c'est mon métier.* Proceed.

AUTHOR.   It's no sort of inference at all. It's, as it were, a *sub*intentional and *sub*computational process; it's a kind of thing that our sort of brain tissue just does. Psychology gets you from the initial state to P2; then neurology takes over and gets you the rest of the way to concept attainment (that is, to locking according to the present assumptions). Intentional explanation can't, in any event, go all the way down on anybody's story. Sooner or later neurology has to take over. (Indeed, sooner or later *physics* has to take over.) Where exactly that happens is not an apriori issue. As it turns out, P2 is one of those places.[24]

SNARK.   Taken all together, that's rather a lot of assuming, hypothesizing, speculating, and, generally, whistling in the dark. Why don't you prove something, for a change?

AUTHOR.   Go chase your tails. I'm not even *trying* to prove anything; not a priori and not a posteriori either. I'm trying to find a straw to cling to. We badly need some ideas about how the various bits and pieces of what we've so far found out about concept acquisition might fit together. I'm suggesting a possible arrangement; specifically, an arrangement that, because it doesn't require that concept acquisition be a kind of learning, might be acceptable even to

---

[24] I don't want to raise general issues about the relations between the two kinds of explanation; only long stories have a chance of being right about that, and this is just a footnote. But it's pretty plausible that intentional processes don't, as it were, float free. They must have implementations that can (in principle) be specified in non-intentional vocabulary; e.g. in neurological vocabulary. And it isn't plausible, in fact it's perfectly obviously not true, that a neurological process that impacts intentional-level phenomena must *ipso facto* itself be an intentional process. Brain damage, for example, regularly plays havoc with psychological states, capacities, and processes; but it doesn't do so via an intentional process. It's (to use a way of talking from an earlier paper) just 'brute causal'. (As, come to think of it, is most of what happens in the world. What's striking about intentionality is, on the one hand, that it's so important, and, on the other hand, that there's so little of it around.)

raving nativists (like me); that is, to nativists who have become convinced by the sorts of arguments we've been considering, that 'concept learning' is an oxymoron. Assuming that forming a stereotype is typically a stage in concept acquisition might do the trick; it has, prima facie, the following attractive features:

Since stereotypes are formed by induction, assuming that learning a stereotype is a stage in concept acquisition starts us on explaining why concepts are typically learned from their instances.

Indeed, it starts us on explaining why concepts are typically acquired in consequence of experiences with their *good* (e.g. statistically modal) instances; whereas if concept acquisition isn't concept learning, there is no a priori reason why they should be. Or, to put it the other way around, even if concept acquisition isn't learning, it would be well if it turned out to involve a learning process *inter alia*.

It would also comport with well-known empirical results suggesting that even very young infants are able to recognize and respond to statistical regularities in their environment. A genetically endowed capacity for statistical induction would make sense if stereotype formation is something that minds are frequently employed to do.

In short, the present proposal would start us on explaining why concept acquisition, though (on pain of circularity) it can't be what HF says it is, nevertheless often has the look of rational inductive inference. By contrast, this apparent rationality of concept learning is a stumbling block for a kind of concept nativist who thinks that concepts are acquired by some sort of triggering.

All that being so, what we need now is just a neurological story about P2; that is, about whatever it is that transforms a mind that has learned a stereotype into a mind that has acquired the concept whose stereotype it is. I have no such story. I'm not even a neurologist.

SNARK. Tell me again why P2 can't be some sort of inference?

AUTHOR. Well, because there are only two kinds of inferential process that it could be; and, pretty clearly, it isn't either of them. One option that's ruled out is that the mind somehow compares stereotypes with candidate concepts and pairs each stereotype with the concept that matches it best. That sort of story would be circular on the face of it, since our problem is how concepts are acquired, and you can't compare a stereotype with a concept that you don't have. The other possibility is that there is a pattern of inference which, given just a stereotype, identifies the corresponding concept. But that does strike me as most implausible. The basic problem is that there are so many different kinds of relations in which a concept and its stereotypes may stand. The cabbage stereotype is related to the concept CABBAGE in one way; but the king stereotype is related to the concept KING in quite a different way. (Cabbages look like one another by and large. By and large, kings don't, except when they are wearing their crowns.) And the triangle concept is related to its stereotype in still quite another way. And the stereotypic odd number[25] is related to the concept ODD NUMBER in another way still. And so forth, I should think more or less indefinitely.

---

[25] Believe it or not, there actually is such a thing. See Armstrong et al. (1983).

I don't believe that one can, as it were, just look at a stereotype and figure out what concept it is the stereotype of. Even if P2 were some kind of inference, I don't think it could be one that runs from a stereotype to the concept of which it is the stereotype.

SNARK. You do, however, acknowledge the bare possibility that P2 is some kind of inference rather than a merely mechanical push-and-pull?

AUTHOR. That is, I suppose, a bare possible. But I'd bet heavily against it as a working hypothesis. P2 must, of course, correspond to some neurological process or other. But it doesn't remotely follow that it also corresponds to any *intentional* process (to a kind of reasoning, for example). Nor is there, as far as I can tell, any empirical consideration that suggests that it does. Rather, the underdetermination of concepts by their stereotypes looks to be very radical. (So much so that the same stereotype can correspond to different concepts; chickens are paradigmatic instances both of FOOD and of BARNYARD FOWL). Given such cases, I'm hard pressed to imagine an inferential process which would reliably produce the right results.

SNARK. I don't suppose you're prepared to tell us anything useful about P2 (other, I mean, than that it isn't inferential)?

AUTHOR. I don't suppose so either. In fact, I can imagine it turning out that there isn't actually much about it to say. I'm assuming that, in the paradigmatic cases, P2 starts with an (inductively derived) stereotype and eventuates in locking to some property of which the stereotype is a particularly good instance. It's a point to keep in mind here that, quite possibly, being locked is itself a very heterogeneous relation;

there are perhaps all sorts of mechanisms that can sustain the connection between a mental represent-ation and the property that is shared by the things in its extension. (See the discussion of Margolis 1999 above.) This suggests the (very unpleasant) possibil-ity that P2 may be heterogeneously implemented at subintentional levels. Since concepts get locked to lots of quite different kinds of things-in-the-world (cabbages, kings, prime numbers, whatever) there might well be lots of different kinds of mind-world mechanism that constitute the locking. That lock-ing is a neurological process would not entail that the process of getting locked is a neurologically natural kind.

SNARK. Can I make a friendly suggestion?

AUTHOR. I doubt it.

SNARK. No, really. Suppose it's true that stereotypes aren't concepts. Why couldn't concepts be stereotypes together with similarity metrics? That's, after all, what psychologists who are into stereotype theory mostly think that concepts are. (See, for example, Osherson and Smith 1981.) If they are right, a reasonable suggestion for a nativist to make is that the similarity metric(s) is, as it were, wired into the neurology. Knowing what the stereotype for a concept is, one then just (noninferentially) sees other things in the concept's extension as relevantly similar to the stereotype. That is, given a concept's stereotype, one just (noninferentially) sees things in the concept's extension as similar to one another. That one does is provided gratis by the innate structure of the brain (or whatever);[26] which is to say

---

[26] Snark remarks that he is abstracting from the phenomenon of 'learned similarity'; this would require attention in a more serious account of the sort of concept-acquisition theory he has in mind.

that it's bedrock as far as intentional explanation is concerned. What's unlearned in concept acquisition is thus one's appreciation of the similarity between the stereotypic instances of the concept and the rest of its extension. Doesn't that even almost sound a little like Wittgenstein? At least a very small little?

AUTHOR. It won't work; the compositionality problem persists. Just as you can't construct the stereotypic female dentist (if there is one) from the stereotypes for FEMALE and DENTIST, so too you can't construct the *similarity metric* for the stereotype of FEMALE DENTIST from the similarity metrics for FEMALE and DENTIST. The respect in which female dentists are like one another isn't the sum of the respect in which females are like one another and the respect in which dentists are like one another. (In fact, it's not obvious what does make female dentists like one another, except that they are all female dentists.) That is not just a passing sneer. A similarity-based theory of concepts is vacuous unless the relevant parameter of similarity can be specified *without making use of the concepts in question.* All Fs are, to be sure, similar to each other in that all of them are F.[27] That is no help and we didn't need cognitive science to tell us about it.

The fundamental problem is the one noted above: the ways in which different kinds of thing are similar to one another aren't, in general, similar to one another. No doubt, there are respects in which

---

[27] It is, for example, true but not edifying to be told that what makes birds similar to one another is that they are all '+bird'; or that what makes artifacts similar to one another is that they are all '+artifact'; or that what makes (physical) objects similar to one another is that they are all +(physical) object; or that what makes the agents of actions similar to one another is that all share the feature '+ agent of an action'. You might be surprised how much of the literature in what's called 'lexical semantics' consists of the learned reiteration of such truisms.

cabbages are similar to one another. Likewise there are respects in which kings are. But that's all just truistic; to turn it into a substantive similarity-based theory of concepts you also need that being similar to a cabbage is similar to being similar to a king. Well, it's not; and, since it's not, you would expect the compositionality of similarity metrics to fail; as indeed it does. (For discussion see Fodor and Lepore 2002.)

SNARK. Here's a thought: Why couldn't similarity between concepts be explicated by some notion of *overlap* of semantic features? Roughly, the more features an x shares with the C stereotype, the more it's likely to be viewed as falling under C.

AUTHOR. Features are useless. They are overdue for extinction. Female dentists have something in common with male dentists, according to the present view; it's that both satisfy (are in the extension of) the feature +DENTIST. But now: do male dentists and female dentists both fall under the *same* feature +DENTIST? That is, are male dentists and female dentists both dentists in the very same sense of 'dentist'? Or are there two (very similar) semantic features +DENTIST, one that applies to dentists who are male and one that applies to dentists who are female? Nothing is gained by replacing the unpromising question 'What makes a thing similar to a dentist' with the equally unpromising question 'What makes a thing similar to a +dentist?' Bother features, here and elsewhere.)[28]

---

[28] It should come as no surprise that features don't really *do* anything. 'Feature' is, after all, just a way of writing 'open sentence'. 'Bachelors share the feature +male' is just a way of saying that—IS MALE' is satisfied by bachelors; there's really nothing to choose between these formulations. (Nor does it help one bit to add that the features in question are 'subsemantic'; or that they are 'distributed'. Compare Smolensky 1995). These remarks

SNARK. Well, if you don't like my theory about similarity metrics being what's unlearned in concept acquisition, how about you tell me your story.

AUTHOR. Don't have one.

SNARK. Why am I so very not surprised?

AUTHOR. But I can conjure you a fantasy. It will help if we start with a very informal introduction to the notion of an attractor landscape. (It's one that comes up frequently in discussions of neural nets, but we mustn't hold that against it. Snarks who require an introduction to this sort of model should see Elman et al. 1996: ch. 2.) So, then: The mind is like a sea.

SNARK. Come again?

AUTHOR. I said: 'The mind is like a sea'. Imagine a sea that's dotted with boats, all sailing along, happy as larks. Lots of sun and just the right amount of wind blowing at a favorable angle. The yard bills are paid. None of the crew is seasick, and the navigational instruments are all working fine. (I said this is a fantasy). There is, however, a catch. Randomly distributed over the sea on which the boats are sailing, there are whirlpools.

SNARK. Whirlpools?

AUTHOR. Whirlpools. That is, holes in the surface of the sea into which things may fall according to the principle that the closer to a whirlpool a thing gets, the greater the force with which the whirlpool tries to suck it in. (The paradigm example of an attractor landscape is a Newtonian universe, where point masses attract one another with a force that varies inversely as a function of their distances.)

---

also apply, *mutatis mutandis*, to the kind of theories that represent concepts (not as feature bundles but) as locations in a 'multidimensional vector space' (compare Churchland 1989). Here, too, the proposal is merely notational. (For discussion see Fodor and Lepore 2002: ch. 9.)

SNARK. I don't wish to play this game. I don't *do* whirlpools.

AUTHOR. That's OK; just so long as you've got the picture. Well, then, here's how the simile applies to concept acquisition: Think of concepts as attractors, each with its location in the sea. Think of stereotypes as boats in the sea located according to the principle that the better the stereotype, the closer it is to the corresponding attractor.

SNARK. Since when do stereotypes come in better and worse?

AUTHOR. I just made it up. The intuition is that there are cases where knowing a stereotype comes pretty close to knowing necessary and sufficient conditions for a thing to fall under the corresponding concept; and there are cases where it doesn't. That is because, to put it roughly once again, there are cases where most (actual or possible) Cs are very like the stereotypic C, and there are cases where many aren't. More or less equivalently: there are cases when the stereotype gives you lots of information about the properties Cs share as such and there are cases where it doesn't. (The stereotype for *triangles* is maybe typical of the former, the stereotype for *thing* or *event* is surely typical of the latter.) It's ones of the first kind that I'm calling 'good' stereotypes. OK?

SNARK. [*growls discontentedly but does not utter*].

AUTHOR. [*continues*]. Well then, the picture is that the better the stereotype, the closer it is to an attractor. And the closer the stereotype is to an attractor, the more likely it is that learning the stereotype is sufficient[29] for acquiring the corresponding concept; that is, for locking to the property that the corresponding concept expresses. To a first approximation, then,

---

[29] *Empirically* sufficient; not, of course, *conceptually* sufficient.

the picture is that *what's innate is the geometry of the attractor landscape.*

SNARK. Come again?

AUTHOR. Look, suppose the metaphysical situation is that to have the concept SHEEP you must be in the locking relation (whatever that is) to the property of being a sheep (whatever *that* is). Well, this discussion has been independently committed both to content being referential, and to reference being some sort of causal/mechanical/nomological relation between (actual or possible) tokens of a concept and (actual or possible) instances of the property that the concept expresses. So, to put these pieces together: Get close to an attractor and you lock to a property. That's a brute fact; in particular, it's a brute fact about the kind of animals we are (presumably about the kinds of brains we have); and it's the bedrock on which the phenomenon of concept acquisition rests.

SNARK. Of course, that doesn't tell us a bit about how the thing works; I mean, it doesn't explain *how* learning the stereotype gets you locked to the right property.

AUTHOR. Nothing is perfect. But it's some comfort that this sort of picture has a respectable provenance. For example, what I've been suggesting is quite close to the standard gestalt treatment of how perceptual closure works. Their idea was that perceptual categorization is biased in the direction of 'good forms'. So, a circle with a small gap is seen as an instance of *circle tout court* rather than as an instance of something-with-a-gap. Likewise, a triangle with a slightly curved side is seen as an instance of TRIANGLE; and so forth. In effect, shapes that have good form function as attractors in the perceptual analysis of things whose shapes are slightly deformed; and the closer a percept is to having a good form, the more likely it is to be caught by the corresponding attractor. Plato was right, plus or minus a bit: to see a figure as a triangle is to see it Under The Form of Triangularity.

So, here's my story about concept acquisition: What's learned (not just acquired) are stereotypes (statistical representations of experience). What's innate is the disposition to grasp such and such a concept (i.e. to lock to such and such a property) in consequence of having learned such and such a stereotype. Experience with things that are asymptotic approximations of The Triangle in Heaven causes locking to *triangularity*.[30]

I wonder whether that makes me a nativist? And, if it does, what kind of a nativist does it make me? On this way of carving the goose, the difference between relatively radical kinds of concept nativism and more modest kinds is mostly in the generality of the principles that map the stereotypes onto the concepts. Here again the analogy to discussions of good form is striking. Is the gestalt account of perceptual closure radically nativist? That depends on the generality of the principles according to which goodness of form is assessed. If they are very specific—if you have to say what counts as good form independently for each kind of percept—then the implied nativism is very strong indeed. If not, then not.

SNARK. I find myself, on balance, deeply unmoved. Haven't all the interesting questions been begged?

AUTHOR. Yes, of course they have. As I said, this is a picture, not a theory. To say that you acquire a concept 'automatically' when you encounter things that are

---

[30] Concepts that don't have instances (TRIANGLE, UNICORN) can be learned so long as they do have stereotypes.

close to an attractor isn't to say how the locking is
achieved; it's just to say that how it's achieved isn't
to be explained at the intentional level. Likewise,
though I think that the geometry of the attractor
space must be innate, I've offered no suggestions
at all about what geometry the innate space would
be required to have in order to account for the
contingent facts of human concept acquisition. For
that matter, even if I'm right that geometry of the
space must be available prior to concept acquisition, I have no reason to deny that it can alter under
the pressure of experience, learning, maturation, or
any other mind-world or mind-body interactions.
Whether, or to what degree, it is labile is an empirical issue; and, as things stand, it's wide open. In
principle, all that's required to be set innately is the
initial layout of the attractor landscape. From there
on, everything is negotiable.

The moral, anyhow, is that the stereotype of a
concept, together with a specification of a creature's
experience, does *not* suffice to determine whether that creature will acquire that concept. You also
need to know the geometry of the creature's attract-
or space. But, quite likely, that a creature's attractor
space has the geometry it does is simply a brute
fact about that creature.[31] That's the sense in which
concept acquisition is an irrational process.

SNARK. Isn't that just a rotund way to say that all concepts
are innate?

AUTHOR. Yes, of course all concepts are innate (if 'innate'
means 'unlearned'). I thought that was clear some
pages back. And, since I suppose it's common

---

[31] Or, perhaps, it's a brute fact about that *kind* of creature. It's an open question to what
extent the taxonomy of creatures by their mechanisms of concept acquisition runs parallel
to their phylogenetic classification.

ground that a creature's innate conceptual endowment must be realized by its neural properties, all I've added is that it might be revealing to think of such properties as determining the geometry of an attractor landscape. In particular, that might be a way of avoiding thinking of them as implementing an HF model of concept acquisition.

SNARK. I think that you've entirely lost track of the topic of this conversation. Let me remind you. I had asked (very long ages ago, it seems to me) how come, if there's no such thing as concept *learning*, our concepts are typically acquired from their instances. You then proceeded to tell a long and not terribly entertaining story about attractor landscapes, the point of which (if I understood you) was to explain how concept acquisition might fail to be an inferential process so long as stereotype formation is a stage in concept acquisition. It's because stereotypes (but not concepts) are learned by 'induction' (or whatever) that concepts are (typically) acquired in consequence of experience with their instances. Is that right so far?

AUTHOR. It'll do for the sake of the argument.

SNARK. But you've left something out. Would you like to know what you've left out?

AUTHOR. No.

SNARK. Then I shall tell you. You say that we jump, by some or other 'automatic' process, from our stereotypes to our concepts. And you also say that these jumps don't count as inferences. All that being so (or, rather, all that being assumed to be so), what explains why the concepts that we jump to typically express properties that are instantiated in the actual world? Stereotypes fit the world because they are formed by a rational, inductive process.

But if the process that gets us from an acquired doorknob stereotype to the concept DOOKNOB is irrational, what explains why *not just the stereotype but also the concept* fits the world? Don't you require some sort of preestablished harmony between the concepts we jump to and the way things are?

AUTHOR. I agree that needs some looking into.

To start with, it's important not to overestimate the extent to which our concepts do apply to things in the world. The moral of Descartes's kind of case is that, strictly speaking, we *don't* learn TRIANGLE from encounters with triangles; nor do we apply it to triangles that we encounter. Strictly speaking, there are no such things. Of course, when we're speaking loosely (which is most of the time) we speak as though there are triangles aplenty. (That we do talk that way is simply patent: It comes as a *surprise* to hear that there aren't any triangles: 'Draw me a triangle.' 'I can't.' 'Because you haven't a pencil?' 'Because I'm a Platonist.') So then: There is a concept (call it X) to which our kinds of mind jump from experiences with things that are, loosely speaking, triangles. Presumably this process is mediated by learning what is, loosely speaking, the stereotype of a triangle. It's only in school that we learn that X *isn't*, strictly speaking, the concept of *triangularity* and that the 'triangle stereotype' is only loosely speaking the stereotype of *triangle*.[32] The usual direction of analysis takes X to be a loose approximation to TRIANGLE. The right direction

---

[32] There isn't, of course, a stereotype for *triangles* strictly so called: strictly speaking, any instance of TRIANGLE is as good an instance of TRIANGLE as any other. Accordingly, there are theorems about instances of TRIANGLE that are strictly so called, but none about instances of TRIANGLE that are loosely so called.

of analysis takes TRIANGLE to be a sophisticated tidying up of X.

SNARK. Well; maybe. But what about DOORKNOB? I hope you're not suggesting that, strictly speaking, there aren't any of those.

AUTHOR. Well, much the same pattern that applies to *loose* talk of triangles applies to *strict* talk of doorknobs. The difference is that whether a thing is strictly speaking a doorknob, but *not* whether a thing is strictly speaking a triangle, *depends on how it strikes us*. Accordingly, what's essential for being a triangle can be specified without reference to us; but what's essential for being a doorknob can't be. To be a triangle is to have three sides which ... etc. But to be a doorknob *just is* to be the kind of thing that makes minds like ours jump to DOORKNOB. As I've put it elsewhere (Fodor 1998), the property of being a doorknob is mind-dependent (whereas, of course, the property of being a triangle *isn't* mind-dependent; it's merely abstract).

I suppose it's the DOORKNOB pattern, rather than the TRIANGLE pattern, that's primordial. Because lots of things strike us as doorknobs, it follows that there are lots of doorknobs. Many things strike us as triangles too, of course, but it doesn't follow that there are lots of triangles; to the contrary, there aren't any. According to the kind of line I've been trying to sell you, this is all as it should be: It's not an objection to concept nativism that concepts like DOORKNOB and the like are acquired from and apply to things in the world; and it's not an objection to concept nativism that concepts like TRIANGLE strictly speaking aren't and strictly speaking don't. That all falls out from differences between the metaphysics of properties like *being [strictly speaking] a doorknob* and properties like *being [strictly speaking] a triangle*; the former, but not the latter, of which is mind-dependent. Plato's mistake was in thinking that the acquisition of DOORKNOB should be modeled on the acquisition of TRIANGLE, with the implausible consequence that the only doorknobs are the ones in heaven. Well, everybody makes mistakes.

SNARK. That you call nativism? Hume thought that it's experience of doorknobs that causes us to form the concept of a doorknob. So Hume was a nativist by you?

AUTHOR. Everybody, Hume included, has to be a nativist about something; out of nothing, nothing comes. Hume's mistake was to assume that DOORKNOB can be *defined* (just like TRIANGLE, except that the definition of DOORKNOB is 'sensory'). Given that assumption, sensory concepts are all that Hume was required to be a nativist about; DOORKNOB could be assembled from them by construction from doorknob experiences.[33] By contrast, I think that doorknobs don't have definitions; you get from experience to DOORKNOB not by construction but by a kind of leap of faith. I'm an empiricist too, but of the existentialist variety.

SNARK. Would you say that there's a moral to all this? Or shall we just stop?

---

[33] Remember that for Hume what we think of as 'logical construction' was an *associative* process. In particular, it wasn't a species of HF. So, Hume wasn't in jeopardy of the argument that learning DOORKNOB requires a (primitive) concept of doorknobs. I've known many psychologists who still want to get out of the kind of paradoxes we've been discussing by opting for some associationist account of concept learning. Because association is supposed to be a causal/mechanical process rather than a rational/computational process, that *would* be a way out if associationism were true. But, of course, it isn't.

AUTHOR. I think the moral is that once having got clear that concepts must not be identified with their stereotypes, it becomes plausible that stereotype learning is a stage of concept acquisition at least for concepts like DOORKNOB and maybe for concepts like TRIANGLE too; that's why concept acquisition so often looks like a kind of induction.

SNARK. That's not a moral, that's just a summary.

AUTHOR. I'm not finished. The pressing research problem is now to understand, in some depth, the relation between concepts and their stereotypes. That, I suppose, is the minimum that's needed if we're eventually to understand why it is that learning the stereotype for C triggers the acquisition of C and not of some other concept (equivalently, why it triggers locking to the property that C expresses and not to some other property). As of this writing (so it seems to me) practically nothing is known about the relation between stereotypes and the corresponding concepts except that they are different things. The following just about exhausts what can be assumed with reasonable confidence: (i) The extension of the stereotype is often (but not always; see TRIANGLE) a subset of the extension of the concept. (ii) Concepts express mind-dependent properties more often than you might suppose; so, if you want to understand concept acquisition, DOORKNOB is a better case to think about than TRIANGLE.

SNARK. Are you finished now?

AUTHOR. I think so.

SNARK. Good!

6

Preconceptual Representation

6.1 Introduction

It's been a working assumption throughout this book that seeing a thing (to say nothing of thinking about one) requires representing it; hence that *seeing* and *thinking* inherit the constraints on *representing*. But (so far at least) nothing precludes the possibility that some of the *representing* that goes on in seeing/thinking is nonconceptual. Well, then are there unconceptualized mental representations? If so, what might they be like? And where might one look for some? And how would you know if you'd found one?

SNARK. And who cares?

AUTHOR. Well, epistemologists care. For example, it's often said (at least since Sellars 1956) that nothing preconceptual is 'given' in experience; there is no such thing as acquaintance with the world 'as it is in itself', in abstraction from the effects of its being conceptualized; in effect, there is no principled distinction between the perceptual realm and the realm of thought.[1] That being so, what is given in experience can't be what justifies perceptual beliefs. This line of argument is sometimes described as 'neo-Kantian'. For all I know, it may be.

---

[1] It isn't really clear to me that Sellars did endorse this sort of thing. But lots of philosophers who take themselves to be Sellarsians do, which is good enough for present purposes (see e.g. McDowell 1994).

SNARK. Why should I care whether epistemologists care whether there is an experiential given? It's one thing to deny that anything in the content of experience shows us how the world is when it's swallowed raw. It's quite another thing to deny that there is anything in the content of experience that isn't conceptualized. I am not an epistemological Snark, I am a psychological Snark. I am therefore content to wonder whether there is preconceptual experiential content and let the epistemological chips fall where they may. Even if what is experientially given isn't what *justifies* perceptual beliefs, it might be what *gets conceptualized* in the course of the formation of perceptual beliefs.

AUTHOR. Good for you, Snark; it is indeed Very Bad Practice to run your psychology with epistemological malice aforethought. People who do so generally make the worst of both. Still, questions about justification aside, a psychologist might reasonably wonder what role experience plays in belief formation. And the question what (if any) preconceptual content experience contains would surely be crucial in that inquiry. Let us, therefore, have a look at it.

SNARK. I think it's time for lunch.

AUTHOR. Later.

6.2 Kinds of representations

For reasons I'll presently set out, I think that at least some of the mental representations that are causally implicated in the formation of perceptual beliefs are indeed nonconceptual. The line of argument I'll have on offer goes like this: On the one hand, it's (empirically) plausible that at least some of these representations are 'iconic' (rather than 'discursive'); and, on the other hand, it's in the nature of iconic representations not to be conceptual. That being my polemical strategy, I had better say something about what I take iconic and discursive representations to be.

To begin with, my usage is idiosyncratic. In the semantics/semiotics literature 'iconic' frequently comports with notions like 'pictorial' and 'continuous'. But it's not always clear just what either of those amounts to, or just what the connections between them are supposed to be. As often as not, they simply take in one another's wash. I'm going to pretend that the slate is blank and just stipulate. So, then, 'iconic' and 'discursive' denote mutually exclusive modes of representation; that a representation is either entails that it's not the other. (I leave it open that some kinds of representation are neither iconic nor discursive. Offhand, I can't think of a good candidate, but it doesn't matter for my present purposes.) I further assume, for the familiar reasons (see Ch. 2), that all the kinds of representations we're concerned with are compositional. To a first approximation, a representation is compositional iff its syntactic structure and semantic content are both determined by the syntactic structure and semantic content of its constituent parts. According to my usage, the distinction between iconic and discursive representations turns on a difference between the ways that they achieve their compositionality.

6.3 Discursive representation

The sentences of natural languages are the paradigms; here again the outlines are familiar. Every sentence is a finite arrangement of constituents that are themselves either primitive or complex. Each complex constituent is a finite arrangement of 'lexical primitives' (words, near enough). Lexical primitives have their syntactic and semantic properties intrinsically; roughly, a word is a triple consisting of a bundle of phonological features, a bundle of syntactic features, and a bundle of semantic features.[2] These are enumerated by the word's 'entry' in the 'lexicon' of the language. A discursive

---

[2] Except that I don't really believe in semantic features (see Fodor 1998).

representation in L is syntactically compositional iff its syntactic analysis is exhaustively determined by the grammar of L together with the syntactic analyses of its lexical primitives. A discursive representation is semantically compositional in L iff its semantic interpretation is exhaustively determined by its syntax together with the semantic interpretations of its lexical primitives.[3] Consider, for example sentence (1) below. Its syntactic structure is (more or less) as shown in (2), and it's semantic interpretation is (more or less) *John loves Mary*. The syntax and semantics

(1) John loves Mary.

(2) (John$_{NP}$) (loves$_V$) (Mary$_{NP}$)$_{VP}$

of the sentence are determined by such facts as that 'John' is a noun and denotes *John*, that 'loves' is a verb and denotes the relation *x loves y*, and that 'Mary' is a noun and denotes *Mary*. Further details are available upon application at your local department of linguistics.

What matters for us is this: the semantic interpretation of a sentence (*mutatis mutandis* of any discursive representation) depends exhaustively on the way that properties of its lexical primitives interact with properties of its constituent structure; and not every part of a discursive representation is *ipso facto* one of its constituents. So, for example, 'John', 'Mary', and 'loves Mary' are among the constituents of (1) according to the analysis (2). But 'John loves' isn't, and nor is 'John ... Mary'.[4] This is part and parcel of the fact that neither the semantic interpretation of 'John loves' nor the semantic interpretation of 'John ... Mary' contributes to determining the semantic interpretation of 'John loves Mary';

---

[3] It helps with the exposition to identify the semantic interpretation of a sentence with its truth-conditions, as I will generally do. This is, of course, wildly tendentious, but I don't propose to trade on it. It is, by the way, important to keep an eye on the ambiguity between, on the one hand, interpretations qua representations that the grammar of L assigns to its sentence types and, on the other, interpretations qua representations that speakers/hearers of L assign to tokens of its sentences in the course of communication exchanges. Which is which will be apparent from context wherever it matters. I hope.

[4] Lexical primitives themselves count as constituents because they have semantic interpretations. Whole sentences are constituents by courtesy.

in fact, neither of them *has* a semantic interpretation in that sentence (though, of course, each of the lexical primitives that they contain does).

I'll say that the constituents of a discursive representation are those of its parts that are recognized by its 'canonical decomposition'. According to me, it is having a canonical decomposition that distinguishes discursive representations from iconic ones.

6.4 Iconic representation

Pictures are the paradigms (but see caveats to follow). I suppose that pictures, like sentences, have a compositional semantics. Their principle of compositionality is this:

Picture principle: If P is a picture of X, then parts of P are pictures of parts of X.[5]

Pictures and the like differ from sentences and the like in that icons don't have *canonical* decompositions into parts; *all* the parts of an icon are *ipso facto* constituents. Take a picture of a person, cut it into parts whichever way you like; still, each picture part pictures a person part.[6] And the whole that you have if you reassemble all the picture's parts is a picture of the whole person that the parts of the picture are pictures of.

So, then, in everything that follows, a representation that has no canonical decomposition is an icon. I will argue (quite soon now) that iconic representations *ipso facto* lack a number of the characteristic features of conceptualized representations; so, the question we started with ('Are any mental representations unconceptualized?') can be swapped for the question 'Are any mental representations

---

[5] I assume, for ease of exposition, that P is of X is the only semantic relation that holds between pictures and things in the world that they are pictures of; a fortiori, that it is the only such relation that is compositional. I don't think it matters to my line of argument whether this is so. I likewise leave it open that some pictures aren't 'of' anything.

[6] Some parts of an icon are too small to have interpretations; the atoms it's composed of, for example. I'll generally ignore such matters of 'grain', but see below in the text.

iconic?' And that, finally, is a question on which empirical evidence can be brought to bear. First, however, I digress for caveats.

6.5 Digression on icons

I've taken pictures as my paradigms of icons, but I don't mean to suggest that they are the only examples. I suppose that graphs aren't pictures, but if you draw a curve that represents the distribution of a property in a population, a part of that curve *ipso facto* represents the distribution of the property in a part of that population (which is to say that it partially represents the distribution of that property in the population). So, graphs are (typically) icons according to my usage. Since icons don't have to be pictures, it can't be assumed that icons *ipso facto* resemble what they represent; not even on the (mistaken) assumption that pictures do.

6.6 How icons work

So far: Iconic representations, like discursive representations, are typically *of* this or that. But the former have no canonical decomposition; which is to say that they have no constituent structure; which is to say that, however they are sliced, there's no distinction between their canonical parts and their mere parts. Here's another way to put this: An icon is a homogeneous kind of symbol from both the syntactic and the semantic point of view. Each of its parts is a constituent, and each constituent gets a semantic interpretation in accordance with the Picture Principle. But neither is true of discursive representations. Only a specifiable subset of the parts of a discursive symbol (namely, its canonical parts) are syntactic or semantic constituents; and it is thus far open that the various constituents of a discursive representation may contribute in different ways to determining the semantics of their hosts.

Our paradigms, the sentences of a natural language, are clearly uniconic in both these respects. Considered syntactically, they contain: nouns, verbs, adjectives, NPs, VPs, PPs, and so on. Considered semantically, they contain: singular terms, descriptions, predicates (including complement structures), and an apparatus of logical terms like quantifiers, variables, and connectives. Correspondingly, both the rules that distinguish sentential constituents from mere sentential parts, and the rules that compose the interpretation of sentential expressions from the interpretation of their constituents turn out to be disconcertingly complex and hard to state; linguists have thus far had only very partial success in formulating either. Compare the unarcane apparatus that sufficed to formulate the Picture Principle.

Because they discompose into syntactically and semantically heterogeneous constituents, discursive representations can have logical forms (maybe all discursive representations do that can express truths). By contrast, because they decompose into syntactically and semantically homogeneous parts, iconic representations don't have logical forms. I take that to be truistic. The logical form of a symbol is supposed to make its compositional structure explicit; that is, it's supposed to make explicit the contribution that each of the interpreted parts of the symbol makes to its interpretation. But each part of an iconic symbol is a constituent, and each constituent contributes in the same way to the interpretation of the whole icon: each part pictures part of what the icon pictures.

Because the interpreted parts of an iconic representation are in this sense syntactically and semantically homogeneous, iconic symbols can't represent things that discursive symbols can. For example, icons can't express the distinction between negative propositions and affirmative ones, which turns (*inter alia*) on semantic distinctions among logical constants. Likewise they can't express quantified propositions; or hypothetical propositions; or modal propositions. They can't even express predication, since doing that requires (*inter alia*) distinguishing terms that contribute individuals to semantic interpretations from terms that contribute sets (or properties, or whatever). For very closely related reasons, pictures don't have truth-conditions. In the root case, for a symbol to be true it has to pick out an individual and a property and predicate the latter of the former; but iconic representations have no way to do either. So, the camera doesn't lie, but nor does it tell the truth.[7]

It's implicit in these sorts of considerations that discursive representations typically carry ontological commitments, but iconic representations don't.[8] In particular, discursive representations do, but iconic representations don't, impose principles of individuation on the domains in which they are interpreted.[9] I don't want to talk about this at length because I'm scared to. So, it would help enormously if you'll just let me assume that what individuals a system of representation is ontologically committed to depends on the census of quantifiers, variables, singular terms, and sortal predicates to which it has access. To a first approximation, systems of representation are committed to the individuals over which they quantify. Conversely, if the available representational system doesn't include quantifiers (or classifiers or something of the sort), there is no right answer to the question 'Which things (how many things?) does this symbol represent?'. (Didn't Quine say something of that sort? I hope he did; I would so like to be in respectable company for a change.) To be sure, a photograph may show three

---

[7] This is continuous with the familiar objection to the 'picture theory' of ideas: There is nothing in John's not loving Mary for a picture to resemble.

[8] It is notoriously moot whether, and under what conditions, the ontological commitments of a system of discursive representations might be unique (for example, whether there's a fact of the matter about what the representations refer to). As far as I can tell, the usual arguments for indeterminacy assume that the data for interpretation(/translation) are exhausted by correlations between the informant's utterances and the situations in which he utters them. The claim is that there is, even in principle, nothing in that sort of data that could distinguish (e.g.) commitment to an ontology of rabbits from commitment to an ontology of undetached rabbit parts. Since, however, I think the correlationist premise is surely false, it strikes me as not terribly important whether the conclusion follows. For discussion see Fodor (1994).

[9] However, it's of prime importance not to read 'principle of individuation' epistemically. If I have the concept CAT, I know the principle of individuation for cats; namely, that each cat is one cat, and nothing else is any. So, if I have the concept CAT, then I know how to count cats; that is, I know that I must count one for each cat and nothing for anything else. But what does not follow is that if I have the concept CAT I am thereby enabled to count aggregations of cats. Likewise, to know that each sheep is one sheep is to command a metaphysical truth of some depth. But it doesn't imply a procedure (an algorithm; a 'criterion' for computing the cardinality of a flock).

giraffes in the veld; but it likewise shows a family (*one* family) of giraffes; and an odd number of Granny's favorite creatures; and a number of Granny's favorite odd creatures; and a piece of veld that's inhabited by any or all of these. No doubt, we can usually agree about how to interpret the ontology of such a photograph; we do so in light of whatever project we happen to have in hand. But what matters to the present issues is that the discursive symbol 'three giraffes in the veld' specifies a scene relative to such concepts as THREE, GIRAFFES, IN, and THE VELD. A fortiori, a mind that lacks these concepts can't read the symbol as representing three giraffes in the veld (or as representing one family of giraffes in the veld, or as representing an odd number of giraffes in the veld, etc.). Contrast iconic representation: you can, of course, see three giraffes in the veld without having the concept GIRAFFE. Nor do you need GIRAFFE to take a picture of three giraffes in the veld; a camera and film will suffice. (Less these days.)

Equivalently (more or less): the context 'iconally represents ... ' is like the contexts 'sees ... ', 'describes ... ', 'points at ... ', and 'photographs ... '. They are all transparent to substitution of coextensive descriptions. But 'discursively represents ... ' is like 'sees as ... ' and 'describes as ... ': it always has an opaque reading (which, in fact, it usually prefers). According to RTM, that's because seeing things as C and describing things as C, like other acts of conceptualization, operate by subsuming the things seen under the concept C. It's thus entirely in the spirit of RTM that 'conceptualizing X as C' and 'predicating C of X' are two ways of saying much the same thing.[10]

6.7 Brief review

We started with conceptualized versus unconceptualized representation, which we then swapped for discursive versus iconic representation. This allowed us to reformulate the question whether

---

[10] Except, of course, that 'C' is used in the first but only mentioned in the second.

there are unconceptualized mental representations as the question whether any mental representations are iconic. We then suggested that (because they lack logical form) iconic representations don't provide principles of individuation for their domains of interpretation. This lead to a final metamorphosis: 'Are there unconceptualized mental representations?' becomes 'Are there (empirical) phenomena in which representation and individuation are dissociated?'. If there are, then that's prima facie evidence of nonconceptual mental representation. We're just about to see what such evidence can look like. But, first, a quick consideration of an a priori objection that many philosophers appear to find persuasive; indeed decisive.

'Look', you might say (or, anyhow, Snark might), there just couldn't be phenomena in which representation and individuation are dissociated. For, if a symbol represents a such and such, it must represent it *as* something or other. There aren't, as it were, two kinds of representing, one of which ignores this maxim (and is thus transparent), and the other of which obeys it (and is thus opaque). Rather, we get the 'transparent' reading of 'represents ... ' by abstracting from some or other opaque reading of 'represents ... '; that's to say, by ignoring the mode of representation in a specification of a representational content. There's a close analogy to two ways that one might read an assertion that John believes the king of France is bored: According to the transparent reading, it's the ascriber who takes responsibility for the definite description; according to the opaque reading it's John who does. (See e.g. Brandom 2000; Dennett 1982.) That, however, is a distinction between styles of belief ascription rather than a distinction between kinds of representing (or, a fortiori, between two kinds of believing). Likewise for the presumptive difference between *representing* and *representing as*. Representing a thing is always representing it as this-or-that. But one has the option, in saying that something is represented, of not bothering to say what it's represented *as*. So, iconic and discursive representations couldn't differ in the way that this discussion has supposed; the difference couldn't be that the latter but not the former conceptualizes, and hence individuates, whatever it is that it represents.[11]

That sort of objection has force on the assumption that all representing implies representing as. But assuming that it does would beg precisely the issue we are discussing; namely, the possibility that some mental representation is nonconceptual. That representing requires conceptualization was supposed to be the conclusion of the argument, not its premise; so we can't take for granted an analysis of either that postulates an inalienable connection between the two. Suffice it for present purposes, then, if we can imagine, even roughly, how X might represent Y without representing Y as falling under some concept or other.[12] That would be representation without individuation according to the present line of thought.

6.8 Informational content

I think, in fact, that there's quite a plausible candidate for representation of that kind: X represents Y insofar as X carries information about Y, where 'carries information about...' is read as transparent. If so, then maybe construing what's given as some sort of information would allow for representation that's not 'under a description' and hence for unconceptualized representing. In particular, the claim would be that tokens of symbols typically

---

[11] If in the case of iconic symbols resembling is sufficient for representing (and if resembling isn't itself description-relative) that would explain how there could be representation without individuation. But I don't believe that preconceptual representations resemble what they represent; nor, I suppose, does anyone else who is party to this discussion. Alternatively, demonstrations ('this' and 'that') might be instances of representation without conceptualization, but the claim that they are is highly tendentious.

[12] SNARK. What on earth are you talking about?

    AUTHOR. The thesis up for discussion is that representation per se needn't presuppose principles for the individuation of what is represented; roughly, discursive representation does but iconic representation doesn't. So, the polemical situation is that if you want to argue against the thesis, you mustn't take for granted that representations are *ipso facto* conceptualized; that would beg the question at issue. Does that help?

    SNARK. Did you really think it would?

carry all sorts of what I'll call 'Dretskian' information. (Come to think of it, so too does practically everything else.) And 'carries information about...', unlike 'represents as...' is transparent to the substitution of coextensives at the '...' position. On the other hand, what information an interpreter can recover from a tokening of a symbol depends on what concepts the interpreter has available. Even though a picture carries information about giraffes, only an interpreter who has the concept GIRAFFE can see that it does (i.e. can see it as doing so).[13] What information a representation contains doesn't depend on how it is interpreted. But what information you can recover from a representation depends (not just on what information it contains, but also) on what concepts you bring to it. The given is unconceptualized representation that is awaiting conceptualization. This differs very much from the traditional empiricist account according to which the concept X is acquired from experiences as-of-Xs (presumably by some sort of process of abstraction). For reasons that connect with the discussion in Chapter 5, that way of thinking about concept acquisition seems to me to be inevitably circular, so it can't possibly be right.

In any event, it can't be right if, as I'm now suggesting, experiential content is the same thing as informational content. You can't abstract DOMESTIC FELINE from experiences-as-of-domestic-felines unless you *take them to be* experiences-as-of-domestic-felines; and you can't do that unless you have DOMESTIC FELINE in

---

[13] Information-construed-as-causal-correlation was introduced into the philosophy of language in Dretske (1981). I think that was a major advance. But, unlike Dretske, I don't suppose 'carries information' is the basic notion in this area; in particular, I doubt that concept possession can be understood in terms of it. Rather, the analysis ought to run the other way around: What concepts are available to the interpreter sets an upper bound on what information he may be able to recover from the tokening. What's crucial is that if a tokening of a representation carries information about F, and only if it does, an interpreter who has the concept F may be able to recover that information. ('He may be' not 'he must be'; since all forms of pragmatism are to be shunned, it mustn't be assumed that to understand a representation type implies being able to interpret its tokens: see Ch. 2.) What's crucial is that if a representation carries information about F, then an interpreter who has the concept F may be able to recover that information from the representation. But if he doesn't, then he can't.

your conceptual repertoire. Taking-X-to-be F and applying-the-concept F to X are two ways of saying the same thing.

I'm endorsing a quite different way of thinking about the relation between concepts and experiences.

The idea is that the role of concepts in the perceptual analysis of experience is to recover from experience information that it contains. (I think this is a Kantian kind of idea. I think Kant would put it that the function of concepts in the perceptual analysis of an experience is to afford a 'rule for the synthesis' of the experience. But I may be wrong to think this. What do I know about Kant?) At very least, this idea is easy to illustrate. What's this a picture of?

Give up? It's a picture of a bear climbing a tree (as seen from the other side of the tree).[14] If you have the concept BEAR (and the concept TREE and so forth) you can, as it were, pull the picture together under this description. But if you don't, you can't. Clearly, you couldn't 'abstract' the concept BEAR from encounters with this sort of bear-picture (or, *mutatis mutandis*, from encounters with the corresponding bear-experience).

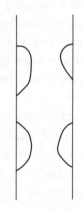

Figure 6.1 *What's this?*

[14] I'm indebted to Lila Gleitman for suggesting this very un-Kantian way to illustrate (what I'm taking to be) a Kantian point. There aren't, if memory serves me, many jokes in Kant.

Well, so there are some interesting implications of thinking about experiential content as informational content, quite aside from the one that's of most present concern: that the notion of carrying information about X seems to offer a way of representing X without representing it as anything; hence a way of meeting what I took to be the Dennett/Brandom objection to a preconceptual given. But I haven't got a worked-out elaboration of this kind of treatment, nor can I prove that one is possible. Whether it is is another of those questions that scare me. I proceed, therefore, to conditionalize: Assuming that an informational construal of the given allows for representation *of* that isn't representation *as* (hence for representation without conceptualization, hence for representation without individuation), the empirical issue is whether there is empirical evidence for such dissociations in the psychology of cognition. I think there's lots of it, and of several kinds. Selected examples to follow.

6.9 The 'items effect'

To test a theory, you need (what used to be called) 'correlating definitions'. Here's one: all else equal, the 'psychological complexity' of a discursive representation (for example, the amount of memory it takes to store it or to process it) is a function of the number of individuals whose properties it independently specifies.[15] I shall call this the 'items effect'.

Consider, as it might be, phone books. They specify properties of individuals (their numbers and addresses), and they are explicit as to both the individuals and the properties. All sorts of things follow: the phone books of big cities are generally bigger than the phone books of small cities; they weigh more and they take

---

[15] That is, the individuals and properties that are enumerated (rather than merely quantified over). De facto, 'All men are mortal' predicates mortality of more men than 'Two men are mortal'. But the relative complexity of these representations doesn't differ in consequence.

up more shelf space; it takes longer to look up an arbitrary number in a big phone book than in a small one; and it's harder to memorize (or even to copy) the contents of a big book than that of a small one; and so forth (these truths being, of course, purely contingent). This is all because the representations in phone books are discursive, hence conceptualized; accordingly, their interpretation presupposes the possession and application of such concepts as X'S NAME IS 'X' and PHONE P HAS THE NUMBER N. Lists, like sentences, are paradigms of discursive representation: on the one hand, they exhibit effects of their content (it's the number that's listed for John that you proceed to dial in consequence of looking his number up); and, on the other hand, they exhibit an effect of the number of items they contain.

Compare photographs: A photograph of 60 giraffes takes no more space in your album (or on the screen) than a photograph of 6 giraffes. For that matter, it takes no more space than a photograph of no giraffes (the one that you made when you forgot to take the lens cap off). Photographs are time-sensitive (since very old ones are generally more degraded than very new ones, token photographs can carry information about their age). But they aren't item sensitive. Photographs of many Xs aren't, in general, more complex than photos of a few Xs; the former don't, for example, have more constituents than the latter. This is hardly surprising in light of the preceding discussion: iconic representations don't individuate; they don't represent individuals as individuals. A fortiori, nothing about them depends on the number of individuals that they represent.

Still, I do want to emphasize that failing to find items effects is not, all by itself, a knock-down test for iconic representation; as usual with empirical inferences, alternative explanations have to be ruled out. For example, tasks that involve searching for an item in a stimulus array ('Where's Waldo?') may be insensitive to the size of the array if the search is carried out 'in parallel'. So, given a search in which there is no items effect, one sometimes can't tell whether that's because it's a search of an iconic representation or because it's a parallel search.

On the other hand, the discursive/iconic distinction is orthogonal to the parallel/serial distinction: Some parallel searches involve conceptualizing the items in an array, and others don't, and empirical evidence can distinguish between the two. For example, the former, but not the latter, requires identifying negative instances as well as positive instances.

A toy example will serve to illustrate the principle. Imagine a page divided into squares each of which contains a letter that's assigned randomly (an 'A' or a 'V' or a 'W' or whatever). Suppose you want to find all the Ks on the page. The search can be carried out either serially or in parallel, but if you find the Ks by a serial search, you ought to acquire, in passing, lots of 'incidental' information about the negative items, and (all else equal) you should be able to identify at least some of them. ('Were there any Ms on the page?'. 'Yes, I think so.') Compare a parallel search. Take a transparency the same size as the stimulus array and ruled into boxes in the same way. Put a 'K' in each box. Place the transparency over the stimulus page and read off every identifiable letter. All and only the items you can read off are Ks. Since the identities of the negative instances aren't registered in this kind of parallel search, the subject can't tell you what negative items there were. ('Were there any Zs?' 'I haven't a clue.') The moral, then, isn't that the item effect is a litmus for iconic representation; rather, it's that there is a galaxy of related indicators of iconicity, and there's no principled reason why, in a given case, they mightn't decide the issue beyond a reasonable empirical doubt if they are taken together. If (to return to an earlier example) you are counting giraffes in parallel, there's no reason why it shouldn't take you longer to count six of them than to count sixty. But, since it usually does, it's a good bet that you don't usually count giraffes in parallel.

6.10 Some facts at last

Can we find, in the perceptual-psychology literature, indications of a mode of representation that exhibits typical effects of icon-icity? If we can, then it's on the cards that such representations are unconceptualized, hence that there is a perceptual given. In fact, relevant examples are the stock in trade of introductory-level cognitive-science texts. The basic idea is that perceptual inform-ation undergoes several sorts of process (typically in more or less serial order) in the course of its progress from representation on the surface of a transducer (e.g. on the retina) to its representation in long-term memory. Some of the earliest of these processes operate on representations that are stored in an 'echoic buffer' (EB),[16] and these representations are widely believed to be iconic. Two consequences of their presumed iconicity should be stressed, since both suggest possible experimental investigations.

First, since iconic representations are unconceptualized, they don't individuate items in the domains they represent; so repres-entations in EB oughtn't to produce item effects. Second, qua unconceptualized, iconic representations don't express proper-ties whose recognition requires perceptual inference. Inferring is in the same basket as saying and thinking; they all presuppose conceptualization. So, in the case of vision, the icons register the sorts of properties that photographs do (two-dimensional shape, shading, color, and so forth) but not 'object' proper-ties like being *an animal* or, a fortiori, being *a cat belonging to Granny*. You can, of course, see a cat as a cat that belongs to

---

[16] Not to be confused with 'short-term memory' (which is supposed to be conceptualized and hence item limited except when rehearsal is allowed). It's STM, rather than EB, to which George Miller's famous 'seven items plus or minus two' is supposed to apply (Miller 1956). The expository problem is partly that there's no settled terminology in the psychological literature, so one just has to muddle along. But there's a substantive empirical issue about whether EB and STM really are identical psychological mechanisms. I don't suppose this issue actually to be settled; but for the present purposes I shall assume that they're not.

Granny; but that requires conceptualization. The present point is that a cat can't be, as it were, *given* as a cat that belongs to Granny.

Correspondingly, in the case of auditory perception, icons in the echoic buffer should specify the sorts of properties that show in a spectrogram: the frequency, amplitude, and duration of a sound, but not whether the sound is a rendering of 'Lilibulero'.

You may have noticed that I stuck in 'register' without telling you what it means. Well, roughly, for a representation to register a's being F is for it to contain Dretskian information about a's being X. In particular, 'registers', like 'contains Dretskian information about' is transparent to the substitution of identicals. If a contains Dretskian information about e1, and e1 = e2, then a contains information about e2. Likewise, if a registers information about e1, and e1 = e2, then a registers e2.[17] Also, it's possible to register the Dretskian information that a is F even if you don't have the concept F. (You get a plausible instance of the registration of Dretskian information if you assume that you can have an experience as of red without having the concept RED.)

> SNARK. Grrr!
> AUTHOR. Be that as it may.

There are two other differences between registering and perceiving. First, a representation token can carry information about anything, but there are constraints on which of its properties can be registered; only 'sensory' or 'transducer detectible' properties can (see above); a mind can register only such properties as it has mechanisms for transducing.

> SNARK. And, what, pray, is a transducer?
> AUTHOR. I thought you'd ask. Here's one way to think about it:

---

[17] I persist in my usual serene impartiality as to what the variables range over. For expository purposes, let it be events; but you aren't allowed to ask me what events are.

Computation (like, for example, thinking) takes mental representations onto other mental representations. Transduction (like, for example, registering impinging redness) takes ambient energy onto mental representations. In the usual case (barring hallucinations and such) perceptual integration starts with the registration of sensory information. Were there no transducers, perception couldn't get started. Will that do?

SNARK. No.

AUTHOR. Very well then; I return to the main line of exposition.

The second difference between perception and registration: Qua unconceptualized, registrations can't express properties whose detection requires inferences. (Inferences need premises and conclusions, and premises and conclusions are *ipso facto* conceptualized; which, by assumption, registrations aren't.)

Bearing all that in mind, we may now return to the question whether there is evidence for unconceptualized representation in perception (that is, evidence of the registration of stimulus properties). Let's start with an anecdote just by way of building intuitions. So: here I am, seated at the keyboard, working hard on a piece for *Mind and Language* (or whatever); at the moment, I vacillate between a semicolon and a comma. A clock begins to chime. 'Chime, Chime, Chime', the clock says. At first I ignore this, but then it seizes my attention. 'I wonder what it may be o'clock', I say to myself (it being my habit to address myself in a sort of pig-Georgian). What happens next is the point of interest: I commence to count the chimes, *including ones that I hadn't previously noticed*. Strikingly (so, anyhow, the phenomenology goes), it's not that I say to myself 'There have been three chimes so far, therefore what I'm now hearing is chime four'; rather, it's that I count chimes that were previously not attended to: 'One chime, two chimes, three chimes', I say to myself, thereby subsuming each chime under the sortal

concept CHIME. Four more chimes follow and I duly add them to
get the total. I think: 'It must be 6: 30' (the clock in the hall runs half
an hour fast).[18] Given such observations a psychologist might well
want to consider, as a working hypothesis, that there is a brief interval during which an unconceptualized (presumably iconic) representation of the chiming is held in the EB. Notice that one's ability to
do this trick is time-bound; it lasts only for perhaps a second or two,
so you can't count unattended chimes that you heard yesterday.
Within the critical interval you can conceptualize (hence individuate, hence count) the chimes more or less at will. After that, the
trace decays and you've lost your chance. I think the psychologist
might well be right to conclude all that as a working hypothesis.

Prima facie objection: 'Clearly there is an item limit on the buffer.
You may be able to count two or three chimes retrospectively, but
I'll bet you can't do seventeen'. First reply (in passing): 'Temporal
effects can mimic items effects, so they must be controlled for.
Suppose representations in EB last three seconds and it takes the
clock four seconds to chime four times. You will then "lose" the
first chime in the sequence before you register the fourth. This
is not, however, an effect of the number of stimulus items that
can be registered in EB; it's just an interaction between the
temporal duration of the input and the temporal capacities of
the buffer'. Second reply (more interesting): 'It's not because the
buffer is item-limited that you can't count seventeen chimes;
it's because counting involves individuation and individuation
requires conceptualization, and it's independently plausible that
conceptualizing is expensive'.

There actually are data that suggest that the second is the right
diagnosis. They come from a deservedly famous series of experiments by George Sperling (1960). Sperling's findings are richer

---

[18] I'm pleased to report that there is (anecdotal) evidence that mine is not the only
head that works this way: '[Molly] found it hard work to attend to kind Miss Phoebe's
ceaseless patter. She came to a point, however, when the voice ceased; and could recall, in a
mechanical manner, the echo of the last words which ... from the dying accent that lingered
in Molly's ear, she perceived to be a question' (Elizabeth Gaskell, *Wives and Daughters*, 1866).

than I have space to summarize, but they support a pervasive phenomenological intuition: 'When complex stimuli consisting of a number of letters are tachistoscopically presented, observers enigmatically insist that they have seen more than they can remember afterwards, that is, [more than they can] report afterwards' (p. 1). In the experiment, 'the observer behaves as though the physical stimulus were still present when it is not (that is, after it has been removed) and … his behavior in the absence of the stimulus remains a function of the same variables of visual stimulation as it is in its presence' (p. 2). Performance in the experiment showed that though, when queried after the stimulus is turned off, S can report only 3 of the letters he's seen, *he can report any 3*. So there appears to be a kind of memory, available for the brief registration of visual stimuli, the item capacity of which is, at a minimum, considerably bigger than what is available for the subject to report. Notice that the items in this memory must have some or other sort of content; that's required to explain why S's report is accurate more often than chance.[19]

One more observation about Sperling's results is especially interesting given that we are committed to representations in EB not being conceptualized: Sperling's 'partial report' effect is *not* found when the items to be recalled are cued by category ('Report the numbers but ignore the letters'). This strongly suggests that representation in EB is indeed preconceptual. You can only report an 'A' token as a letter token if you have categorized it as a letter token. So, if the 'given' is what has content but isn't conceptualized, it's thus far plausible that the iconic representations in EB qualify as given. But I do want to emphasize the 'thus far' part. The argument just set out is empirical; it suggests that there is iconic representation in perception, but it certainly doesn't demonstrate

---

[19] In the basic 'partial report' experiment S receives a brief visual exposure to an alphanumeric matrix. After a controlled interval S is cued as to the location of the items to be reported ('top row', 'middle row', etc). On average S is able to report any 3 of the cued items from a matrix of at least 12 stimuli. 12 stimuli is considerably more than S is able to report when asked to recall all of the items he can remember.

that there is. Demonstrations are ever so much nicer than suggestions; their level of confidence is so much higher. But there isn't
one, either pro or con the given, nor will there be. There is, I
think, less apriority in heaven and earth (or anywhere else) than
philosophers have dreamed of. On the other hand, I also want to
emphasize that Sperling's study, though particularly elegant, is only
one of a plethora of straws in the wind. Effects of content without
items effects are actually easy to find when you know where to
look.[20] I'll mention one other example because it makes the point
dramatically.

Béla Julesz and his colleagues studied the perception of computer-
generated displays of matched pairs of visual stimuli, each of which
consists of an array of dots, which were identical except that some
of the dots on one are slightly shifted from their location on the
other. Under conditions of stereoscopic presentation (one member
of a pair is presented to each eye), such stimuli produce a powerful
illusion of three dimensionality. The area containing the displaced
dots appears to emerge from a shared background.

From our point of view, several considerations are germane.
First, the displacement of the dots must somehow be registered by
the subject's sensory representation of the stimulus. After all, the
sensory representation is the only information about the stimulus
that's available to affect what the subject sees. In particular, the
subject has no relevant background beliefs about the stimuli of the
kind that a 'top-down' account of the depth illusion might appeal
to. (Testing top-down accounts of depth perception was, in fact,
Julesz's main interest in experimenting with random dot stimuli.)
So, if S's experience failed to preserve the information that some
of the dots have been displaced, there could be no illusion of
stereopsis. To effect the illusion, the visual system must compare a

---

[20] Sperling is very conservative in estimating how much information a visual icon can
contain. But he does remark that 'it seems probable that the 40-bit information capacity
observed in these experiments was limited by the small amount of information in the stimuli
rather than by a capacity of the observers (1960: 27).'

representation of the left-eye stimulus array with a representation of the right-eye array and somehow determine which dots have been moved. These to-ings and fro-ings are, it goes without saying, entirely subpersonal.

I won't bother you with the received account of how the Julesz illusion works; it's complicated, and I only think I understand it on alternate Tuesdays. What's important is that the mechanism that detects the displacement couldn't possibly have access to a list of the dots with their positions in each array. Once again, the lack of an items effect is a relevant consideration. You can get the stereo illusion with arrays of thousands of dots. The amount of information that would need to be registered and processed to make the estimates of displacement by comparing such lists would thus be orders of magnitude too large to be feasible. (In fact, within a large range, the fewer dots there are, the *harder* it is to obtain the illusion; reducing the number of dots below a certain threshold makes the effect go away.) What happens is apparently that the displacement is computed over iconic representations from each of the two eyes. It is presumably because these representations are iconic rather than discursive that the optical relation between the retinal images is critical in producing the illusion.[21]

There are lots of other experimental results in the literature that point to much the same kind of conclusions I've been drawing here; but perhaps the ones I've cited will do to give a sense of the thing.

6.11 Conclusion

I think there is quite likely a perceptual given. In any case, it would seem that the issue is empirical; finding out whether there is is no philosopher's business. On the other hand, the experimental out-comes should be of professional concern to philosophers who argue

---

[21] You can get the stereoptic effect from Julesz patterns if you look at them with your eyes crossed just right. Why on earth should that be so if what is being compared are lists?

a priori that there can't be a given because it's a priori that all content must be conceptualized. Such philosophers are now required to sketch alternative explanations of the sorts of empirical results towards which I've been gesturing. I am not holding my breath.

But does whether there is a given matter philosophically in any other way? Does it, in particular, matter to epistemology? I offer two epistemological reflections.

6.10.1 First epistemological reflection

If what is given is supposed to ground perceptual judgements, as in foundationalist versions of epistemology, then it must be both noninferential and introspectible; the former in order to avoid a regress of grounding, the latter in order that the content of one's experience should be available for the justification of one's perceptual beliefs. But the empirical evidence is very strong that there is no psychologically real level of mental represent-ation that meets both these conditions. Rather, it appears that what can be introspected is always the product of subpersonal and encapsulated inferences and, conversely, what is a plausible candidate for being uninferred (e.g. the representations in EB) is almost never available to introspection. So, for example, it holds without exception as far as I know that the deliverances of perception become accessible to the perceiver only after the operation of the perceptual constancies; hence the elliptical plate that looks round, the 'correction' of perceived color for changes in the ambient light, the failure of retinal size to predict apparent size, and so forth through a very long list of familiar examples. And (I think again without exception) all varieties of CTM treat the perceptual constancies as paradigm examples of the products of subpersonal inferences; that is, they imply that, invariably, mental representations that exhibit the effects of constancy are inferred. It is, in short, empirically implausible that what is giv-en could be what grounds perceptual beliefs. That being so, a foundationalist epistemologist has two options: either to ignore the psychology of perception or to stop being a foundationalist epistemologist.

I sometimes wonder whether our epistemology has quite caught up with the Freudian revolution in psychology. There is every sort of evidence that a great deal of the reasoning involved in the causal fixation of quotidian perceptual beliefs is unconscious and hence unavailable for report by the reasoner; in particular, either what justifies our perceptual judgments isn't introspectively available or most of our perceptual beliefs aren't justified. I'm unclear that it matters much (from, as one used to say, a world-historical point of view) which of these epistemology chooses.

6.10.2 Second epistemological reflection

It's often suggested, especially by philosophers in the Sellars tradition (like Brandom, McDowell, and Davidson in some of his moods) that the given can't be what grounds perceptual judgments because justification is a relation among *contents* and whatever isn't conceptualized *ipso facto* has no content. The horrific consequence is the isolation of the psychology from the epistemology of justification (as McDowell puts it, the separation of the 'realm of reasons' from 'the realm of causes'). In particular, the kind of causal explanations of perceptual judgments that psychologists seek can at best provide 'exculpations where we wanted justifications'. This is notoriously a long question; but I do hate a priori arguments that such and such a kind of discourse can't be naturalized; and 'realm' talk makes my skin crawl. So, I can't resist a couple of points under this head.

The first is that discussions of the justification of perceptual belief simply mustn't take for granted that all the perceptual content that's available to perceptual justification is *ipso facto* conceptualized. I suppose that it would be safe to assume so if *belief* content were the only kind of content there is; since it's plausible that beliefs are *ipso facto* conceptualized. But if, as I've been arguing, there's a plausible case for preconceptual, iconic representation, the truism that justification is a relation among the contents of representations does not entail that justification is a relation among conceptualized representations.

Accordingly, the epistemological question that needs settling is whether the content of an unconceptualized representation might be the datum that grounds (e.g. makes rational) a perceptual judgment. Well, I'm damned if I see why it can't be. A picture of three giraffes in the veld carries information about there being three giraffes in the veld. (It carries all sorts of other information too, of course. But so what?) Somebody who has the concepts GIRAFFE, THREE, VELD, and so on (and only somebody who does) is to that extent in a position to recover that information from the picture; and his reason for believing that there are three giraffes may well be that the picture shows three of them and that he sees that it does. His reason, notice; not his mere exculpation. As far as I can see, none of that is under threat from the consideration that judgment requires conceptualization.

The question how (for example, by what computational processes) unconceptualized iconic representations might get 'collected under a concept' is, of course, very hard; and the answer is unknown for practically any of the interesting cases. On the way of looking at things I've been trying to persuade you of, it's a large part of what the psychology of perception is about. But, as far as I can see, there's nothing to suggest that it's unanswerable in principle. Pragmatism is, of course, always and everywhere false, so if there are rules for the conceptualization of experience, they can't be a priori (or, anyhow, they can't be semantic). There aren't, for example, any 'criteria' for recognizing giraffes. What I'm after is therefore a version of Kant's view that concepts synthesize what's given in perception that does without adopting Kant's pragmatism (or, indeed, anybody else's).

I end with a short methodological homily. I don't see how the epistemology of perception can simply ignore the empirical question of how perception works. Quite generally, justifying a belief can't require a thinker to do such and such unless the thinker has the kind of mind that can do such and such. It can't require him to introspectively access the noninferential, preconceptual grounds of his beliefs unless he has the kind of mind that has introspective access to the noninferential, preconceptual grounds of his beliefs. I've heard it said that how perception actually works doesn't matter to epistemologists because theirs is a normative not a descriptive enterprise. But how could one be bound by norms that one is, in point of nomological necessity, unable to satisfy? And what's the conceivable interest, even to epistemologists, of norms that don't bind us?

7

The Metaphysics of Reference

Only matter has causal powers. I don't know exactly what that means, but the underlying metaphysical intuition is perhaps clear enough to be getting on with: Whatever enters into causal interactions is constituted of the sort of stuff that basic physics is about. Call that the 'physicalist' thesis (PT); I suppose it's at least part of what one has in mind when one speaks of basic physics as basic.[1] The development of science has been driven by the physicalist thesis at least since Lucretius. Unlike many of my colleagues, I think PT functions as an a priori methodological constraint on scientific practice; 'a priori' in the sense that any theory that fails to conform to PT to that extent counts as disconfirmed. This applies to intentional psychology *inter alia*: Only matter can think. If I believed in implicit definitions and the like, I would say that the physicalist thesis partly defines the scientific enterprise as we have come to understand it so far. But I don't, so I won't.[2]

Now, the main goal of this book is to help make science out of commonsense intentional psychology (my life's work, I

[1] Basic physics is, of course, a moving target; our estimate of what the material world is made of has changed a lot since Lucretius proposed atoms and the void. No doubt it will change still more before we're finished. That doesn't, however, make the physicalist thesis vacuous, nor does it write a blank check on the ontology of future science. For example, PT implies that there is a *unique* basic science (in effect that the special sciences are arranged in some sort of hierarchy, a claim for which plausible evidence is already in hand) and it requires that how the ontology of basic science turns out determines the ontology of all the rest of science. None of that is truistic; maybe none of it is even true.

[2] I guess what PT really is, is *synthetic* a priori: In principle it's subject to change under empirical pressure, but de facto it's universally presupposed in empirical theory construction.

suppose, if you don't include feeding the cat). So, I'd better say something about what philosophers call the 'naturalization' of intentional psychology. (For present purposes, a naturalized psychology, intentional or otherwise, is just one that comports with PT.)

What makes intentional psychology problematic from the point of view of the physicalist thesis is, of course, its commitment to intentional states and processes; that is, to states and processes that are both endowed with causal powers and susceptible of semantic evaluation in respect of their truth, reference, aboutness, content, and the like. It is not immediately obvious that something with those sorts of properties could be constituted entirely by the sorts of things that the ontology of basic physics recognizes.[3]

But, despite its having a plausible claim to centrality, PT actually isn't much discussed these days either in the philosophical literature or in cognitive science. Not in cognitive science because, in their deepest heart of hearts, the great majority of psychologists think that talk of *truth* is unscientific (not to say vulgar) and that they already know how to naturalize reference. Namely, it's got to turn out to be some sort of association, either among ideas or between ideas and the world (or between stimuli and responses in case the psychologist in question is a behaviorist); and it's not hard to imagine a machine that can form associations. Imagining such machines is what connectionists do for a living.

By way of ironic contrast, philosophers, at least since the Wittgenstein disaster, don't worry much about naturalizing intentional psychology because they think it's known to be impossible. (This is one of the very important ways in which the mainstream of

---

[3] Come to think of it, it isn't *entirely* clear that *any* middle-sized objects (mountains or typhoons, to say nothing of cabbages or kings) really are constituted entirely by things of the sort that the ontology of basic physics is prepared to recognize. But intentional psychology is especially worrisome since (presumably) none of the other special sciences invokes semantic/intentional properties as part of its explanatory apparatus. Presumably we don't need notions of truth, reference, content, and the like to tell the scientific story about mountains, typhoons, or even cabbages. Kings, however, seem to be a different kettle of fish. In short, it's conceivable that everything *except* intentional/semantic states and processes is material. Naturalism about psychology sets its face against this possibility.

contemporary 'analytic' philosophy departs from the historical mainstream of empiricist theorizing.) What makes the naturalization of intentional psychology impossible is, putting it very roughly, that semantic content inheres, in the first instance, in the expressions of public languages,[4] and their metaphysics is essentially connected to conventions, norms, and the like. Since conventions, norms, and the like are themselves up to their ears in intentionality, the application of PT to intentional explanations couldn't but breed circularities. The suggested moral is either that intentional explanations constitute an 'autonomous' realm of discourse or that they are merely *façons de parler* eventually to be displaced by discourse that is explicitly about brains. In neither case could intentional psychology be a science in the sense that geology is.[5]

The unsurprising consequence of these ways of thinking is that, even by the usual standards, the geography of this part of the woods is very badly understood. It is even depressingly unclear just what problems a successful naturalization of intentional/semantic properties would have to resolve. That being so, I see no way to proceed except by assuming lots of things, and what I'll have to say about the naturalization of the intentional/semantic is unlikely to be of much interest unless the assumptions are correct. Oh well.

Some assumptions.

1. To begin with, I assume, in the spirit of the preceding chapters, that the semantics of thought is prior to the semantics of language. So, for example, what an English sentence means is determined, pretty much exhaustively, by the content of the thought it is used to express. The corresponding implication is that semantics is essentially a theory of thoughts, the contents of which are, I suppose, *not* determined by norms and conventions. Quite possibly

---

[4] Or, perhaps, in speech acts that such expressions are used to perform; the distinction doesn't matter for present purposes.

[5] Or perhaps geology is also a *façon de parler* and there is actually no science except basic physics. People have been known to say that. People say the oddest things.

English has no semantics, some appearances to the contrary notwithstanding.

2. I assume that reference is compositional; the reference of a complex expression is a construction out of the referents of its parts. (In fact, something stronger; reference is *reverse* compositional: see Fodor and Lepore 2002).

3. I assume, in the spirit of the preceding chapters, that referentialism is true. There is no problem about naturalizing meanings, senses, and the like because there aren't any such things.[6]

4. I assume that there are two kinds of reference: reference to individuals and to properties. This means, from the syntactic point of view, that the vehicles of reference are exhaustively singular terms and predicates.

5. I assume that some sort of causal theory of reference is true, both for predicates and for singular terms.[7] The residual question is then: 'which sort?'. The rest of this chapter is a claim that some of the most important standard arguments purporting to show that there can't be a causal theory of reference are unsound. (If I'm right about that, then perhaps one should stop assuming in the philosophy of language and/or the philosophy of mind that naturalization isn't possible.)

6. I assume that the crux of the problem of naturalizing reference is to provide a theory of perceptual representations. The

---

[6] This leaves open as the semantics of 'logical' expressions: connectives, quantifiers, and so forth. For what it's worth, I'm inclined to think that 'and' is defined by its truth-table (and not, for example, by its 'inferential role'). I don't think this view commits a circularity, but I won't try to convince you of that.

[7] Assuming this helps with PT of course; but there's another, more parochial reason why it would be nice to have a causal account of the semantics of LOT. It's an argument that's been raised against the LOT picture very many times (indeed, against RTM as such) that Mentalese formulas themselves require an internal interpreter if they're to be meaningful. The immediate implication would be a homuncular regress, which is not a pretty thought. This line of argument has proved remarkably resilient over the last couple of decades; it has survived repeated decapitation. Patently, however, it is defanged if the content of a mental representation is determined not by the results of its interpretation but by its causal connections to things in the world.

paradigms of such might well be present-tense demonstrative thoughts (thinks: *That's a cat*). Having got a substantial number of cases of perceptual reference under control, the rest of the story might appeal to some or other sort of definite description to fix the reference of Mentalese terms that don't occur in present-tense perceptual thoughts (*the cause of that grinding sound; the guy I saw in the kitchen yesterday; and so forth*).

SNARK. 'Cheater, cheater | Pumpkin eater.'

AUTHOR. *Really*, Snark; at your age. And with so respectable a publisher.

SNARK. Sorry; it slipped out. But I had thought you said there are at most hardly any definitions.

AUTHOR. I had thought I said that too.

SNARK. Then tell me, please, how you get from a vocabulary that is (by assumption) only rich enough to refer to (some? many? whatever?) things that *are* current objects of perception to a vocabulary that is sufficient for reference to things that are *not* current objects of perception? Tell me that. Go on. I can hardly wait.

AUTHOR. Suppose E is an expression in a vocabulary of the latter kind. You're quite right that I can't assume that it has a definition in a vocabulary of the former kind. I can't, given the things I've been saying, assume that it has any definition at all. But I don't need to if the metaphysics of reference is to be understood in terms of the causal locking of a term to its referent. All I need is something in the perceptual vocabulary that I can use to establish the locking. It might, for example, be a definite description of the referent of E that is (as one says) 'rigid'.[8] If so, then by definition it isn't a definition of E.

---

[8] For this and related notions see Soames (2002).

In fact, come to think of it, what locks E to its referent needn't even be a description that's *true* of E's referent. It's pretty widely recognized that new expressions can be introduced by descriptions that are *false* of their referents (see especially Donnellan 1972). My guess is that that sort of thing happens all the time. In particular, my guess is that that sort of thing is at the heart of our capacity for transtheoretical reference. It explains why I can use the vocabulary of my theory to criticize assertions that you make in the vocabulary of your theory even if (as is surely the usual case) neither of our theories is actually true. I don't imagine you could do science lacking some such arrangement. Or anything else much either. This is as far as you can get (at least, it's as far as I can see how to get) from the view that the semantics of a theoretical term has to be relativized to the theory that it's a term in (either in the manner of Kuhn or in the manner of Ramsey). Good. Semantic relativism, besides being false, is a pernicious and immoral doctrine which I would not wish even on a snark.

Well, so I'm making these six assumptions,[9] all of which (except perhaps the last, which is loosely in the tradition of empiricism[10]) are tendentious. Some of them are *very* tendentious. So be it. With all of them in force, we turn to the main business of this chapter, which is to consider the prospects for constructing a naturalized, causal theory of reference. To my knowledge, there are three prima facie objections to the project which, severally and collectively, have convinced many—maybe

---

9   SNARK. That's rather a lot, don't you think.
    AUTHOR. I'd make more if I could think of any that might help. Since I have to start somewhere, it might as well be somewhere close to where I'm going.
[10] The resemblance, though, is pretty superficial. I'm not claiming that the inside-the-perceptual-circle vocabulary is rich enough to *define* the outside-the-perceptual-circle vocabulary, nor am I claiming that it is restricted to terms that express 'sensory' properties (whatever exactly those are), or that it is in any way epistemologically privileged. I don't believe any of that; nor should you. In-the-circle vocabulary is just the sort of stuff you learn from Mummy when she says, as it might be, 'That's a duck, dear'. Still, if the things I've been saying are right, there's *something* to the empiricist view that facts about perception have a special role to play in concept acquisition. Let us all praise famous persons.

most—philosophers that it's a dead end; there may be others, but these are iconic.

The first I've already mentioned; namely, the putative groundedness of content, including referential content, in a metaphysics of norms, conventions, and the like. It suggests that a causal account of reference would presuppose the naturalization of intentionality at large, which, though perhaps not impossible in principle, is also not likely to be achieved by next Tuesday. In any case, I'm interested in the idea that a naturalistic metaphysics of content proceeds *from* the reduction of reference to causation *to* a general, naturalistic treatment of the intentional/semantic; if so, the former mustn't presuppose the latter.

The second familiar worry involves not naturalistic theories of reference in general but causal theories of reference in particular. It concerns a tangle of issues about how, if reference is a kind of causation, it's possible to think about, or speak about, anything except the current cause of one's thought or utterance. The paradigm here is what I'll call the problem of 'wild tokenings' (of which the notorious 'disjunction problem' is a special case).

Finally, there is the 'Which link' problem: If referents are in some way causes of the utterances/thoughts that refer to them, then each of the former must belong to a *chain* of events that eventuates in the tokening of one of the latter. But causal chains extend (presumably) indefinitely in both directions. So, the question arises what determines which link in such a chain of events is the referent of the thought or utterance.

I wouldn't bother you with these worries except that the project of this book is, after all, to help make respectable science out of content, and I do think (see Introduction) that naturalism is part of what the respectability of a science consists in. That being so, I would feel better and sleep more soundly if there are prima facie replies to the prima facie arguments against the reduction of reference to causation.

7.1 Normativity

Everybody goes on about norms. Cows go 'moo!', philosophers go 'norm!'. The idea, roughly, is that contents of symbols emerge from conventions that control their use, thereby determining what it is to use them *correctly*. Since causation per se is neither correct nor incorrect, content can't reduce to causation; and that applies to referential content *inter alia*.

But though this line of thought is simply ubiquitous in the literature of analytic philosophy (cf. Wittgenstein, Sellars, Davidson, Dennett, Brandom, etc.), we can safely ignore it. For better or worse, we're committed to LOT; and LOT, though it is a system of representations, isn't a system of representations that anybody *uses*, correctly or otherwise. One doesn't use thoughts, one just has them. Having thoughts isn't something that you *do*; it's something that happens to you. There are speech acts (maybe); but there aren't any thought acts. And so forth. These are all ways of saying much the same thing; they're part and parcel of the idea that LOT is a system of representation that mediates thought, not of one that mediates communication.

SNARK. Doesn't that make LOT a private language? And didn't Wittgenstein prove that there can't be such a thing?

AUTHOR. I *think* that what Wittgenstein meant by a private language is one the referents of whose expressions are epistemically accessible only to its user; and, of course, LOT isn't one of those; we use the concept COW to think about cows; and cows are public objects. If, however, Wittgenstein did use 'private language' to mean something like LOT, then I can't imagine what he had against them. They look all right to me.

7.2 'Wild tokens and the disjunction problem'

Purblind on a dark night, John mistakes a large cat for a small cow. He thinks, as it might be, *there goes a small cow*. So his having the thought is, *inter alia*, an instance of his thinking of something as a cow; in particular, it is *not* an instance of his thinking of something as a cat or as a cat-or-cow).[11] Or, in the course of a daydream about cows John comes to have a thought about cats; so a thought about cats is caused by a thought about cows, but neither cats nor cows are causes of either. How is this possible if reference reduces to causation?

I haven't much to say about the 'wild tokens' problem that I haven't said elsewhere. Here's the basic proposal (for lots of discussion see Fodor 1990; Loewer and Rey 1991): By assumption, if John is referring to anything at all, he is referring to something that caused his thought; and, of course, everything caused by a cat is *ipso facto* caused by a cow-or-cat. Thus the disjunction problem. But there is (so I claim) nonetheless a difference between the case where John is thinking of a cat as a cow-or-cat and the case where John is thinking of a cat as a cow. It resides in the counterfactuals: John couldn't have thought of a cat as a cow-or-cat unless he could have thought of it as a cat and could have thought of it as a cow. But this doesn't go the other way around: being able to think of a cow as a cow or as a cat does not require being able to think of it as a cow-or-cat. So, being able to think about cows-or-cats is, as I've sometimes put it, 'asymmetrically dependent' on being able to think about cows and being able to think about cats. Because of this difference in the counterfactuals (so I further claim), a causal theory of content can, after all, accommodate our intuitions

---

[11] This kind of example is especially exasperating if you're the sort of philosopher who believes that charity is constitutive of interpretation. Since, in the circumstances imagined, interpreting John as referring to a cow-or-cat makes more of his thoughts true than interpreting him as referring to a cat, it appears that the charitable interpretation will be the wrong one. There is a close connection between the claim that no causal theory of reference can cope with the wild-tokens problem and the claim that no causal theory of reference could offer an adequate account of false assertion or false belief.

about the content of John's thought: Since the concept that John (mistakenly) applied to a cat was one that he could have had even if he didn't have the concept CAT, it must have been a token of the concept COW that John's encounter with the cat caused him to entertain, and not the concept COW-OR-CAT. So everything comes out right. (Unless I've made a mistake. Which is perfectly possible.)

Suppose this sort of treatment really does capture our intuitions about John. The question remains whether it works for wild tokens at large. I have my suspicions, but I'm not going to foist them on you. Further research is, as one says, required. Still, if I've got it right about John, that would seem to put a dent in what has been widely considered an impregnable argument against such theories; namely, that they can't (indeed, *demonstrably* can't) provide an account of what it is to say or think something false (to misapply a concept, etc.). It is, I'm suggesting, simply a fallacy to argue that since there can't be such thing as a miscause, there likewise can't be such a thing as a causal theory of mistakes. And, notice that although 'mistaken', 'incorrect', and maybe even 'false' are indeed normative notions, the sort of treatment of the disjunction problem that I've suggested doesn't invoke the norms in question. Or any others.

7.3 Which link in the causal chain?

It's common ground that any instance of a perceptual thought comes at one end of a causal chain. If such a thought refers at all, then, if the causal theory of reference is true, we must suppose that what the thought refers to is some or other link in such a chain of causes. The problem is: Which link?

The sequence of events that causally connect ones thoughts about cats to cats typically includes, for example, one's cortex becoming active in various interesting ways. Now, one might be prepared at a pinch to live with a little semantic indeterminacy if that's the price of a naturalized theory of reference. But 'There's a cat' refers to a cat, not to a cortex; if that's not common ground, what would be? Worse still: For all I know, the causal chain that leads to one of my CAT tokens reaches all the way back to the big bang; for all I know, every causal chain there ever was reaches all the way back to the big bang. If so, it may seem that no causal theory can rule it out that the big bang is all that anybody ever thinks about. But, surely, nobody thinks about the big bang *all* of the time; not even Woody Allen. Something must be done.

Here's where we start to get some use out of the assumption that the core cases we have to deal with are *perceptual* thoughts (more or less equivalently, that they are demonstrative thoughts, since, I suppose, what you're in a position to perceive is pretty much what you're in a position to demonstrate). So, the big bang is out as the referent of my thoughts about Mr James the cat; and so is everything that happened yesterday and so is everything that will happen tomorrow; and so is everything that didn't happen; and so forth. None of these is currently perceptually available. Also, as we'll see presently, if the core cases are perceptual, that willy-nilly drags in the notion of a perspective, and that helps too. What you can (currently, visually) perceive depends on what's visible from your current point of view. Things beyond your visual horizon are out, and so are things that are within your horizon but that are eclipsed by things between you and them.

So, for various reasons, we can picture you as being situated at the center of a circle that includes all but only the things you can now see from here, and as being at the end of a causal chain which intersects the circumference of that circle. By assumption, whatever your current perceptual thought refers to must be among the links of that chain that are in the circle. The question, to repeat, is: Which such link? The best we've done so far is to reduce the number of candidates.

Actually, I think a notion that Donald Davidson introduced (for, however, a rather different purpose) provides the answer. That I do think this rather surprises me, since I haven't, by and large, much sympathy with Davidson's views about the content of beliefs, perceptual or otherwise.

7.4 Triangulation

As I read Davidson, he was deeply involved in trying to find a transcendental argument that there can be no intentional content without (at least the possibility of) radical interpretation;[12] a thesis from which, as I remarked above, the autonomy (irreducibility, whatever) of the intentional follows pretty directly, as does the claim that languages must be epistemically public objects.

I think Davidson thought he might ground the argument he wanted in the epistemological conditions for radical interpretation: Any content that an informant's utterance(/thought) can have must *ipso facto* be accessible to a 'radical interpreter'; that is, to an interpreter who starts off with nothing but (say) a priori principles of logic and methodology, and whose empirical data consist of information about the informant's observable interactions with the environment in which he is situated.[13] I think Davidson thought he could rely on this because interpretation from the radical interpreter's epistemic position would be a condition for a language to be *learnable*, and he took for granted that learning its semantics is an essential part of learning one's first language. In short, since the epistemic position that the radical interpreter is supposed to occupy is presumed identical to the epistemic position from which children actually do learn language, it *must* be possible to learn a language from that position. All that being so, any transcendental consequence of the possibility of radical interpretation must be

---

[12] This is not, perhaps, the way that Davidson intended to be read; I have heard him say that he had no truck with transcendental arguments. So either my parsing of his texts is wrong or Davidson was wrong about what he had any truck with. The present considerations don't depend on choosing.

[13] In particular, Davidson's radical linguist can't make any very rich assumptions about the content of the native informant's propositional attitudes, since, for Davidson, the problem of the radical interpretation of an informant's language is essentially identical to the problem of identifying the content of his beliefs, desires, and so forth.

true. (I once asked Davidson why only semantics, among all the various empirical disciplines, labored under this sort of a priori epistemic constraint; it isn't plausible, after all, that whether there's a cave in the middle of a mountain depends on whether someone in the epistemic position of a radical geologist could find one there. Davidson replied that 'language is special'. I suppose what he meant was that theories about languages are tied to theories of learnability in a way that geological theories aren't. Taking it for granted that there is some epistemologically interesting sense in which first languages are *learned* has brought many a philosopher and many, many a psychologist, to grief. See Ch. 5.)

Let's just stipulate that all that is more or less correct, or that it could be made more or less correct by appropriate tinkering.[14] Now, since the sort of theory of radical interpretation that Davidson had in mind was a species of causal theory of reference, it has the usual 'Which link?' problem (as, indeed, Davidson fully recognized). How, then, is that problem to be solved on an account of content that says that the possibility of content entails the possibility of radical interpretation?

Suppose I am a linguist bent on interpreting Adam's utterances on a certain occasion when we are both puttering about in the garden. Suppose that a large, hairy, ugly snake suddenly swings into view.[15] (To simplify, we may stipulate that nothing else of interest happens at the same time.) Adam thereupon emits an utterance in his native tongue and I likewise emit an utterance in mine. The scene is now ripe for what Davidson called 'triangulation'.

Here, very approximately, is how I take it that triangulation is supposed to work. I'm aware that the vocable I uttered in the situation imagined means (in my home language) something like *Go away large, hairy, ugly, snake*. Indeed, the intention with which

[14] Perhaps I should repeat that I believe no such thing. What I'm doing is to sketch the galaxy of assumptions from which Davidson's story about triangulation seems to have emerged.

15   SNARK. Snakes have hair?

AUTHOR. This is a philosopher's snake. A philosopher's snake has hair if the philosopher whose snake it is says that it does.

I uttered that form of words was precisely to express my desire that the large, hairy, ugly, snake in question should go away.[16] So, what I was talking about lies on a causal chain from the snake to me, just as a causal account of reference requires. OK so far. But notice that the same sort of reasoning that I've just applied to me qua interpreter also applies to Adam qua informant; or at least it's reasonable for me to suppose that it does in my attempt to interpret Adam's utterance. After all, given that Adam is much the same sort of creature I am, it's thoroughly plausible that, like me, he said what he did with the intention of expressing the desire that the snake in question should go away. All that being so, it's thoroughly reasonable for me to suppose that the form of words Adam uttered is one that speakers of his language use when a desire to be rid of a snake comes upon them.

So I can triangulate. That is, I can reasonably suppose that a causal chain that runs from the perceptual horizon to my utterance would intersect a causal chain that runs from the perceptual horizon to Adam's utterance, and that it would do so *at the snake*. Put very schematically, the idea is that the link that's the object of a speaker's thought(/the referent of his utterance) is the one where the causal chain from the world to the speaker(/thinker) intersects the causal chain from the world to his interpreter when the speaker and the interpreter are caused to utter tokens of the same type. *Ceteris paribus*, to be sure.

The essence is that, in the situation imagined, I have a lot more information available with which to interpret Adam's utterance than had at first appeared. Together with my observation of the form of words he used and the circumstances in which he used it, I also have what I know about *my own reaction* to being in the situation that he was in. Because I do, I can infer what Adam is likely to have said by using the form of words that he did, and hence what that form of words is likely to mean in his

---

[16] It seems Davidson doesn't think a problem of radical interpretation with respect to *one's own* utterances. It is unclear to me that he has any right not to think that.

language:[17] It's likely to mean the same thing that my utterance in my language did; namely, *Go away large, hairy, ugly snake*. And, given that Adam and I are both referring to the snake, the causal theory allows me to infer that the snake is on both the causal chain that leads to his utterance and the causal chain that leads to mine. In particular, it's at the link at which those chains intersect. Were this chain of inference unsound, there would be (in point of both metaphysics and epistemology) no way that I could have interpreted what Adam said, and no way that a child in my position could have figured out what the form of words Adam uttered means; quite generally, there could be no matter of fact about the referential semantics of Adam's language. So I suppose Davidson to suppose.[18, 19]

Here are some characteristic passages.[20]

This much should be clear [*sic*] the basic triangle of two people and a common world is one of which we must be aware if we have any thoughts at all. If I can think [at all] I know that there are others with minds like my own, and that we inhabit a public time and space filled with objects and events ... (p. 86) The triangle I have described stands for the simplest interpersonal situation. In it two (or more) creatures each correlate their own reactions to external phenomena with the reactions

[17] It is, however, an empirical question whether interpreters really are able to draw that sort of inference in those sorts of circumstances with any significant reliability; and, in fact, the evidence is that they can't. S's are surprisingly bad at guessing what a speaker might be saying even when it's plausible that the speaker is saying something about the situation that he and the interpreter share; this is especially true for the interpretation of verbs (see Gleitman et al. 2005).

[18] Hence the philosophical joke: 'Q. How many philosophers does it take to see a tree? A. Infinitely many: one philosopher to look at the tree, another one to interpret the one who looks at the tree, and still another one to interpret the one who interprets the one who looks at the tree, etc. I don't suppose you found that joke hilariously funny. Philosophical jokes generally aren't.

[19] It seems Davidson also thinks that the significance of triangulation for interpretation provides a transcendental argument for the essentially 'social' character of language: a sort of 'private language' argument after the fact. I'm not going to consider this proposal, since it's patently incompatible with the computational account of cognition to which this book is for better or worse committed.

[20] Davidson offers, as far as I know, no fully worked-out theory of triangulation. The quotations in the text are culled from a scattering of his essays reprinted in 2001, to which my citations refer.

of the other ... interaction, triangulation ... gives us the only account of how experience gives a specific content to our thoughts. Without other creatures with whom to share responses to a mutual environment, there is no answer to the question what it is in the world to which we are responding ... (p. 129) The child finds tables similar; we find tables similar. It now makes sense for us to call the responses of the child responses to tables. Given these patterns of response, we can assign a location to the stimuli that elicit the child's response ... It is a form of triangulation: one line goes from the child in the direction of the table, one line goes from us in the direction of the table, and the third line goes between us and the child. (p. 119)

There's much more of the same kind in the Davidson corpus, but that should suffice to give the feel of the thing.

Well, as the reader will have predicted, I think just about every word of that is false. In particular, I don't think that learning a language has anything much to do with correlating linguistic responses to publicly available stimulations; and I doubt that there is, or could be, a theory of interpretation in anything like the sense that Davidson appears to have in mind. And (this is important) I don't see why any *actual* interpreter has to be involved in the process of fixing meanings. Wouldn't a counterfactual interpreter who shares Adam's psychology do just as well?[21] In fact, wouldn't it do for this other person to be *Adam himself*, only situated in counterfactual circumstances?[22] In which case, the a priori demand for an interpreter, even if it can somehow be justified, wouldn't suffice to show that the ontology of interpretation must require more than one-person states. In particular, referential content might be no more intrinsically 'public' than is talking to oneself.

---

[21] I like counterfactuals, but many philosophers doubt they can bear much weight. I don't think, however, that Davidson could himself have avoided resting a lot upon them. Many thoughts don't actually get uttered; and many utterances don't actually get interpreted. There is no Great Interpreter in the sky to do for their intentional contents what God did for Berkeley's tables and chairs; namely, sustain them when nobody else is around to do so. Counterfactuals look like being the only candidates for an ontology of interpretation. Some of the implications of this are far afield and very surprising (see Fodor 2008).

[22] Or a 'counterpart' of Adam himself if you prefer that way of doing business.

We'll return to this last line of thought presently. Suffice it that, although what Davidson says about interpretation depending on triangulation appears to leak in several places, I think that something like triangulation may help solve the 'Which link' problem; which is, as we've seen, a problem that any viable causal theory of reference, Davidsonian or otherwise, must contrive to solve somehow or other.

OK. So there's Adam and there's the snake, and Adam utters, as it might be 'Gavasnake'. I'm taking for granted (as per assumptions previously announced) that Adam's utterance expresses a perceptual belief and that the perceptual belief it expresses refers to a link in a causal chain that starts at Adam's perceptual horizon and eventuates in his utterance. To which such link does it refer? Suppose it refers to the snake, or to the snake's appearance on the scene.[23] What, metaphysically speaking, determines that it does? I do no more than follow Davidson (though not, I imagine, to any place where he would wish to lead).

Suppose that we represent the causal history of Adam's utterance by a line that runs to it passing through its referent intersecting the perceptual horizon somewhere or other. Call this 'Adam's line'. Every point on Adam's line corresponds to a (more or less remote) cause of his utterance. The present question is: which of the links in this causal chain is its referent? I take Davidson's intuition to be that the answer depends on the value of at least one further parameter; a parameter that isn't (fully) determined by Adam's line. And, notwithstanding that I think much of what Davidson says about triangulation isn't true, I think this intuition is spot on. To (metaphysically) determine the referent of Adam's thought, we need another line.

---

[23] I propose not to worry about the ontology of reference; e.g. about whether Adam's reference is to an event, or to an object, or to both, or to neither. I think, in fact, that answering that question requires more information than my story about Adam has thus far supposed his interpreter to have. But never mind. (Or, if you do mind, see Fodor 1994 for some discussion.)

Which other line? Well, to start by tidying up a bit; since we are assuming an RTM model of perceptual belief, we can stop worrying about the referent of what Adam *said* and ask about the referent of the mental representation a tokening of which (in his 'perceptual belief box' as it were) caused Adam to say it:[24] Call this 'Adam's representation'. And, since we are trying to fix the referent of a *perceptual* belief, we can speak literally of Adam's perspective on the scene that confronts him. Call that 'Adam's perspective'.

Here, then, is the proposal in a nutshell: Imagine there is not just the actual Adam with the perspective that he actually has, but also a counterfactual Adam ('Adam2') who is, say, three feet to the actual Adam's right. Adam2 has a (counterfactual) perspective on the (actual) visual scene; one that differs from Adam's perspective in accordance with the usual (i.e. the actual) laws of parallax. Assume that Adam2 tokens a representation of the same type that Adam does. Draw a line that starts at Adam2's token and represents its causal history (i.e. the causal history that Adam's token *would have had* if Adam had been at the position that Adam2 occupies in the counterfactual scenario). Call this Adam2's line. The metaphysical problem is: given the two causal histories, solve for the referents of the tokens. RTM allows us to do so. It says that the two tokens have the same referent iff Adam's line and Adam2's line intersect at a link; and that their referent is the link at which they intersect.

So, what Adam's utterance referred to depends on counterfactuals about the causal chains that would have caused it at the various positions that Adam *might have* occupied when he uttered it. At a minimum, this story must work at least as well as Davidson's; if Davidson is right to claim that the (actual) Adam's chain intersects his (actual) interpreter's line at the snake, then I am justified, and for the same reasons, in claiming that Adam's actual line would likewise

---

[24] This helps, since, of course, what you actually *say* (like what you are actually disposed to say) depends not just on the content of your perceptual belief, but on how that belief interacts with a background of your other beliefs, desires, and so forth. This is one of the ways that framing the issue as the interpretation of a speaker's *utterance* (rather than the interpretation of the speaker's *thoughts*) drags you into holism. I take it for granted that holism is a place to which it is good not to be dragged.

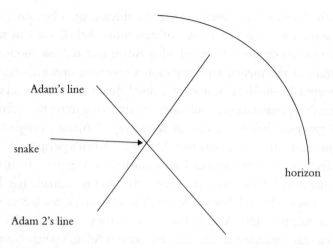

Figure 7.1 *Adam and his counterpart triangulate on a snake.* Given the causal chain that the referent belongs to, one can figure out which link on that chain the referent is. Thus, by assumption, the referent of Adam's thought is somewhere on Adam's line, and the referent of Adam 2's thought is somewhere on Adam 2's line. The snake is the unique link which satisfies both conditions, so it is the referent of both thoughts.

have intersected the (counterfactual) line of Adam2 at the snake. In fact, my story is just Davidson's story about triangulation, only stripped of extraneous posits. I need no interpreter as a condition of Adam's thought having content; counterfactuals about Adam himself will do. Correspondingly, I don't need to admit that interpretable languages are *ipso facto* epistemologically public; all that's required is that what a speaker(/a thought) refers to needn't change with (actual or counterfactual) changes in perspective. My proposal, unlike Davidson's, is thus compatible with the view that people think in a (de facto) private language. As, indeed, I fully believe that they do.

There are various caveats with which I more or less won't bother you. For example, the procedure just outlined doesn't generalize to fix the referent of beliefs that *aren't* perceptual. Roughly, that's because in Adam's case, but not in the general case, we can use shifts in perspective to pick out the relevant counterfactuals; the counterfactuals that count are the ones which would be true if Adam had had a different point of view. But, as previously remarked, I'm quite prepared to assume that if the triangulation procedure can provide a rich enough vocabulary of perceptual representations, Adam's other concepts can be introduced by definite descriptions.[25]

I've given no argument that the 'Which link?' problem is the only objection to the possibility of a causal-chain account of the metaphysics of reference that would be left over if the normativity problem and the disjunction problem were solved. Never mind; we'll deal with the others as they come along.

So where, if anywhere, does this discussion leave us? Come to think of it, where, if anywhere, does this whole book leave us? It might be useful to enumerate some of the theses that are probably false if referentialism is true and a causal account of Mentalese reference can, in fact, be given. They include just about all of the views of mind and language that are currently in fashion in either philosophy or cognitive science.

1. Practically all recent philosophers to the contrary notwithstanding (in particular, all pragmatists to the contrary notwithstanding; hence, Quine, Davidson, Wittgenstein, Dummet, Sellars, etc. and their followers to the contrary notwithstanding), *reference is ontologically prior to truth*; which is, of course, just what the proper treatment of compositionality, productivity, systematicity, and the like independently require. Philosophers who deny that reference is ontologically prior to truth have confused their metaphysics with their epistemology. It may be that, in the course of language learning, radical interpretation, radical translation, etc.

---

[25] It perhaps bears repetition that the definite descriptions in question needn't provide analyses of the representations they introduce; indeed, the representations they introduce may perfectly well be primitive, hence not analyzable. So, the distinction between representations whose referents are fixed by triangulation and representations whose referents are introduced by description need not be principled and, in particular, may have no particular relevance to questions about the individuation of the representations.

truth-conditions on (some, simple) sentences are *established* prior to establishing what refers to what. (Or maybe not. If, like me, you doubt that languages are learned, and you doubt that there could be a theory of radical interpretation/translation, you will not wish to spend much time debating this.) But nothing about ontological priorities would follow.

2. There is no particular reason to believe that reference is a social phenomenon. At no point in the preceding sketch was a 'second person' interpreter invoked; whenever it began to look like we might need one, it turned out that the same speaker(/thinker) in a counterfactual situation would do just as well. It is therefore unsurprising that some languages turn out to be private; what's perhaps surprising is that not all of them do.[26]

3. There is no particular reason why supposing that mental representations have semantic properties should lead to a homuncular regress. Excepting perhaps neurologists, *nobody ever* interprets mental representations. Nor, in any case, could such interpretations be what bestows content on mental representations. The content of a mental representation is its referent, and what fixes its referent is the character of its causal connections to the world.

4. There is no particular reason to believe that the content of expressions in public languages is metaphysically prior to the content of propositional attitudes. In fact, there's every reason to think that it mustn't be, on pain of making an utter mystery of how public languages could be learned. Generally speaking, learning requires thinking. Wittgenstein's (and Skinner's) suggestion that learning a first language is somehow a matter of 'training' is preposterous on the face

---

[26] *Using a language for communication* requires implementing some sort of procedure that its speaker/hearers can use for translating it into and out of the language of thought. But it doesn't follow that there must be such a procedure in order for there to *be* a language of thought.

of it (not to say strikingly lacking in detail). Who trained you, for example?

5. There is no reason to believe that the content of a mental representation (that is, its referent) has anything to do with its role in inference (insofar as its role in inference is identified with its role in mental processes; that is, with its role in mental computations). There is likewise no reason to believe that the content of a mental representation has anything much to do with its causal relation to other mental representations; all that counts is its causal connections to the world. A fortiori, there is no reason to believe that the metaphysics of meaning imposes a 'charity' condition, or a 'rationality' condition upon ascriptions of beliefs.

6. There is no reason to believe that the content of one's concepts is determined by (e.g.) the character of one's behavioral capacities. Pragmatism is false. It does remain open, however, that content-determining mind–world causal connections are mediated (sometimes or always) by the exercise of such capacities. If so, then what actions one can perform is (contingently but not metaphysically) relevant to the content of one's concepts.[27]

7. There is no particular reason to suppose that cognitive development comes in 'stages'. So far as I know, all the classical versions (including, most notably, Piaget's) depend on assuming that the content of mental representations is what changes from stage to stage, and that content supervenes on inferential role. Neither of these is true according to the present treatment.

---

[27] But there's a caveat. It remains open that although there are no rationality (etc.) constraints on what contents a propositional attitude can have, there may well be such constraints on a propositional attitude with that content being a belief. *Believing* may be functionally defined even though *believing that P* is not. You need two parameters to specify an attitude: roughly, *believing that P* versus *desiring(/preferring, intending, etc.) that P* and *believing that P* versus *believing that Q*. It has never been very clear how conditions of charity, rationality, and the like would apply in the case of attitudes that don't have truth-values.

8. There is no reason to suppose that 'how you think' or 'what you can think about' depends on what language you speak. Nothing but the semantics of Mentalese determines what one can think, or think about, and the semantics of Mentalese is prior to the semantics of English.

9. There is no reason to suppose (as, however, many philosophers appear to do) that demonstration presupposes conceptualization; for example, that you can only demonstrate something if you have a concept that subsumes it (or, perhaps, that you believe subsumes it). In fact, the whole thrust of the discussion has been that the priorities go the other way around: relations depend on causal relations, not vice versa. This is, of course, essential if any reductionist program along the lines of PT is to get off the ground.

10. In fact, the story I've been telling you comports rather nicely with the story that Zenon Pylyshyn likes to tell about FINSTS. FINSTS are preconceptual pure demonstratives of Mentalese. The visual system uses them to effect a primitive sort of reference; in particular, to pick out distal objects in the course of very early[28] visual processes. The way FINSTS work is: they get 'grabbed' (in circumstances that are presumed to be specifiable in purely psychophysical terms and thus do not presuppose conceptualization)[29] by ambient things and events, which they then 'stick to' in ways that frequently tolerate changes in the target's location, speed, trajectory, color, apparent shape, and even its disappearance due to visual occlusions. Since you can, if Pylyshyn is right, achieve this primitive sort of reference without the application of concepts to the

[28] Computationally early, not (or not necessarily) ontogenetically early. Still less phylogenetically early.

[29] Somebody lights a cigarette in a dark room; all eyes move reflexively to foveate the light and a FINST is reflexively assigned. No conceptualization of the stimulus is required to mediate the process; not even conceptualization of the stimulus as a light. In this sort of case the direction of causation is, as it were, from outside in, not from inside out; so it's the reverse of what I suppose happens when a concept is assigned to a percept.

referent, the idea that there is an internal connection between referring and conceptualizing would turn out not to be true. I don't know whether Pylyshyn's story about how pure demonstration works in early vision is even approximately true, but it's certainly very attractive; and I would be vastly surprised if it could be refuted by an appeal to a priori constraints on the relation between reference and conceptualization.[30]

11. There may be no good reason for supposing that English has a semantics at all; perhaps the only thing that does is Mentalese. If that's right, then what are usually called 'semantic level' representations of English sentences (or representations of their 'logical form') are really no such things. Rather, they should be taken as representing translations of English into Mentalese. The translation of a sentence in Mentalese is, of course, no more a representation of that sentence than is its translation in French. To suppose otherwise would be to commit what in the old days they called a 'category mistake'.

The implications for linguistic theory (if not for linguistic practice) might be quite interesting. For example, it could turn out that there is no such thing as the 'interface' between semantic-level representations and syntactic-level representations (because there is no such thing as semantic-level representation). We might also want to reconsider the conventional view, embraced for expository convenience in the preceding chapters, that the content of English is compositional. (By contrast, the content of Mentalese representations had better be for all the familiar reasons: productivity, systematicity, and so forth.) If it turns out that Mentalese is compositional and English isn't, then, very likely, not every Mentalese sentence has a translation in English. That's

---

[30] Still less by appeal to a priori constraints on the relation between demonstration and consciousness. Compare Campbell (2002).

perfectly fine. Who but a philosopher of the pragmatist persuasion would claim that you can say whatever you can think?[31]

And so forth. I'd be very surprised if there aren't many other things that most philosophers and cognitive scientists believe but that a serious, naturalizable, computational version of RTM would refute.

    SNARK. If only we had one.
    AUTHOR. If only we had one.

---

[31] Still less plausibly that it's a priori that you can say whatever you can think; that would imply, for example, that animals can't think anything at all. Mr James, who is the domestic feline currently in residence here, takes the slight to heart.

'But animals can't think in the same sense of the term that we do.' 'Well, in what sense of the term *do* we think? Presumably it's the sense of "think" in which "think" means *think*. Surely, if animals think at all, they too must think in that sense of the term. How else?'

References

Aizawa, K. (2003), *The Systematicity Arguments* (Dodrecht: Kluwer).

Armstrong, S., Gleitman L., and Gleitman, H. (1983), 'What Some Concepts Might Not Be', *Cognition*, 13:263–308.

Block, N. (1986), 'Advertisement for a semantics for psychology', in French et al. (1986).

Boghossian, P. (1997), 'Analyticity reconsidered', in Wright and Hale (1996).

Brandom, R. (2000), *Articulating Reasons* (Cambridge, Mass.: Harvard University Press).

Campbell, J. (2002), *Reference and Consciousness* (Oxford: Oxford University Press).

Carey, S. (1985), *Conceptual Change in Childhood* (Cambridge, Mass., MIT Press).

Carruthers, P. (2001), Review of Fodor, *The Mind Doesn't Work That Way*, *Times Literary Supplement*, 5 October, p. 30.

Carnap, R. (1956), *Meaning and Necessity* (Chicago, Ill.: University of Chicago Press).

Churchland, P. S. (1987), 'Epistemology in the age of neuroscience', *Journal of Philosophy*, 84: 544–53.

Churchland, Paul (1989), *A Neurocomputational Perspective: The Nature of Mind and the Structure of Science* (Cambridge, Mass.: MIT Press).

Connolly, A., Fodor, J., Gleitman H., and Gleitman L. (2007), 'Why stereotypes don't even make good defaults', *Cognition*, 103/1: 1–22.

Cowie, F. (1999), *What's Within* (Oxford: Oxford University Press).

Davidson, D. (2001), *Subjective, Intersubjective, Objective* (Oxford: Oxford University Press).

Dennett, D. (1982), 'Beyond belief', in A. Woodfield (ed.), *Thought And Object* (Oxford: Clarendon).

Deutsch, J. A. (1960), *The Structural Basis of Behavior* (Chicago, Ill.: University of Chicago Press).

Devitt, M., and Sterelny, K. (1987), *Language and Reality* (Cambridge, Mass.: MIT Press).

Dewey, J. (2002), *Human Nature and Conduct* (Mineola, NY: Dover).

Donnellan, K. (1972), 'Proper names and identifying descriptions', in D. Davidson and G. Harman (eds.), *Semantics of Natural Language* (Dordrecht: Reidel).

Dretske, F. (1981), *Knowledge And The Flow of Information* (Cambridge Mass.: MIT Press).

Dreyfus, H. (1978), *What Computers Can't Do* (London: Harper Collins).

Elman, J., Bates, E., Johnson, M., Karmiloff-Smith, A., Parisi, D., and Plunkett, K. (1996), *Rethinking Innateness* (Cambridge, Mass.: MIT Press).

Fodor, J. (1968), 'The appeal to tacit knowledge in psychological explanation', *Journal of Philosophy*, 65: 627–40.

——(1981), *Representations* (Cambridge, Mass.: MIT Press).

——(1990), *A Theory of Content* (Cambridge Mass.: MIT Press).

——(1994), *The Elm and the Expert* (Cambridge Mass.: MIT Press).

——(1998), *Concepts* (Oxford: Oxford University Press).

——*The Mind Doesn't Work That Way* (Cambridge, Mass.: MIT Press).

——(2001), 'Doing Without What's Within', *Mind*, 110/437: 99–148.

——(2008), 'Against Darwinism', *Mind and Language*, 23/1: 1–24.

——(2004), 'Language, thought and compositionality', *Mind and Language*, 16/1: 1–15.

Fodor, J., and Lepore, E. (1992), *Holism* (Oxford: Blackwell).

——'The Emptiness of the Lexicon', *Linguistic Inquiry*, 29/2: 269–88.

Fodor, J., and Lepore, E. (2002), *The Compositionality Papers* (Oxford: Oxford University Press).

——(2007), 'Brandom Beleaguered', *Philosophy and Phenomenological Research*, 74/3: 677–91.

——(2002) (eds.), *The Compositionality Papers* (Oxford: Clarendon).

Fodor, J., and McLaughlin, B. (1990), 'Connectionism and the Problem of Systematicity: Why Smolensky's Solution Doesn't Work', *Cognition*, 35: 183–204.

Fodor, J., and Pylyshyn, Z. (1988), 'Connectionism and Cognitive Architecture: A Critical Analysis', *Cognition*, 28: 3–71.

Forster, K. (1998), 'The Pros and Cons of Masked Priming', *Journal of Psycholinguisic Research*, 27: 203–33.

French, P., Uehling, T., and Wettstein, H. (1986) (eds.), *Midwest Studies in Philosophy*, 10 (Minneapolis, Minn.: University of Minnesota Press).

Gibson, J. J. (1966), *The Senses Considered as Perceptual Systems* (Boston, Mass.: Houghton Mifflin).

Gleitman, L., Cassidy, K., Nappa, R., Papafragon, E., and Trueswell, J. (2005), 'Hard words', *Journal of Language Learning and Development*, 1/1: 23–64.

Glymour, C. (1996), 'Why I am Not a Baysean', in Papeneau (1996).

Harris, Z. (1988), *Language and Information* (New York: Columbia University Press).

Hume, D. (1739/1985), *A Treatise of Human Nature* (London: Penguin).

Jackendoff, R. (1993), *Languages of the Mind* (Cambridge, Mass.: MIT Press).

Kim, J. (1992), 'Multiple Realization and the Metaphysics of Reduction', *Philosophy and Phenomenological Research*, 52: 1–26.

Koffka, F. (1935), *Principles of Gestalt Psychology* (New York: Harcourt).

Kripke, S. (1979), 'A puzzle about belief', in A. Margalit (ed.), *Meaning And Use* (Dordrecht: Reidel).

Ledoux, J. (2002), *The Synaptic Self* (NY: Viking).

Lewis, D. (1972), 'Psychophysical and Theoretical Identification, *Australasian Journal of Philosophy*, 50: 249–58.

Loewer, B., and Rey, G. (1991) (eds.), *Meaning In Mind: Fodor And His Critics* (Oxford: Blackwell).

Macdonald, C., and Macdonald, G. (1995), *Connectionism* (Cambridge, Mass.: Blackwell).

Margolis, E. (1999), 'How to acquire a concept', in E. Margolis, and S. Laurence (1999).

Margolis, E., and Laurence, S. (1999), *Concepts: Core Readings* (Cambridge, Mass.: MIT Press).

Mates, B. (1951), 'Synonymity', in *Meaning and Interpretation*, University of California Publications in Philosophy, 25: 201–6.

McDowell, J. (1994), *Mind and World* (Cambridge, Mass.: Harvard University Press).

Miller, G. (1956), 'The magical number seven plus or minus two', *Psychological Review*, 63/2: 81–96.

Miller, G., Galanter, E., and Pribram, K. (1960), *Plans and the Structure of Behavior* (New York: Holt, Reinhart & Winston).

Miller, G., and Johnson-Laird, P. (1987), *Language and Perception* (Cambridge, Mass.: Belknap).

Murphy, D. 'On Fodor's Analogy', *Mind and Language*, 21/5, 553–64.

Osgood, C., and Tzeng, O. (1990), *Language, Meaning and Culture* (Westport, Conn.: Praeger).

Osherson, D., and Smith, E. (1981), 'On the adequacy of prototype theory as a theory of concepts', *Cognition*, 9: 35–58.

Papineau, D. (1996) (ed.), *The Philosophy of Science* (Oxford: Oxford University Press).

Pears, D. (1990), *Hume's System* (Oxford: Oxford University Press).

Pigliucci, M., and Kaplan, J. (2006), *Making Sense of Evolution* (Chicago, Ill.: University of Chicago Press).

Pinker, S. (2005), 'So how does the mind work?', *Mind and Language*, 20/1: 1–24.

Prinz, J. (2002), *Furnishing the Mind* (Cambridge, Mass.: MIT Press).

Putnam, H. (2000), *The Threefold Cord: Mind, Body and World* (New York: Columbia University Press).

Pylyshyn, Z. (2003), *Seeing and Visualizing* (Cambridge, Mass.: MIT Press).

Pylyshyn, Z. (1987) (ed.), *The Robot's Dilemma* (Norwood, NJ: Ablex).

Reid, T. (1983), *Thomas Reid's Inquiry and Essays* (Indianapolis, Ind.: Hackett).

Rhees, R. (1963), 'Can there be a private language?', in C. Caton (ed.), *Philosophy and Ordinary Language* (Urbana, Ill.: University of Chicago Press).

Rosch, E. (1973), 'On the internal structure of perceptual and semantic categories', in T. Moore (ed.), *Cognitive Development and the Acquisition of Language* (New York: Academic).

Ryle, G. (1949), *The Concept of Mind* (London: Hutchinson).

Sellars, W. (1956), 'Empiricism and the philosophy of mind', in *Minnesota Studies in the Philosophy of Science*, 1 (Minneapolis, Minn.: University of Minnesota Press).

Smith, E., and Medin, D. (1981), *Categories and Concepts* (Cambridge, Mass.: Harvard University Press).

Smolensky, P. (1988), 'On the proper treatment of connectionism', *Behavioral and Brain Sciences*, 11: 1–23.

—— (1995), 'Connectionism, Constituency and the Language of Thought', in C. Macdonald and G. MacDonald, (1995).

Sperber, D. (2002), 'A Defense of Massive Modularity', in Depoux (ed.), *Language, Brain and Cognitive Development: Essays in Honor of Jacques Mehler* (Cambridge, Mass.: MIT Press).

Sperling, G. (1960), 'The Information Available in Brief Visual Presentations', *Psychological Monographs*, 74: 1–29.

Treisman, A., and Schmidt, H., 'Illusory Conjuction in the Perception of Objects', *Cognitive Psychology*, 14/1: 107–42.

Wright, C., and Hale, B., (1996) (eds.), *A Companion to the Philosophy of Language* (Oxford: Blackwell).

Index

AI 8, 15–16
Aizawa, K. 56n
analyticity
  and constituency 30
Aristotle, 5, 67, 88
Armstrong, S. 154n
associationism, 62n, 63n 96, 98
  and productivity, 103–105

behaviorism 36n
Block, N. 19
Boghossian, P. 33, 36, 38
Brandom, R. 11, 19, 53n, 109n, 178
Brunner, J. 11

Campbell, J. 219n
canonical decomposition 173
Carey, S. 28
Carnap, R. 69n
Carruthers, P. 117–118
Cartesianism 9, 12, 14
Chomsky, N. 19, 53n, 102, 103, 105n
Churchland, Patricia 8, 12, 15
Churchland, Paul 159n
cognitive architecture 37, 106, 118n
compositionality, 17, 56n, 106, 171
computation 5, 70
concepts 20
  primitive, 28
  sensory, 28
  basic, 64
  learning of, 132
connectionism 7, 103, 112–13, 122
Conolly, A. 46
constituent structure, 58, 105
Cowie, F. 143n
Cowie, F. 54n

Darwin, C. 149
Davidson, D. 19, 193
Definitions in use (objections to) 32–4
Denett, D. 103n, 178
Descartes, R. 9, 149
Deutsch, J. A. 6

Devitt, M. 54n
Dewey, J. 11, 114
direct realism 6
Dretske, F. 141, 180, 182
Dummet, M. 11, 215

echoic buffer 185, 188
Elman, J. 159
empiricism, 11
evolution, 12, 15

files 92–100
FINSTs (Fingers of Instation), 218
Fodor, J. 7, 14, 54, 56n, 58n, 65n, 73,
    143n, 158, 159n, 77n, 104n, 107n,
    166, 171n, 176n
frame Problem 116–121
Frege, G, 16, 56n, 62n, 82, 89, 90n
functionalism 8, 90–91

Gibson, J. J. 6
globality 121–4
Glymour, C. 136

Heidegger, M. 11
holism 5–6, 50–87
Hume, D. 11
Hume, D. 7–58, 103, 131, 167
Husserl, E. 52n

Inferential Role Semantics (IRS) 25,
    32–48, 53, 70n
information 180–182
instrumentalism, 5
intensionality, 10–12
isotropy, 115
items effect 182

Jackendoff, J. 29
James, H. 47, 146
James, W. 11
Julesz, B. 190

Kant, I. 93, 149, 194
Kant, I. 181
Kaplan, J. 9
Katz, J. 4n
Kim, J. 90n
knowing how (/that) 35
Kripke, S. 76n
Kyburg, H. 117–118

Ledoux, J. 103
Lepore, E. 56n, 65n, 158, 159n
Locke, J. 103
locking 141, 151
logical form 175
Lormand, E. 117
LOT 1 11–18

Margolis, E. 140–4m, 156
McDowell, J. 6, 193
Medin, D. 150n
Mental processes 8, 61–2
Mill, J. S. 96
Miller, G. 15, 16
Murphy, D. 114

nativism, 11, 94n
naturalism, 18
Newton, I. 104
normalcy conditions 43

Operationalism, 142
Osgood, C. 106n
Osherson, D. 156

Paderewski 71–3
Pears, D. 31
Peirce, C. S. 41
Piaget, J. 11, 217
picture principle 173
Pigliucci, M. 9
Pinker, S. 113
Plato 6, 6
pactical syllogism, 15
pagmatism, 8–12
Prinz J. 28, 59n, n
productivity 19, 20
Propositional attitudes 5, 11 (publicity of 9–90)
publicity 89–92

rule following 38–48
Putnam, H. 6, 11
Pylyshyn, Z. 56n, 58n, 60n, 218–19
104, 107n, 117, 218

Quine, W. V. 11, 55n, 90n, 176, 215

ramsey sentences 140n
referentialism, 16, 18, 53
Reid, T. 6
relevance 115
representation 171–7
    distributed 20
    discursive 58n
    iconic 5
Representationalism 139–144, 139
    Lewis, D. 140n
Rhees, R. 81n
Rosch, E. 28
RTM 5, 7
rule following 37–41
Ryle, G. 11, 14, 103n, 120

Sellars, W. 11, 193, 215
semantic ascent 20
semantic level (of a grammar) 31
skepticism, 9–10
Skinner, B. F. 102, 216
sleeping dog strategy 117–20
Smolensky, P. 158n
Sperber, D. 118n
Sperling, G. 188–90
Sperling, G. 188–9
stereotypes 149–51
Sterelny 54n

transduction, 186–7
Turing, A. 21, 125–6
twin Earth 17
Tzeng, O. 106n

Vygotsky L. 11

Watson, J. 103n
Waugh, E. 21n
Wittgenstein, L. 11, 19, 36 40 , 120, 142, 152n, 216
Wurzburg school 96n